SEX-POSITIVE
SOCIAL WORK

SJ DODD

SEX-POSITIVE SOCIAL WORK

Columbia University Press / *New York*

Columbia University Press

Publishers Since 1893

New York   Chichester, West Sussex

cup.columbia.edu

Copyright © 2020 Columbia University Press

Library of Congress Cataloging-in-Publication Data

Names: Dodd, Sarah-Jane, author.
Title: Sex-positive social work / SJ Dodd.
Description: New York : Columbia University Press, [2020] | Includes
bibliographical references and index.
Identifiers: LCCN 2019051989 (print) | LCCN 2019051990 (ebook) |
ISBN 9780231188104 (cloth) | ISBN 9780231188111 (trade paperback) |
ISBN 9780231547666 (ebook)
Subjects: LCSH: Social service—Practice. | Sex. | Sexual health.
Classification: LCC HV10.5 .D626 2020 (print) |
LCC HV10.5 (ebook) | DDC 361.3/2—dc23
LC record available at https://lccn.loc.gov/2019051989
LC ebook record available at https://lccn.loc.gov/2019051990

Cover design: Elliott S. Cairns
Cover image: Private collection / Bridgeman Images

For Emma and Jack, who fill my life
with meaning and light

CONTENTS

ACKNOWLEDGMENTS

This project was two decades in the making, so please forgive me if there are a lot of thank-yous! When I was a doctoral student, my good friend Mary Andres and I developed and cotaught a human sexuality elective course for social work students. I still think back fondly on the hours we spent prepping and debriefing, in a collaborative effort to ensure our students really grasped the concepts we were trying to convey. I am so grateful we decided to take that leap together. The foundation of that original course is present within this volume.

In the twenty years between that first course and today, I am so lucky to have taught sexuality to literally hundreds (getting close to thousands!) of students at the Silberman School of Social Work, Hunter College, City University of New York, in New York City. Our students are a unique group—diverse, committed, thoughtful, challenging, and focused on social justice. Their engagement with this material in the classroom and beyond has helped me grow as a social worker and teacher. This book is fully informed by our classroom interactions and activities, which have pushed me to think deeply about each topic. I look forward to growing even more as our students interact with this content.

ACKNOWLEDGMENTS

After many years of percolating as an idea, this book became a reality because of the generous support of the deans of the Silberman School of Social Work. I am especially grateful to Dean Mary Cavanaugh, whose unwavering belief in the project, as well as guidance, and concrete supports were the difference in making this work possible. Additionally, Associate Dean Gary Mallon, a generous colleague and friend since even before I arrived in New York City, has been instrumental. His ongoing generosity extended this time to connecting me with Columbia University Press and my editor for this work. He also regularly checked in to see how the book was going and to offer encouragement. I have loved all the opportunities we have had to work together so far, and I look forward to many more. Associate Dean Caroline Gelman also has offered unwavering support and encouragement throughout and continues to be a valued colleague.

I am extremely appreciative of my editor, Stephen Wesley, at Columbia University Press, who has been enthusiastic from the beginning. He helped me lay out a clear timeline, nudged me at just the right moments to keep me moving forward, and provided excellent editorial support throughout. He also managed to tighten up my writing without losing my voice and got rid of almost every superfluous "that" I had sprinkled throughout! I want to thank Christian Winting, my assistant editor, who worked in tandem with Stephen to make sure the final product was put together as smoothly as possible. I appreciated his responsiveness and attention to detail. I am grateful for the support of the entire Columbia University Press team. I am also grateful to the anonymous reviewers who provided feedback on both the proposal and the full draft. I have no doubt that their thoughtful suggestions strengthened the final product.

I want to extend a special thank-you to Julia Bartz, whom I was lucky enough to have as my research assistant through the main part of this project. Julia went above and beyond, not only gathering literature and assembling references but also editing early drafts and offering thoughtful critiques and insights. I think without Julia this book would still be only half finished! In the final stages of the project I was very grateful to have another student, Ren Lee, provide assistance and even some computer graphics to make sure I met my deadline.

ACKNOWLEDGMENTS

I'm a firm believer that it "takes a village." I have a very special village supporting me in this and every endeavor. My colleagues at the Silberman School of Social Work provided the perfect mix of support and intellectual challenge. Maddy Petrow-Cohen offered encouragement as she listened to weekly progress reports over lunch with patience and enthusiasm. Julie Petrow-Cohen also cheered me on at every opportunity. Barbara Bickart and Bridget Hughes grounded me while making me laugh as we sat in front of their fire. Kathleen Bailie, Andrea Erickson, Ally Cherins, and Liz Hochberg ("Big Guts") were amazing cheerleaders, nourishing me with food, drink, and laughter all along the way. Simon, my brother, and Susie, Alex, and Lucy were encouraging from afar. Mum and Dad beamed with pride, even if they weren't exactly sure what it was I was writing about. And even though I moved to the United States over thirty years ago, I still feel their love and support as though they lived next door. Finally, to the family I am lucky enough to have created: Teddy, the newest addition, sat on my lap or lay next to me hoping crumbs from my chocolate chip scone (thank you, Able Baker) would drop on the floor. Emma and Jack are really the best kids anyone could wish for—full of love, caring, and compassion, with a good dose of adventure thrown in. They are even pretty good-humored about mom having books that say "sex" on them all over the dining room table. When I first came out as gay, the very idea that I could have children was beyond my imagination. The fact that I get to be a parent is the single greatest gift of my life. Laura made that gift possible. She has been on this journey with me since before that first class was taught. She is my rock and my joy. She challenges me to reach outside my comfort zone and take risks, yet she always makes me feel right at home. I feel so blessed to get to do life's journey together—the Bo-Dos are my world.

SEX-POSITIVE SOCIAL WORK

INTRODUCTION

Sex is everywhere—on television, in movies, on social media, in advertising, and even in politics. Sex and sexuality are central to our lives. Social workers come across them in almost every practice setting and almost every client population. We routinely engage with clients experiencing sexual- and gender-identity issues, reproductive concerns, sexual abuse, sexual violence, troubled relationships, and sexually transmitted infections.

Yet active conversations about healthy sexuality and sexual well-being are missing from social work literature, education, and practice.[1] The "conspiracy of silence" identified by Jean Gochros almost half a century ago is still very much with us.[2] My students often tell me they avoid topics of sexuality whenever possible, and their supervisors often admit the same. Part of the problem is too little information, knowledge, and experience with sex education in social work education. That's why I wrote this book. *Sex-Positive Social Work* is meant to address this silence, challenge social workers to embrace rather than avoid questions about sexuality in practice, and articulate a sex-positive frame for social work.

Twenty years ago, I started teaching a course called Human Sexuality to social workers, after I discovered that there was no such course available during my master's in social work program. I had taken Human Sexuality as part of my graduate work in education, so it seemed odd to me that there was not even an elective course on the subject offered in the social work curriculum. During my doctorate program at the University of Southern California, I joined forces with a colleague from the Campus Student Counseling Center to develop a three-credit elective. The response to our first course was overwhelming: full enrollment and fully engaged and inquisitive students. We both learned a tremendous amount, and now twenty years later, we both still teach Human Sexuality, though we've moved on to different faculties and are at different schools.

When I got to the Silberman School of Social Work, Hunter College, City University of New York, in New York City in 2000, I was met with the same situation—no class on human sexuality. Luckily, this time there was one in the catalogue, which the administration supported me in resurrecting. We have offered the Human Sexuality elective regularly ever since, and this academic year (2020) we have added extra sections to support the ever-growing interest in the content.

Along my journey teaching human sexuality, I've always been amazed by the willingness of my students to share their experiences, vulnerabilities, and fears about sexuality in practice and through their own experience. And I am always equally disappointed by how little attention is paid to sexuality—especially positive sexuality—within the social work curriculum and literature.

In my two decades of teaching sexuality, I have relied almost exclusively on textbooks written by psychologist, psychiatrists, and physicians. But the social work lens is different. That is precisely why we all chose social work. It addresses the holistic person-in-environment. It pays attention to the biological, psychological, and social. And it champions social justice. Social work centers the values of our profession as it explores sexuality and gender from a nonjudgmental, self-determination-focused perspective.

So I wrote this book. I wrote it to fill a gap in the literature and the curriculum—giving us a social work lens on sexuality and gender and shifting from a deficit focus to a positive, strengths-based one across the whole curriculum. I also hope it challenges you to look at some of your own assumptions about your clients' relationships, gender, and sexuality and to begin to test those assumptions by engaging the subject in practice.

The goal of this book is to survey key topics around sexuality for social workers from a strengths-based, sex-positive perspective. A sex-positive perspective encourages agency in sexual decision making and embraces consensual sexual activity as healthy, something to be enjoyed without stigma or shame.[3] It embraces sexuality as a human right. Despite sexuality's prominence in social work practice settings, many social work professionals have internalized sociocultural taboos about discussing sexuality, so they tend to avoid the topic in practice. While social workers have embraced the notion of working from a strengths-based perspective, sexuality is still predominantly approached from the opposite direction— focusing on risks and possible harms. A strengths perspective does not focus on the client's deficits or limitations but instead on their strengths, skills, aptitudes, and resources.[4] It does not pathologize consensual sexual activities like paraphilias or fetishes unless they cause distress. And it does not assume that someone's sexual- or gender-minority status is the key to their presenting problem.

The purpose of this book, therefore, is to offer a sex-positive approach to sexuality for social workers with illustrative case examples. It is designed to encourage you, as social work practitioners, to embrace rather than avoid issues of sexuality within your practice, incorporating the sexual dimension into the biopsychosocial assessment and engaging in conversations about sexuality regularly with clients as appropriate. The book encourages sexual fulfillment, attention to desire, intimacy, arousal, and overall sexual well-being without judgment or assumptions. Too often, substandard sex education and the cultural taboos related to sex leave people unsure of their sexual selves, filled with shame and guilt rather than excitement and joy. They do not understand their own likes and dislikes and are unable to ask about those of their partners.

This book provides you with the tools to develop a vocabulary for sex-positive conversations with your clients so they can engage with their sexual selves and explore who they are as sexual beings. It is also an opportunity for them to unlearn sex-negative messaging and replace it with affirming, nonjudgmental internal dialogue.

Sexual well-being is critical to overall well-being. This book will give social workers the tools to approach sex and sexuality actively and positively with clients. It is designed to embolden you to engage in discussions of sexuality with clients, and it is written to provide an opportunity for self-reflection and professional growth. The book includes foundational-level content on a range of topics related to sexuality: developing your own comfort; avoiding assumptions; considering cultural context; setting the environment (physical space and inclusive intake forms); taking a sexual history; understanding physiology; differences in arousal; variations in sexual identity; experiences of gender identity; intimacy; communication; understanding relationships (attachment theory and relational theory); sex in older adulthood (expectations, physical issues and enhancements, residential settings, and sexually transmitted infections and diseases); BDSM (bondage and discipline, dominance and submission, and sadism and masochism) and kink; consensually nonmonogamous and polyamorous relationships; and ethical considerations, including erotic transference. It is by no means complete. In some cases I can raise only some of the most basic issues of a subject. And just as in class, in some cases the book raises more questions than it answers. But it will provoke conversations, encourage you to think, and introduce topics you may explore more fully.

In class, my students challenge me by presenting a wide range of experience levels—from comprehensive to almost nonexistent. Some of my students have significant experience working as sex educators or in sex stores or running groups for teens in schools. Some have taken a number of courses on sexuality and gender in high school and college. However, others come to class knowing almost nothing about sexuality and with no experience in discussing sex. Some grew up in strictly religious households where sex was not discussed (especially with girls). Some came from places within the Caribbean, the Middle East, or Latin America, where cultural taboos about sex prevailed. My readers are an equally diverse audience. Some of you will be left wanting to explore topics more fully. Others will find the information a little uncomfortable to digest and may move through the book slowly, taking time to process the information. Whatever your particular level of familiarity and comfort, I hope you will find things in this book to challenge your assumptions, give you new ways to think about a topic, or additional skills to engage clients more fully in relation to sexuality.

Each chapter is designed to provide an overview of foundational content about the specific topic as well as references and resources for you to explore more deeply if you desire. In many ways the book mirrors my classroom process by first providing clear and straightforward descriptions of key concepts using theoretical frameworks and then emphasizing the application of that knowledge through case illustrations and specific examples. At the end of each chapter, a summary provides an overview of the key issues raised. Discussion questions are also provided to stimulate further dialogue and promote self-reflection. Resources offer suggestions for further investigation into particular topics. Student learning outcomes identified in the Council on Social Work Education's "2015 Educational Policy and Accreditation Standards" are highlighted at the beginning of every chapter. Some are cited only in particular chapters. For example, competency 1—to "demonstrate ethical and professional behavior"—is featured in chapter 10, which addresses sexuality and ethics. Others are universal themes, like competency 2—to "engage diversity and difference in practice"—which crops up in every chapter.

This book can help you build a framework from which to discuss sexuality in your practice. Sex positivity affirms the centrality of sexual well-being to overall well-being, including increased life satisfaction and improved relationship quality. I encourage you to fully attend to the sexual dimension of your clients, acknowledging its importance in their lives as critical context whether it is related to the presenting problem or not. The goal is to integrate a central notion of sex positivity even in situations where there has been trauma or experiences typically aligned with a deficits model (e.g., sexually transmitted infections). The sexual dimension should be an integral part of all social work practice, regardless of setting or practice method, and should be included in the initial assessment and ongoing evaluation of all clients. Ignoring the sexual dimension of our clients' lives diminishes our understanding of who they are as people.

Gender and sexuality are constantly evolving, as is the language we use to discuss them. Thus, some of the expressions, terms, and definitions used in this book may become outdated while the book is at the printer. Please give me the benefit of the doubt that my goal was to be inclusive and affirming. I hope you find *Sex-Positive Social Work* an informative and engaging addition to your social work library.

1

CREATING A SEX-POSITIVE ENVIRONMENT FOR YOUR CLIENTS

RELEVANT CSWE COMPETENCIES

Competency 1: Demonstrate Ethical and Professional Behavior
Competency 2: Engage Diversity and Difference in Practice
Competency 3: Advance Human Rights and Social, Economic, and Environmental Justice

Most social workers in the United States, like most Americans, grew up with the cultural norm that talking about sex is taboo.[1] The only place where this taboo may be broken is among a small peer group of one's closest friends. Often, major institutions—including family, school, and religion—reinforce the idea that sexuality is off-limits in conversation. This view is typically reinforced during social work education, where topics of sexuality are only rarely raised within the curriculum.[2] In fact, none of the top twenty-five schools of social work require a course in human sexuality, and almost 24 percent don't offer any human sexuality courses. And whereas 75 percent offer one or two elective courses focused on sexuality, sexual-minority populations, or at-risk groups, the majority of students can earn a master's in social work without studying any in-depth content on sexuality at all.[3]

But by being silent about sex in the social work curriculum, schools of social work are saying implicitly that there is no room for sex in practice.[4] Several decades ago, Richard Roberts pointed out that this construction of silence around sexuality in social work education is mirrored in the clinical setting.[5] Clients are asked to explore deeply personal aspects of their lives during an assessment, including their emotional status, their income, family composition, work history, and trauma history, but they are not asked about their sexual history. Thus, this "conspiracy of silence," noted in the introduction, leaves a potentially important gap in assessment and treatment.[6] The goal of this book is to fill in what the social work curriculum leaves out, giving you the tools to break the silence and integrate sexuality into your practice.

Sexuality is central to an individual's overall well-being. This chapter will discuss how to create a sex-positive environment for your clients. Creating a physical and emotional space that gives clients permission to talk about sex is crucial to developing a sex-positive practice. But the work actually begins with you. Beyond learning about issues related to sexuality, you can also develop your awareness of and comfort with your own relationship to sexuality. After all, knowing about specific sexuality issues does not guarantee your comfort with them, nor does it guarantee that you will engage with them effectively in practice.[7]

Reluctance to engage sexuality in practice may leave you with only part of the picture and may even be detrimental to treatment. For example, James is a twenty-eight-year-old single man who comes to see you about being "stressed out" at work. He feels that despite working long hours his productivity at work is decreasing; he feels isolated socially and is experiencing anxiety. During the intake, you have an opportunity to ask him about his sexual relationships but figure he is isolated socially, so there is no need to ask. Besides, you prefer not to bring up sex unless the client does so first. You are more comfortable that way, and you reason that your clients are as well. It turns out that one of James's coping mechanisms for his stress and isolation is seeking out sex through sex apps. Since you did not ask him whether he was sexually active or sexually satisfied or had any concerns related to sex, James did not feel it was safe or appropriate to raise the issue. By avoiding the topic, you missed an opportunity to get a more complete picture of James's situation and may have intensified his feelings of isolation or even shame related to his situation. Opening the door for James to raise his use of sex apps and sexual encounters to alleviate feelings of isolation might have given you both an opportunity to explore the strengths and challenges of the behavior and the ways in which it serves to enhance or detract from James's well-being.

Steven Harris and Kelli Hays found that therapists' perceived sexual knowledge did not directly increase the likelihood that they would start discussions of sexual concerns with clients.[8] Instead, knowledge had only an indirect effect on the initiation of sex-related discussion when mediated by sexual comfort. So it is not enough to have factual knowledge about sex; therapists must also be comfortable with the sexual content if they are to integrate it into therapy. Harris and Hays concluded that "therapist comfort with sexual content had the greatest influence on therapist-initiated sexuality discussions," and sexuality education and supervision had the second greatest.[9] This chapter will first make suggestions about how to become comfortable talking to clients about sex and then offer concrete steps that you can take to elevate sexuality within your practice, creating the physical and emotional space for your clients' explorations.

UNDERSTANDING YOUR RELATIONSHIP TO SEX AND SEXUALITY

There are two key steps in this process of getting comfortable talking to clients about sex: increasing your knowledge and developing your comfort with a range of sexual issues. If you are like most social workers, you grew up with either very little or perhaps inaccurate information about sexuality. If that is the case, you likely learned about the physiological maturation that occurs during adolescence, and even the mechanics of heterosexual reproductive intercourse, from your slightly flustered seventh-grade health teacher.

Past and present sex education rarely is sex-positive or considers individual agency related to pleasure—particularly for cisgendered females (those for whom gender identity and chromosomal sex are consistent).[10] And sex education often leaves out notions of desire, arousal, and attraction across a range of sexualities and gender identities, which can play out in many different kinds of relationship configurations. For example, sex education is rarely inclusive and affirming of sexual- or gender-minority students. If you did receive adequate, inclusive, and affirming training, then consider yourself in the lucky minority. If not, then this book and its supplemental resources can begin to fill in the gaps.

Your first job, then, is to learn about the wide array of topics related to sexuality. This book will cover some of these: anatomy and physiology, sexual identity, gender identity, nonmonogamous and polyamorous relationships, and BDSM (bondage and discipline, dominance and submission, and sadism and masochism) and kink. Having a basic understanding of these can help you provide a safe, nonjudgmental, welcoming space for your clients. Along with reading this book, you can review the recommended resources, explore related websites, attend relevant conferences or continuing education courses, and practice bringing up sexuality with your supervisor.

For example, we briefly cover anatomy and physiology, which may seem beyond the scope of a social work textbook. However, a surprising number of clients come to therapy with questions about their anatomy and how it compares to "the norm." Penis size is definitely often asked about, and concerns about the color and size of the breasts, nipples, or labia are often raised. Even questions about basic reproductive functions and hormones come up. Being familiar with the body parts and comfortable saying their anatomical names is an important responsibility.[11] You can model this for your clients, who can then take their questions and concerns to their medical provider. As their social worker, you can provide basic information and even look up information on the web with your client (see the discussion of the permission, limited information, specific suggestions, and intensive therapy model in chapter 6) so your client isn't overwhelmed and doesn't end up down a rabbit hole of ads for penile implants and vaginal reconstruction. Then, if necessary, you can role-play with your client so that they feel comfortable raising their concerns with their doctor.

DEVELOPING YOUR COMFORT DISCUSSING SEX

Learning is only part of the equation: to practice effectively you must also develop a comfort with sexual issues. Harris and Hays suggest that Murray Bowen's concepts of anxiety and reactivity are helpful in understanding the role of comfort around discussing issues of sex with clients. They suggest that therapists often perceive their client's anxiety about discussing sex and avoid the topic to relieve that anxiety. Harris and Hays propose that a client who is anxious about sex needs a therapist who is not anxious about initiating conversations on sexual issues that need attention.[12]

Conversely, clients are often in tune with our anxiety and may avoid addressing sexuality with us if they perceive our discomfort. Therefore, it is a fundamental need of social workers to develop comfort with these topics if we are to pass along that comfort to clients. As you delve deeper into the field of sexuality, pay attention to your relationship to the content and try to get in tune with what Justin Sitron and Donald Dyson call your sexological worldview.[13] That is, understand your perspective on sexuality as an individual and a professional.

Sitron and Dyson expanded on Francoeur's notion of a sexuality worldview, which focused on an individual's experiences of and perspective on sexuality.[14] The sexological worldview not only takes into account individual experiences but also adds the professional perspective. Sitron and Dyson's definition evolved in consultation with sixteen experienced sexologists. Perhaps the most important (and, interestingly, least contested) part of their definition is the notion that we do not explore our sexological worldview in the same way that we may scrutinize our other worldviews, like the religious or political ones. The definition begins: "Sexological worldview is the often unexamined but changeable perspective held by each person about the world around them with regards to sexuality."[15] This notion that we do not scrutinize our sexological worldview is not unique to social workers. In fact, the authors found in interviews with thirty sexologists, graduate students of sexology, and new sexology students that one-third could not describe their perspective.[16]

Consistent with the *Code of Ethics* of the National Association of Social Workers and the imperative to practice without judgment, it's important to understand your attitudes and values toward sexuality so that you can recognize and avoid your own biases. Self-reflection is a critical aspect of the therapeutic process and an important part of your professional development process. Given cultural taboos about sex, reflection about sexuality is particularly important. Do some topics feel more familiar to you than others? Are there topics that make you feel particularly uncomfortable? For example, in one study a small proportion (5.5 percent) of social work students reported that they were homophobic—indicating a strong need for them to reflect on their personal and professional values.[17] Pay attention to your relationship to sexuality and the information that you are studying. How does it make you feel? Are there certain topics that you avoid more than others? Are you especially uncomfortable when masturbation is covered, infidelity is broached, sex trade is revealed, or sexuality in older adults is raised? Similarly, pay attention to areas that you are more comfortable with so you can develop a clearer sense of your strengths and areas of potential growth. For example, how do you feel when you find yourself working with someone who identifies as bisexual? Or someone who has rape fantasies, erectile dysfunction, or vaginismus? Or someone who has never had an orgasm, is considering having a child independently, or has a child who identifies as gender creative? Certainly, if there is a situation where you feel that you cannot be nonjudgmental or a client that you are unequipped to deal with, then you should refer the client to someone who can provide appropriate treatment (as we will discuss in chapter 10, on ethics). However, if the problem is simply unfamiliarity or discomfort, then that is a signal that you should learn more about a particular area to serve your clients more effectively.

You can also gauge your willingness to engage with the sexuality issues raised by your clients. If a client mentions that they do not feel as connected to their husband as they had been, do you avoid asking questions about their sexual connection? If your clients raise other topics that have a sexual undertone, do you change the subject and hope it doesn't come up again? Pay attention to your inner dialogue and press through the initial discomfort. Asking follow-up questions permits your clients to delve deeper into their sexual concerns. And even if they do not choose to do so at that moment, you have clearly conveyed permission for them to open the door for a deeper conversation about sexuality in the future.

PRACTICE, PRACTICE, PRACTICE

Once you have strengthened your knowledge foundation and challenged yourself to create an open and nonassuming stance, the next important step in becoming comfortable is through practice. Through practice you will become comfortable asking questions about sex or body parts or hearing complicated and sexually explicit material using appropriate language. Develop your comfort, extending rather than diverting conversations with a sexual undertone so that you can uncover the underlying issue.

There are many ways to strengthen your skills in discussing sex with clients, including watching videos of sexual intakes. Watching videos that purposefully highlight problems can allow you to critique the examples and compare your style with those of other social workers. It can be informative to evaluate the qualities that seem less helpful or are ineffective and even off-putting or damaging in some way. Looking beyond the phrasing of questions, pay attention to body language, posture, tone, and intonation to see how they affect the exchange. Here is an example of two different ways to interview a client about their sexuality.

During an intake, after conversations about the presenting problem and some background characteristics, a social worker ("SW") began to ask a few sex-related questions:

SW: Now we are at the sex part of the form—do you like sex?
Maria: Er . . . yes.
SW: Don't we all! Do you have a boyfriend?
Maria: No.

SW: Who do you have sex with then?

Maria: Um . . .

SW: Well, do you have sex or not? Because if you don't, we can skip these questions.

Maria: I don't.

SW: Oh good. We can move on.

In this example, the social worker felt uncomfortable engaging Maria in a conversation about sex, made awkward and inappropriate statements, and was eager to be let off the hook and move past sex and on to other questions. It is unlikely that Maria would feel comfortable in the near future raising issues related to sex with this social worker.

Just as we can learn from bad examples, it is also helpful to watch positive examples to evaluate good techniques and effective rapport. You can then adopt and adapt the positive aspects of the examples into your own practice. Watching TED talks or interviews with well-known experts like Suzanne Iasenza, Esther Perel, and Tristan Taormino can also provide helpful models for effective and comfortable communication regarding sex.

For example, in the same situation, the social worker and Maria might have had this exchange:

SW: Now I am going to ask you some questions about your sexual health. Are you currently sexually active?

Maria: Yes.

SW: Is your sexual activity interactive (with a partner or partners) or solo?

Maria: Interactive and solo.

SW: Tell me a little bit about your current sexual relationships.

Maria: I broke up with my boyfriend about six months ago and haven't been seeing anyone regularly since then.

SW: You aren't in a specific "relationship" right now, but are there people that you are sexual with?

Maria: Yes. I have a good friend that I have known since high school, and he and I hook up sometimes for fun.

SW: How regularly do you hook up?

Maria: A couple of times a month.

SW: Do you have other people that you are sexual with?

Maria: I hook up with people occasionally if I am out or online once in a while, but nothing much.

SW: Do you have any issues or concerns related to sex with your friend or anyone else that you want to address in our work together?

Maria: No, I don't think so.

SW: OK. Well, if you think of something that you want to discuss, let me know. I wonder—when you are sexual, are there ways that you protect your sexual health?

Maria: Er, yeah.

SW: Such as?

Maria: Well, I mostly get the guys to wear a condom.

SW: OK. Anything else?

Maria: Sometimes I ask if they've been tested.

SW: OK. Do you ever worry about your sexual health?

Maria: Sort of.

SW: We can talk about that more, if you'd like.

In this example, the social worker adopted a curious stance, did not make assumptions about sexual partners or behaviors, asked direct questions, and left the door open for future conversations. Look out for these features when you watch some examples and then begin to develop your own confidence by practicing in a nonthreatening setting. Role-play an intake that includes questions about sexual relationships and sexual health so you can try out different language, different phrasing, and different question orders to see what feels most natural. Obviously, the appropriateness of language and questioning may vary depending on the client and your relationship with them, but practicing different types of interactions can be helpful. Alternatively, you can volunteer to be the client while a colleague role-plays being the social worker and asks sexual-health questions. Taking on the role of client can give you different insights than those you get when you are role-playing the therapist.

You may also get real world opportunities to practice. For example, when you are the client, you can pay attention to whether health and mental-health care providers make it comfortable or uncomfortable for you to ask sexuality related questions. From this you can try to determine what is helpful and unhelpful in the interactions. Additionally, raising client issues around sexuality in both individual and group supervision gives you an opportunity to get support for your work, unpack your countertransference, practice finding the right language, and understand how your own lens on sexuality influences your work (see chapter 10 for a discussion on supervision as well as countertransference).

Some example role-play topics are:

- A twenty-four-year-old cisgender female who is reluctant to have sex with her boyfriend of three years.
- A lesbian couple who are having different levels of sexual desire following the birth of their second child. They previously had a strong sexual connection and very compatible levels of desire.
- A fifty-six-year-old cisgender male who is struggling with the decrease in his libido since turning fifty.
- A heterosexual couple who are having difficulty communicating clearly with each other about their sexual desires, fantasies, and fetishes. As a result, both feel a great deal of intimate connection but are dissatisfied with their sexual connection.

CREATING A SEX-POSITIVE PHYSICAL SPACE

While developing your own sense of comfort and ease talking about sexuality with clients and creating a sex-positive foundation for practice, you can also pay attention to the physical space in which you practice. Check your space for both the explicit and implicit messages that it sends to clients.

When clients visit your office or your agency, they take in the environment and decor. They pay attention to how they feel, and they learn from the space and how it is maintained. Your messaging is important. Are things well kept or shabby? Is the paint new or chipping? What does this say about

FIGURE 1.1 A welcoming sex-positive space

Source: SJ Dodd

the clients' value and of the well-being of the organization? What is the age, gender identity, race, ethnicity, language of origin, and sexual identity of the people who work there? Are the people welcoming and open or hurried and brusque? Do clients see themselves and their relationships represented in the pictures on the wall or the magazines in the rack? It is important that the physical decor reflect a range of diversity. Clients will notice whether they feel welcome.

I always recommend that my students have at least one book that says "sex" or "sexuality" in large letters on the spine, placed so that it is easily visible to their clients—preferably on a shelf above the student's right or left shoulder (see figure 1.1). In this way you use visual cues to communicate that sex is something open for discussion, you are comfortable with it, and it is not off limits. Use books, magazines, posters, postcards, and buttons to create a sex-positive physical space that lets your clients know they are welcome and have your permission to discuss sexuality. Including books related to sexuality or LGBTQ (lesbian, gay, bisexual, transgender, and queer/questioning) issues on your bookshelves or similar magazines in waiting areas is an important way to nonverbally communicate sex positivity to clients.

SEX-POSITIVE INTAKE FORMS
AND PROCEDURES

Once clients have noticed how they feel about the pictures on the wall and the magazines on the table, they will turn their attention to the intake forms and the questions they ask—and clients will note the messages implied here, too. They will notice, for example, how demographic questions are phrased, such as those on race, ethnicity, gender identity, and sexual orientation. They will notice whether they feel represented by the categories provided and if there is room for them to define themselves. They will also notice whether you include questions about sexual history, relationships, body image, sexual identity, and gender-identity concerns. If a long list of topics excludes sexual health issues, it implies that sexuality cannot or should not be discussed.[18] An adolescent with concerns about relationships, sexual health, or sexually transmitted infections may feel unable or reluctant to raise their concerns with you because they see no signals that they can do so. Similarly, an older adult who feels unsure about how to navigate the dating scene after the death of their husband may focus on discussing feelings of isolation rather than nervousness about dating or the physical part of potential new relationships. For this reason, make sure that questions related to sexual health appear on initial assessment forms, along with websites that describe your services.

Some sex-positive examples are included in boxes 1.1, 1.2, and 1.3. Box 1.1 provides examples of sex-positive and inclusive demographic questions related to gender and sexuality in a close-ended format. Box 1.2 includes those demographic questions in an open-ended format. The questions are based on recommendations made by the Joint Commission and the Williams Institute.[19] Both organizations recommend a two-part gender-identity question that asks first about sex assigned at birth and then about current gender identity. The organizations also provide examples of a one-step question regarding transgender identity. Both options are included here for your review. Box 1.3 gives examples of ways to incorporate questions related to sexual health questions into the intake form.

Box 1.1

EXAMPLES OF CLOSE-ENDED DEMOGRAPHIC QUESTIONS

Gender Identity (Two-Part Question)

How do you identify your gender (check all that apply)?

Male

Female

Androgynous

Gender expansive

Gender nonbinary

Gender nonconforming

Gender queer

Transgender male

Transgender female

Transgender, do not identify as male or female

Two-spirit

Other noncisgender identity (please specify)

What sex were you assigned at birth?

Male

Female

Both

Neither

Transgender Identity One-Item Question, Including a Definition

Some people describe themselves as transgender, gender nonconforming, nonbinary, or gender expansive (as well as other descriptors) when they experience a different gender identity from their assigned sex at birth: for example, a person born with a penis who feels female

Box 1.1 (*continued*)

and lives as a woman or a person born with a vagina who feels neither male nor female.

How do you experience your gender?
Do you consider yourself transgender? Yes/No
If yes, how do you describe your gender?

Sexual Identity

How would you describe your sexual identity (check all that apply)?
    Straight (heterosexual)
    Gay
    Lesbian
    Queer
    Bisexual
    Pansexual
    Asexual
    Demisexual
    Omnisexual
    Other sexual identity (please specify)

Sexual Behavior

In the past six months, with whom have you had sex (check all that apply)?
    People who identify as:
        Male
        Female
        Androgynous
        Gender expansive

Gender nonbinary

Gender nonconforming

Gender queer

Transgender male

Transgender female

Transgender, do not identify as male or female

Two-spirit

Other noncisgender identity (please specify)

Not applicable—do not engage in sexual behavior

Other not identified here (please specify)

Box 1.2

**EXAMPLES OF OPEN-ENDED SEX-POSITIVE
DEMOGRAPHIC QUESTIONS**

What name do you use?

Which pronoun do you use (e.g., he/she/they/ze/fe)?

How do you define your gender identity?

How do you define your sexual identity?

Are you currently sexually active?

If yes, what is/are the gender identity(ies) of the people with whom
you have sex?

If no, have you ever been sexually active?

If yes, what is/are the gender identity(ies) of the people with whom
you have had sex?

What is your age?

Box 1.3

**EXAMPLES OF SEX-POSITIVE QUESTIONS
RELATED TO SEXUAL HEALTH**

Are you currently sexually active?

Do you have any sexual partners?

How many sexual partners do you have?

Are you currently sexually satisfied?

What is the gender identity and sexual identity of your partner(s)?

How would you describe this/these relationship(s)?

What is the level of commitment in those relationships?

Is/are your relationship(s) monogamous?

How long have you been sexually involved with this person or these
people?

How would you describe your sexual history?

Describe your most influential sexual relationship.

Note: It is anticipated that you would use a few of these questions at once.
These questions are not designed to be asked all together; rather, they offer
a range of suggestions.

ADDING THE SEXUAL DIMENSION
TO THE BIOPSYCHOSOCIAL

After the initial intake form—which should provide an open, sex-positive
opportunity for clients to define their race, gender, and sexual identity—
the next phase of assessment, the biopsychosocial, should be comprehensive when considering the sexual dimension. The biopsychosocial assessment is a defining characteristic of social work practice as it takes a holistic
look at the client's experience, including biological, psychological, and
social characteristics. Biological considerations include physiological and
genetic factors that may be influencing a client's situation, such as an underlying medical condition like diabetes or a current acute issue like a respira-

tory infection. Psychological factors to be explored include mental health issues, mood disorders, and attachment concerns, such as depression or schizophrenia. And though some mental health professionals stop after the biopsycho portion of the assessment, social workers see the social factors influencing a client's situations as fundamentally important as well. Social factors include cultural, socioeconomic, or community influences that may be relevant, such as the demands of extreme poverty, the stressors of feeling unsafe at home, or expectations of marrying within a certain religion. Adding questions about sexuality to the biopsychosocial(sexual) assessment allows for an even more comprehensive assessment of the client's situation.[20] There are several dimensions to sexuality that are relevant to sexual health and well-being, which in turn affect overall health and well-being and should be considered for inclusion in the assessment.[21] This is true not just in adults but also in adolescents, and particularly in older adults, people with acute or chronic health conditions, and people with disabilities.[22] In fact, as we will discuss in chapter 6, several sexually transmitted infections are rapidly spreading in the older adult population.[23] Therefore, it is critical that you put aside assumptions about who is sexually active (and with whom) and who is not and start to routinely ask a battery of questions related to sexuality that will help you develop a fuller biopsychosocial assessment.

Perhaps you are reluctant to discuss issues of sexuality with a client because talking about sex is culturally inappropriate, or you believe that raising the topic of sex with a client, especially someone who is your elder, is disrespectful. Often, addressing these concerns directly with a client can lead to surprisingly rich conversations (see chapter 3, related to taking a sexual history).

Asking close-ended questions or questions that assume information, such as the gender of the partner under discussion or the number of partners involved, can shut a client down. For example, a common mistake is to assume that a cis-female talking about her sexual relationship with a cis-male identifies as heterosexual. It is better to maintain a curious stance and ask questions that give clients room to describe and create their own narrative. When a client says they identify as queer or are sexually adventurous, asexual, or submissive, do not assume you know what each of these things mean. Instead, ask what that concept means to your client. By giving the client room to describe their own experience without jumping in to overlay your understanding of their experience, you convey openness and give permission for wider exploration. Including questions related to sexuality within the biopsychosocial will simultaneously send the sex-positive message to your clients that sex is an important dimension of their overall selves that needs attention and nurturing in the pursuit of general health.

CHAPTER SUMMARY

This chapter acknowledged that social workers are socialized into the same cultural norms and taboos surrounding sexuality as the general population. Thus, social workers are often uncomfortable with topics related to sexuality and avoid them with their clients. To combat the sex-negative education and socialization process, this chapter asserted that the underlying foundation for creating a sex-positive space begins with you and your knowledge of and comfort with sexuality. Learning and in some cases unlearning, disrupting, or deconstructing myths or beliefs about sexuality learned in childhood are steps in the process of becoming a sex-positive social worker.

This chapter focused on the importance of creating a sex-positive environment for your clients that honors sexuality as a critical aspect of the biopsychosocial assessment. It encouraged you to pay attention to the explicit and implicit messages that you communicate to your clients—from the art on the walls of your office to the questions on your forms—and especially to the questions you ask clients directly. By attending to what is included and what is excluded, we can recognize the fact that silence about sexual issues on forms or during intake and assessment perpetuates the belief that talking about sex is taboo.[24] Sexuality is a dynamic phenomenon as our language, beliefs, and common practices are constantly evolving—which means that our learning journey is ongoing. Enjoy the ride!

DISCUSSION QUESTIONS

1. How did you first learn about sex?
2. What were the dominant cultural influences on your sexuality?
3. What positive or negative messaging did you receive about sex?
4. Were there gendered differences between the messaging you received and that received by other members of your household, living space, or community?
5. Think back on your own past experiences with health or mental health care providers. What messaging did you receive from the way their offices looked or how their forms were worded?

RESOURCES

Planned Parenthood: www.plannedparenthood.org
SIECUS: Sex Ed for Social Change: www.siecus.org
Silberman Center for Sexuality and Gender: www.SilbermanSCSG.com

2

ANATOMY, PHYSIOLOGY, AND AROUSAL

RELEVANT CSWE COMPETENCIES

Competency 2: Engage Diversity and Difference in Practice

Competency 3: Advance Human Rights and Social, Economic, and Environmental Justice

Competency 8: Intervene with Individuals, Families, Groups, Organizations, and Communities

THE SOCIAL WORKER'S ROLE AS AN EDUCATOR

You may be wondering why there is a chapter on anatomy and physiology in a social work textbook. This is not a biology class, and medical school is not in your plans. However, a significant role of the social worker is to be an educator. As we discussed in chapter 1, most people have not had a comprehensive education about sex.[1] They have usually had only a cursory review of the reproductive organs with a heavy emphasis on menstruation, abstinence, pregnancy prevention, and possibly nocturnal emissions. Often educators make a significant effort to dissuade people from heterosexual intercourse by stressing the seemingly inevitability of sexually transmitted infections or pregnancy.

Even for those who had more education about sex, what they learned might have become a little fuzzy over time. So for most people, there are significant gaps in what they know about their own bodies, their physiological responses related to cycles of hormones, and what does and does not arouse them. The purpose of this chapter is to fill in some of those gaps and help you develop a sense of what you do not know so that you may follow up with additional resources if necessary. Specifically, the chapter provides foundational information on sexual anatomy, physiology, and arousal. It also describes reproductive characteristics and addresses some of the myths that clients might believe about their bodies. Finally, it recognizes the limits of our knowledge and stresses the importance of referring clients to physicians for medical consultation or testing when appropriate.

A SPECIAL NOTE ABOUT THE USE OF "MALE" AND "FEMALE"

Please note that in places this chapter refers to the "male reproductive system" and "female reproductive system," as well as to "men" and "women," as a reflection of the way in which medical information is disseminated. However, it is important to remember that all people with penises are not male or men, and that all people with vaginas are not female or women. This is true for people with a range of gender identities and people who are intersex. Please keep this in mind when reading the chapter. Avoid assumptions and generalizations in practice as well.

UNDERSTANDING ENOUGH TO DISPEL MYTHS

Given poor sexuality education and a lack of accurate information, many clients have questions related to whether their anatomical or physiological experience is "typical."[2] In fact, when writing about the clitoris, Lisa Jean Moore recalled the two most frequent questions she encountered while working on a national sex information switchboard were "What is the normal size of a penis?" and "Where is the clitoris?"[3]

Media influences and social norms have set up a situation in which we teach people to be self-conscious about their appearance from a young age.[4] You can't be too tall or too short, or too fat or too thin, and your nose or ears can't be too big or too small. While girls seem to be affected more than boys, both adolescent girls and boys struggle with body image issues and eating disorders.[5] This struggle, explained by Amy Slater and Marika Tiggemann through "objectification theory," seems to be universal and occurs across racial and ethnic groups.[6] It makes sense then that anxiety and body self-consciousness often present themselves in practice. In fact, Pepper Schwartz and Martha Kempner devote the first section of *50 Great Myths of Human Sexuality* to "body parts" for just this reason.[7]

When clients present with body-image or sexual-organ anxiety, the social worker's role can be to provide information and offer reassurance, as well as to refer the client to a medical practitioner when appropriate. General anatomical and physiological information represents an average that actually applies to hardly anyone. Therefore, it is possible to help clients to understand that the information is a very rough guide and that the range of "typical" is very broad.

For example, Shirley is a forty-three-year-old, cisgender, African American woman who has been with her husband since she was twenty-two. Shirley comes to you because her two kids are both in college, and she is worried that she and her husband are drifting apart without the kids to focus on. During your third session, you ask Shirley about her and her husband's sexual relationship to see how it has changed over time. Shirley shares that they have always had a somewhat limited sexual relationship. She was raised to be modest about her body and has been uncomfortable with nudity. After some exploration of her discomfort with her body, Shirley reveals that she has always been reluctant for her husband to see her naked, especially her bare chest, because she is self-conscious about her "unusually large" nipples. Shirley looks at you and asks, "How big should nipples be?" You take the opportunity to talk to Shirley about the many different body types and the wide variety in nipple size, sensitivity, and coloring. You begin to explore how Shirley's relationship with her body, her discomfort with nudity, and her self-consciousness about her nipples may be preventing her and her husband from experiencing physical, and possibly emotional, intimacy.

Shirley's situation reflects a cultural preoccupation with physical perfection, which has given rise to a multi-million-dollar industry. Proliferating advertisements offer surgeries to make one look younger and thinner or have bigger or smaller breasts. This notion of physical perfection is exemplified in genital modification (for both men and women) and vaginal-rejuvenation surgeries, or what Virginia Braun and Leonore Tiefer call the "designer vagina."[8] In fact, labioplasty (making the labia, smaller, plumper, or more symmetrical), breast implants or reductions, and penis circumcisions collectively constitute a big business.[9] As a social worker, you must possess a basic understanding of real-life physiology and be able to access additional information or provide appropriate medical referrals for your clients. You also need to navigate the binary nature of the anatomical and physiological information available. Until you have accurate information relevant to your client, use nongendered inclusive language such as "people with penises" or "people with vaginas," so that men who have vaginas, women who have penises, and people who identify as gender nonbinary, gender queer, or neither male nor female will feel included and comfortable.

REPRODUCTIVE CHARACTERISTICS WITH A VAGINA

In the United States both public and private nudity are "culturally regulated."[10] With a few exceptions, all people—especially adults—are typically expected to cover their genitals. There is a wide variation in comfort with and knowledge of genitalia. Physically, people with penises have greater access to their genitals than people with vaginas and therefore tend to have greater familiarity. Breasts are easily accessible, but you have to take steps

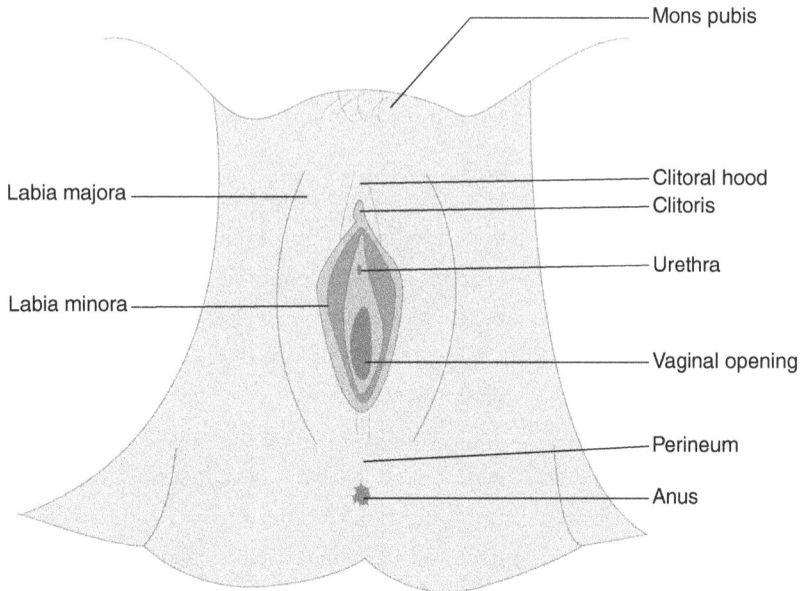

FIGURE 2.1 External reproductive organs with a vagina

to visually explore a vulva. Therefore, many people are unfamiliar with the shape, form, and function of their vulva. They may also be uncertain about the location or existence of the clitoris or G-spot (see later in this chapter for descriptions). Social workers can encourage their clients to become familiar with their genitals so that they can appreciate their structure, better understand their functioning, and monitor them for changes that may signal health problems.

Figures 2.1 and 2.2 are typical representations of the external and internal reproductive organs. The external structures include the mons, mons pubis, or mons veneris (literally, the mound of Venus), which is the fatty mound covering the pubic bone that houses some nerve endings and can be sensitive to touch or pressure (pubic hair develops on the mons during puberty); urethral opening; labia majora (larger outer lips); labia minora (smaller inner lips); prepuce or clitoral hood; clitoris (about the size of a pearl, under the clitoral hood); vaginal opening (or introitus); perineum, which sits between the vaginal opening and the anal opening (or anus). To-

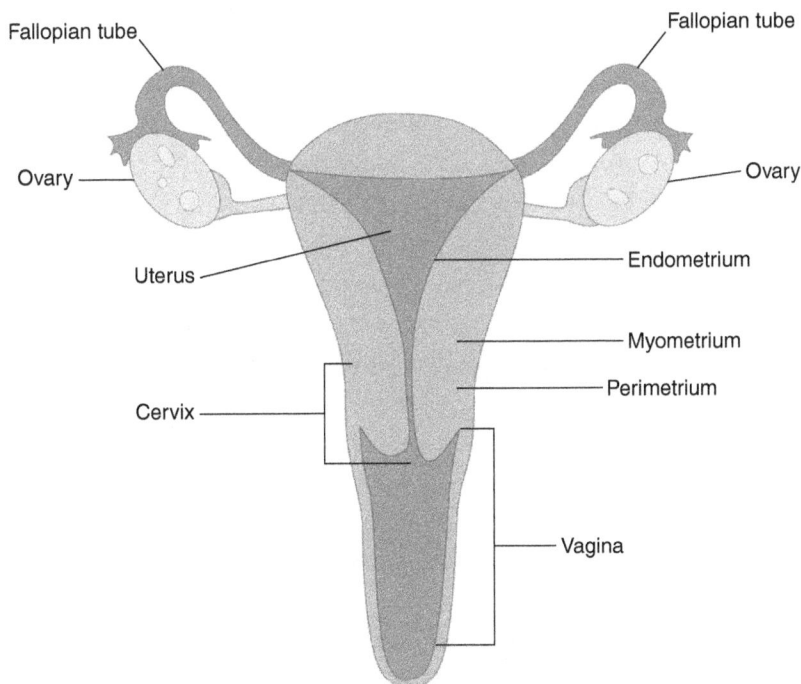

FIGURE 2.2 Internal reproductive organs with a vagina

gether the mons, labia, clitoris, clitoral hood, and urethra are called the vulva. It is not uncommon for people to call the vulva the vagina, but "vagina" refers solely to the internal structure.

The internal structures include two ovaries (one on each side), which produce and release eggs; two fallopian tubes (also one on each side), which carry the egg to the uterus (or womb); the uterus, where a fertilized egg embeds itself and grows; the lining of the uterus, which has layers of membranes like the endometrium, myometrium, and perimetrium; and the cervix.; At the back of the vagina is the tip of the uterus. Sperm travels from the vagina through a small hole in the center of the cervix (called the os) into the uterus. In addition, the Grafenberg, or G-spot, is a spongy mass on the front of the vagina; and the hymen is a thin layer of skin across part of the vagina. Symbolically, the hymen was thought to represent virginity, but it may break for a number of reasons, such as horseback riding or other vigorous exercise. The hymen may also be quite thick and may even require surgery to break it.

There are three typical types of hymen: the annular hymen surrounds the vaginal opening; the septate hymen stretches across the vaginal opening and has a gap on each side, like a bridge; and the cribriform hymen has holes in it, creating a sieve-like appearance.[11] Many cultures place great emphasis on virginity at marriage, and an intact hymen is often used as a marker of virginity, signaling that the vagina has never been penetrated. An intact hymen is so important that some women, especially in Japan and the Middle East, have had their hymens reconstructed (hymenalplasty) to disguise the fact that they have engaged in premarital sexual activity.[12] It is important for social workers to be aware of the range of different cultural traditions related to sex and sexuality and to be open and inquisitive when working with clients.

One clear sign that Western culture has focused sex education on reproduction, not pleasure, is that the clitoris—the only sexual organ with a function purely related to pleasure—was omitted from most anatomy diagrams until the 1980s. In "Polishing the Pearl: Discoveries of the Clitoris," Moore traced the cultural history of the clitoris, including its explication by Realdo Colombo in 1559, its removal via the controversial practice of female circumcision (or clitorectomy), its dismissal as a "purposeless" and inferior penis, and its elevation as the center of female pleasure.[13] While the famed sex researcher Alfred Kinsey (discussed in chapter 4) acknowledged the clitoris to be the focus of female sexual pleasure and orgasm, he and his team omitted it from diagrams because of the social and political constraints in the 1950s that defined sex, sexuality, and pleasure through a very male-centric lens.[14] In fact, Moore concluded her essay by acknowledging that "based on who is defining the *clitoris*, it can be classified as an inverted and diminutive penis, a small erectile sex organ of the female, a love button, an unhygienic appendage to be removed, a site of immature sexual expression, a key piece of evidence of sexual perversions, or a vibrant subject of pornographic mediations."[15]

Scientists have discovered there is more to the clitoris than originally thought. It was once considered to be a small collection of nerve endings that sat under the clitoral hood. We now know that the clitoris has more nerve endings than the glans of the penis. Like the penis, the clitoris has two corpora cavernosa and one corpus spongiosum about an inch long, all of which fill with blood when aroused, creating a type of erection. In addition, the crura are two three-inch internal extensions of the clitoris, which run down and backward away from the clitoral shaft, creating a wishbone structure. There is tremendous variation in the physical anatomy of the clitoris, which means that different people prefer different types of stimulation during sex—some more direct, others more indirect. As Jerrold Greenberg, Clint Bruess, and Sara Oswalt point out, there are potentially both positive and negative consequences of having partners who know about the clitoris: "Those who carefully and delicately stimulate the clitoris may sexually arouse their partner; but those who rub incessantly will only irritate the clitoris and thereby irritate their partners."[16] Ideally, people with a clitoris can communicate to their partners what type of touch they prefer. Besides knowing basic anatomical information, it is important for social workers to identify and correct the omission of the clitoris from diagrams and information, since omitting it mirrors the invisibility of pleasure in sex education—especially education provided to adolescents.

There are also fads and trends that have centered around genitalia, many started by Hollywood celebrities. Genital piercings have become popular, especially piercing the clitoral hood, which some proponents argue increases stimulation and pleasure during sex. Some people "vajazzle," adding sequins, crystals, and sparkly jewels to the vulva. Hair removal trends are also popularized by the media, movies, and pornography. According to a study from 2010, only 12 percent of college-aged women (ages 18–24) did not remove any pubic hair. Fifty-nine percent removed all the hair, while the remaining 29 percent removed some hair. Women in their forties were less likely to remove their public hair, with 50 percent choosing partial hair removal and 28 percent removing no hair.[17] It is important for social workers to know about current trends in genital adornment and surgery to connect clients to resources that explain the possible beneficial and harmful side effects. It is also important to create a safe and judgment-free space where clients can explore their decisions about such practices without feeling that the social worker has an agenda.

Let's consider Jennifer, a twenty-one-year-old Latinx college student from San Francisco who is studying queer theory. She comes to see you in the aftermath of an eighteen-month relationship that ended painfully. During one session, Jennifer wonders if her physical attractiveness was a reason for the relationship's failure. She laughs and articulates her struggle between wanting to live according to strong feminist values by rebuffing the social norms around feminine grooming habits and wanting to conform and manage her physical appearance to be "attractive." She realizes that she has internalized cultural norms about body hair—especially leg, armpit, and pubic hair—but hates the fact that she cares how she is perceived. As a sex-positive social worker, you can provide a space for her to hold both of these truths at the same time: that she has strong feminist values and that she was socialized in a strongly patriarchal culture, where she has been bombarded with messages about how she should look. Creating a space for Jennifer's internal dialogue is a positive first step. Helping her realize that most choices that she makes now are not permanent may leave room for her feelings and habits to change. By shifting the focus from external pressures and redirecting her thinking toward her own feelings of sexual satisfaction and well-being, you can start to focus the conversation on exploring what makes her feel sexually confident and satisfied.

Jennifer's example indicates that social pressures related to sexuality may emerge in a number of different ways. For example, from a social justice perspective, social workers must be aware of the religious and cultural practices of female circumcision and genital cutting, which can have critical implications for sexual health and agency. It is estimated that 80–120 million women worldwide, predominantly in Africa and the Middle East, experience some kind of genital mutilation or circumcision.[18] Genital mutilation has been illegal in the United States since 1996, but it is still practiced illicitly in certain circumstances for religious or cultural reasons. And clients who were born or lived in other countries may have witnessed or experienced the practice firsthand. Female circumcision and female genital-mutilation practices are often performed by people with no medical training or in facilities that are not sterile, and complications can arise that create serious health concerns and even death.[19]

Earlier we discussed how it's more difficult for people with vaginas than people with penises to view and explore their genitals. But this lack of personal knowledge runs deeper and is affected by the overall secrecy and shame about female genitals in Western society. The stigma has had adverse effects. One of the sections in Schwartz and Kempner's book about sexual myths is titled "Vaginas Are Dirty, Ugly, and Smell Bad," which represents another common concern raised in therapy.[20] Vaginas are quite sensitive environments that must maintain a particular, slightly acidic pH level (3.5–4.5) to maintain optimum health. At this pH level the right balance of good bacteria (lactobacilli) can survive. Schwartz and Kempner highlight the taboos associated with sexuality described in chapter 1, noting the use of euphemisms when discussing the vagina and the need to address the "embarrassing odors and the need for special products to take care of 'down there.'" They also make the very good point that "the myth that women's genitals need special attention and products in order not to smell bad is truly problematic. . . . It has perpetuated a cultural perspective that female genitals are something to fix and hide which has psychological implications for women as well."[21] Social workers can encourage their clients to pay attention to the smell of the vulva and vagina, because any change in smell may indicate an infection. Similarly, clients should pay attention to vaginal discharge and become familiar with the arc of discharge through the menstrual cycle, so they can recognize changes in their typical patterns. As we will discuss in the section on arousal, many people find the smell of the vulva to be arousing. However, many women still buy into the myth that the vagina is dirty.

While there is variation based on age, race, and ethnicity, research has found that 79.4 percent of women of college age have used a douching product, and many do so regularly.[22] Women whose mothers or trusted female relatives introduced them to douching were more likely to douche themselves and so were African American and older women.[23] The younger generation and women whose doctors have alerted them to the dangers of douching tend not to douche.[24] Cultural norms around cleanliness are so strong that women continue douching even when they know that they risk decreased fertility or increased risk for a multitude of infections and

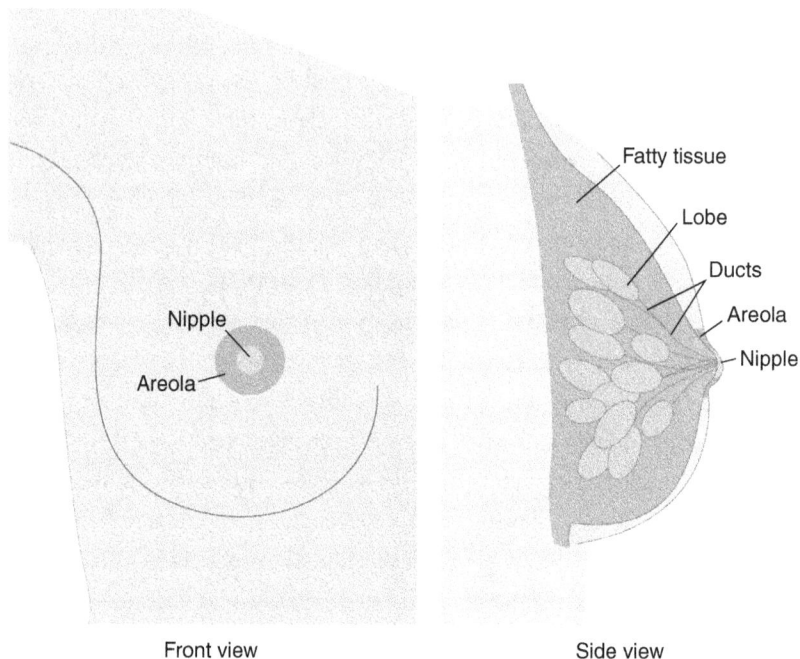

Fatty tissue

Lobe

Ducts

Areola

Nipple

Nipple

Areola

Front view

Side view

FIGURE 2.3 A breast

diseases—including those as serious as HIV and cervical cancer.[25] Yet douching remains a multi-million-dollar industry. Social workers can empower their clients to embrace themselves as they are and to be wary of the potential health effects of douching.

The breasts are secondary sex characteristics that develop during puberty (figure 2.3). Breasts are composed of fatty tissue and mammary glands and vary dramatically in size and appearance. The breast contains 12–20 sections called lobes. These lobes are themselves made up of many smaller lobules, which are the glands that produce milk for nursing. It is these mammary glands and not the fatty tissue that produces breast milk, so breasts tend to produce about the same amount of milk regardless of size. On the outside in the center of the breast is the areola, a darker area of oil-producing glands that keep the nipple lubricated during breast-feeding. The nipple sits in the middle of the areola. The muscles beneath the areola contract and make the nipples erect when they are aroused or cold. As with the genitals, some people become aroused when their breasts or nipples are stimulated, and others do not. As we saw with the example of Shirley, to help clients, a social worker should understand that there is a great variety of breast and nipple shapes, colors, and sizes. Some breasts point up while others point down, and some are firm and dense while others are softer. Social workers can encourage clients not only to embrace the uniqueness of their own breasts but also to regularly examine their own breasts or have their partners do so to maintain optimal sexual health and facilitate the early detection of health problems.[26]

Social workers may encounter clients who are experiencing not only anatomical concerns but also a range of reproductive health issues at various points in their lives. Fertility and infertility issues can cause significant distress and are commonly presented in practice. For example, it is not uncommon for clients to seek emotional support for myriad reasons if they are unable to conceive a child easily when they want to do so. They may seek support when charting ovulation or having sex on demand while trying to conceive has turned sex into a somewhat pedestrian, mechanized imperative rather than a pleasurable expression of emotional or physical connection. Alternatively, some clients may seek advice about whether it is safe to have sex during pregnancy. Others may need help navigating decisions about birth control, such as whether to select an IUD (intrauterine device) or a birth control pill, and may wish to explore the practical, emotional, and physical pros and cons of each type. Others may explore physical or emotional changes in their relationship to sex after giving birth (especially after a vaginal birth) or after a pregnancy has been terminated. As the social worker, you can recommend that clients talk to their physician or other medical provider as appropriate. You can also provide a safe space for clients to explore their options, emotions, and relationship to sexuality—especially ways in which that relationship may have changed at a particular time.

Another key social work role related to anatomy and physiology is to normalize and explain physical and emotional changes that occur during perimenopause and menopause. Providing information about common symptoms of perimenopause (which occurs before menopause) and menopause, like hot flashes, fatigue, difficulty concentrating, and vaginal dryness, can be reassuring and informative for clients. Other physical changes may include a reduction in blood supply to the vagina, reducing its sensitivity. The nipples may become less sensitive as well. Providing clients with straightforward information about what to expect and how to understand physical changes can provide much-needed reassurance.

A sex-positive social work approach recognizes the opportunities as well as the costs of postmenopausal sex. Many women describe experiencing freer and more satisfying sex after menopause since the fear of pregnancy is removed and the focus shifts from reproduction (or concern about accidental reproduction) to pleasure and intimacy.[27] Some women try to diminish the experience of menopause and its negative symptoms through hormone replacement therapy (HRT). Your clients may come to you to explore the pros and cons of using HRT. While clients should get full information from their medical provider, you can help them sort through their feelings about taking the medication, as well as their reactions to both the benefits and the potential negative side effects, such as increased risk of breast cancer and cardiovascular disease (for a full consideration of the impact of menopause and the medical intervention options available, see chapter 6). You should also have access to the *Physicians' Desk Reference* to get some sense of potential physical and emotional side effects of these and other medications for your clients.[28] The push by pharmaceutical companies eager to profit from the medicalization of menopause seems to have lessened somewhat, but there is still much money to be made from pharmacological or surgical interventions sold to people who strive to attain impossible physical ideals.

REPRODUCTIVE CHARACTERISTICS WITH A PENIS

In contrast to reproductive organs with a vagina, reproductive organs with a penis are predominantly externally visible and easily accessible for inspection. Figure 2.4 is a typical representation of the external and internal reproductive organs with a penis. The external features include the scrotum,

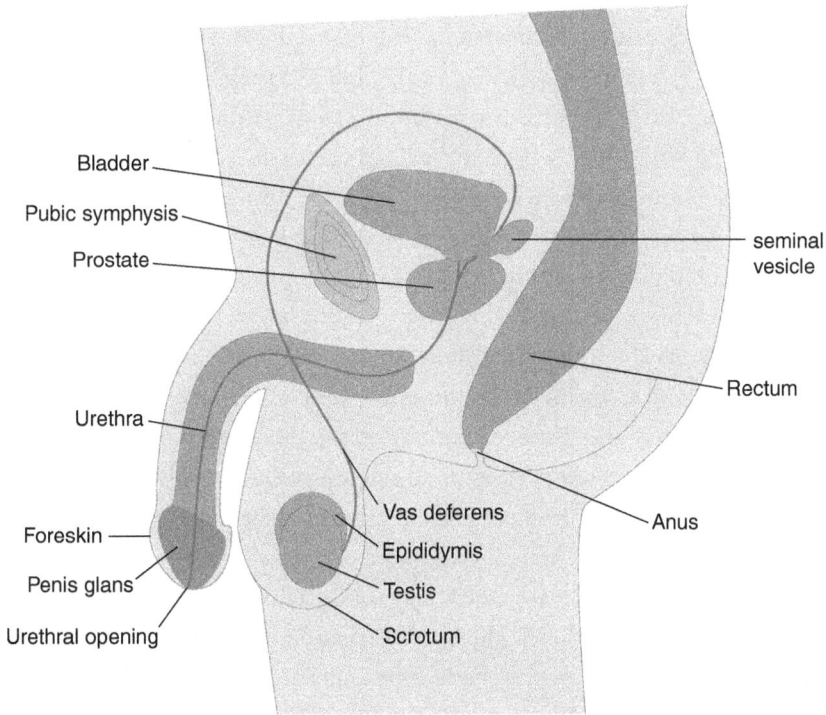

FIGURE 2.4 Internal and external reproductive organs with a penis

two sack-like pouches containing the testes (or testicles) that sit under the penis and generate semen; the shaft of the penis, which engorges when aroused; the penis glans or "head," which is at the top of the penis and is the site of a concentration of nerve endings; the prepuce or foreskin, a flap of skin that covers the head of the penis but that can be retracted easily and may be removed through surgical circumcision, often for religious reasons; the corona, a ridge on the underside of the nonerect penis at the rim of the glans; the frenulum, which connects the corona to the shaft and which is very sensitive and has a cord-like appearance; the perineum, a sensitive strip of skin between the scrotum and the anus (the opening of the rectum) that is an erogenous area to many people, regardless of sex; and the urethral opening, which sits at the very tip of the penis and is where urine and semen leaves the body.

Internal structures include the root of the penis; the urethra, which carries semen or urine; the prostate, a walnut-sized gland sitting below the bladder; the Cowper's gland, a small gland that sits below the prostate; and the seminal vesicles. Within the shaft of the penis are three cylindrical bodies that fill with blood when aroused and create the erection: one corpus spongiosum, spongy tissue along the front of the penis; and the *corpora cavernosa*, two parallel tubes. With sufficient arousal, sperm leaves the testes, travels through the epididymis and vas deferens to the urethra, and is released.

Arousal may be caused by manual, oral, or object stimulation or by sensual sensations. Cognitive thoughts with erotic or arousing content, such as fantasies, may also cause arousal. Erections also occur during the rapid eye movement part of the sleep cycle and are not necessarily the result of erotic dreams. Sometimes during an erotic dream there may be ejaculation—known as a nocturnal emission or, more colloquially, a wet dream. Wet dreams are common in teenagers and young adults, but their frequency slowly decreases over time. Much to the chagrin of adolescents, erections are involuntary (that is, they cannot be controlled). However, changing thought patterns and focusing on unarousing content may diminish erections caused by thoughts and fantasies.

In an effort to maintain a consistent temperature suitable for sperm production, which is approximately six to twelve degrees Fahrenheit cooler than the internal body temperature, when the scrotum is cool it appears to "shrink" by pulling close to the body. Conversely, when the scrotum is hot, it hangs away from the body. If the temperature in the testicles becomes too high, sperm production stops but resumes when the testicles cool back down. Semen, colloquially called cum, is alkaline to offset the acidity of the vagina. Semen is constituted of sperm produced by the testicles mixed with fluid from the seminal vesicles, the prostate, and Cowper's gland. Seminal fluid is a thick, cloudy liquid when ejaculated. Approximately fifty thousand sperm are produced per minute by typically functional testicles, and approximately three hundred million sperm are released per ejaculation.

The social emphasis on male sexuality and virility generates anxiety in a number of men, and it is not unusual for issues related to this anxiety to present in treatment.[29] As already mentioned, it is also not unusual for people to be concerned about their penis size. However, erect penises are often comparable in size, with penises that are short when flaccid gaining more length when erect than those that are longer when flaccid.[30]

Other common concerns in treatment are issues related to the prostate. Inflammation of the prostate (prostatitis) can cause lower back pain, pain during a bowel movement, and pus in the urine. Prostate cancer is a leading cause of death in men, with rates one and a half times higher in African American men than in white and Latinx men (American Cancer Society Cancer Statistics Center).[31] Symptoms of prostate cancer include a frequent need to urinate, pain or burning during urination, weak or interrupted urine flow, and lower back or pelvis pain. Testicular cancer is a much less frequent concern, with incidence rates of 5.5 per 100,000 men compared to 123.0 per 100,000 for prostate cancer, but it can cause significant distress. Just as clients can learn to examine their own breasts, clients can learn to examine their own testicles to screen for lumps, bumps, or other irregularities. Instructions are available through the Testicular Cancer Society or the Testicular Cancer Awareness Foundation.[32] Clients should regularly receive prostate exams as part of their overall positive sexual health habits. Quickly addressing any issues that arise can help reduce the severity and spread of a problem. It can also prevent harmful sex-related habits and patterns, such as those related to the avoidance of sexual activity that may arise out of accompanying discomfort—especially when avoidance becomes ingrained over a long period of time.

As is the case with vaginas, a variety of genital modifications and mutilation practices involving the penis and scrotum exist worldwide, including circumcision, superincision (a partial splitting at the top of the foreskin), and piercing. Thirty percent of men are circumcised worldwide, including 58 percent of U.S. males—with circumcision more common in the United States among whites than among African Americans, Latinx, and Asians.[33] There is also a push for voluntary medical male circumcision to help reduce the female-to-male spread of HIV.

Consider Roberto, a forty-six-year-old Latinx man who grew up in Mexico and moved to the United States when he was fifteen. Roberto comes to you because he has been feeling progressively depressed, and this was affecting his relationship with his girlfriend of three years. You begin your work with Roberto by exploring recent work stressors and financial stress from the tightening job market. As a freelance contractor, Roberto has been increasingly anxious about maintaining enough business. While the increased demands and concerns seemed like a logical cause for his depression, this doesn't seem to be the whole story. On further exploration, Roberto reveals that he is not feeling the same sexual desire as he used to. He is dismayed that it is taking him longer to become aroused and achieve an erection. Having felt great pride in living up to the sexual expectations of Latin males, he is disheartened that he is no longer able to instantly generate arousal and erection. You suggest that Roberto consult a medical provider to determine whether there is an underlying medical condition. If there is none, given Roberto's age and life stage, you can discuss the concept of male menopause (andropause or climacteric) with Roberto. You can also discuss some of the key signs and symptoms that he might expect, including slightly lower sex drive and erections that are slower to occur and don't last as long. Roberto is frustrated with the effect of aging on his sex drive but may take solace in the knowledge that he is not alone. You can also take the opportunity to help Roberto think of a fuller range of ways he can express his sexuality, shifting some of the focus to sensuality and possibly intimacy to enhance the physiological and cognitive experience.

Roberto's case reveals that men experience anatomical and physical changes over time similar to those in women. Much less is known about male menopause, but there is evidence that sperm production and testicular tissue both decrease. There is also a very gradual (approximately 1 percent per year) drop in testosterone levels.[34] Men also report symptoms similar to those found in menopause, including a decrease in energy, sexual desire, and cognitive functioning; difficulty sleeping; hot flashes; night sweats; depression; and bone loss. Researchers in Portugal have developed an andropause symptom-severity inventory based on items from a menopause symptom inventory.[35] The increased visibility of andropause has captured the attention of pharmaceutical companies, which have been eager to capitalize on interest in testosterone replacement therapy (TRT) and the more famous Viagra to enhance erections. However, when exploring the pros and cons of TRT with your clients, be aware that research on its side effects is still limited. The risks appear to be similar to those for HRT: increased risks of cancerous prostate enlargement, sleep apnea, blood clots, and strokes.[36] However, there is no evidence of increased incidence of prostate cancer after andropause.[37] Since it is also likely that you will have clients who take erectile dysfunction medications like Viagra and Cialis, you may also be called upon to discuss the pros and cons of these medications, so stay abreast of the latest developments. As with HRT, the *Physicians' Desk Reference* can provide helpful information about potential physical and emotional side effects of these and other medications.[38] Always encourage your clients to discuss potential side effects with their physician and role-play with them potential conversations in advance if you think such preparation is needed.

THE ANUS AS A SEX ORGAN

In their comprehensive *Discovering Human Sexuality*, Simon LeVay, Janice Baldwin, and John Baldwin appropriately include the anus in their description of sexual organs.[39] Regardless of gender or sexual identity, many people include the anus in their sexual activities, such as penetration and manual or oral stimulation. As a sex-positive social worker, it is important to challenge your assumptions about who participates in or enjoys anal sex. For example, a range of people engage in and enjoy the practice of "pegging," where a person without a penis performs anal sex on a partner (regardless of gender identity) using a strap-on or handheld dildo.

The anal opening is at the back of the perineum. The anus is a tight opening lined with muscles that leads to the rectum, a wider cavernous opening. While the anus has a lot of nerve endings, making touch and penetration pleasurable, the anal sphincter muscles are typically contracted, which creates a tight opening that it may be difficult to penetrate. In addition, there is no natural lubrication that occurs within the rectum, so using a lubricant may be advisable to make penetration more comfortable and enjoyable.

INTERSEX: AVOID THE BINARY IN CONVERSATIONS ABOUT ANATOMY

One drawback of the diagrams and section headings presented in this chapter so far is that they reinforce a binary norm of sex characteristics—when in reality, as already stated, there is variation in genital configuration, shape, color, and size. In addition, the wide range of variations in chromosomes means that 2 percent of people have characteristics of both male and female anatomy to some extent.[40] People with either both sets of reproductive organs or with nondistinctive genitalia[41] are referred to as intersex. Some of the more common chromosomal variations are 45,XO, or Turner's syndrome; 47,XXY, or Klinefelter syndrome; 46,XY, or androgen insensitivity syndrome); and 46,XX, which produces fetally androgenized females and congenital adrenal hyperplasia). More information about each chromosomal variation is available through InterACT, an organization that focuses on advocating for intersex youth (www .interactadvocates.org).

Sex-positive social workers can push back against the dichotomizing that commonly occurs by not using binary language when referring to anatomy or having conversations about sex.[42] Keep in mind that not all people who have vaginas identify as women, and not all people with a penis identify as male. Adjusting your language to ask about behaviors rather than sexes or genders can avoid this problem. For example, if your client is talking about penetration, you can ask what body parts or objects are used for penetration, rather than assuming that you know based on the partner's sex or gender identity. It is also important not to make assumptions about the anatomy of clients or their partners and to allow room for clients to fit outside the anatomical binary. As we will see in chapter 5, the expression of gender identity may not match anatomical characteristics, so working without assumptions allows clients to define themselves.

THE POWER OF LANGUAGE

When I cover reproductive anatomy and physiology in my class, I always include a small group activity that involves listing names for the penis and vagina. I purposefully randomly assign groups of four or five, so that students are not only with people that they know well or with whom they feel comfortable. My students are a diverse group in terms of age, ethnicity, race, cultural heritage, languages spoken, gender identity, sexual identity, and comfort with sexuality, so the lists of slang terms for penises and vaginas are always varied. Every year I challenge students to come up with a name that I have not already heard. They usually succeed.

I purposefully ask them to list names for the penis first, since they tend to find this easier. Words for the penis are somehow more accessible and less offensive, and they tend to be more upbeat and less derogatory. Often they're strong, powerful, active, and even glorifying. The main categories are often weapons—rod, shaft, sword, prick, pipe, and stick (including magic stick, meat stick, love stick, joy stick, and disco stick); foods—wiener, sausage, eggplant, banana, popsicle, cucumber, and lollipop; euphemisms—junior, johnson, little buddy, wee wee, pee pee, private part, and member; names—dick; and serpents—snake, anaconda; or monsters and giants—one-eyed monster, or one-eyed Cyclops. There is also the glorifying term "family jewels." Several words are also culturally specific, including schmeckle, mandingo, and schlong. These powerful and penetrative descriptors reflect the fact that the penis is widely acknowledged to be the "most important sexual body part" that has been "socially constructed to be the 'actor' in the sex act."[43] The status of the penis stands in stark contrast to the dirty, ugly, and smelly status of the vagina. The privileging of the young, white, able-bodied, heterosexual male at the top of the social sexual hierarchy is an important phenomenon that social workers can acknowledge and help disrupt.[44]

Students tend to have a harder and less playful time coming up with names for the vagina. The names tend to mirror the virgin-whore dichotomy with either very delicate terms such as flower, rose (bud), cherry (pie), and doughnut, or very derogatory and offensive terms such as cunt, twat, snatch, pussy, and cum dumpster. Some terms refer to the vagina's appearance, color, smell, or lubrication: lips, (fish) taco, tuna, clam, roast beef, meat curtains, beaver, rug, keyhole, slot machine, slip 'n slide, wet-wet, and velvet underground. As with the penis, there are several culturally specific names for the vagina, including coochie, poonani, poontang, poso, pousiorre, pum pum, and toto. And there are several euphemistic names, including no-no place, who-ha, lady garden, and vajayjay. There are also clearly gendered messages about power and penetration when the names present the vagina as a receptacle, such as box, love tunnel, and entrance. My students describe the words used as a combination of cute, sweet, passive, distasteful, and receptive. There is also significant messaging related to appearance and smell. Sex-positive social work helps clients (and social workers) acknowledge, address, and unpack the shame-based, negative taboos about our reproductive organs. It's also important to help clients move from institutional messaging about cleanliness, hairiness, or appearance to embracing the uniqueness of their sexual selves.

UNDERSTANDING AROUSAL

William Masters and Virginia Johnson fought the medical establishment to study patterns of arousal during heterosexual intercourse. The study of sex and the field of sexology were seen as illegitimate medical pursuits, so funding and opportunities were limited. Fighting hard to maintain a small lab space at Washington University in St. Louis, Masters began studying the sexual arousal response to help people experiencing sexual dysfunction. Joined by Johnson originally as an administrative assistant and eventually as a research partner, Masters left the university in 1964 to establish the Reproductive Biology Research Foundation. The organization was renamed the Masters and Johnson Institute in 1978, but it closed in 1994. Masters and Johnson gathered data via in-depth interviews and their visual observations of participants engaged in sexual activity. After gathering hours of data, in 1966 Masters and Johnson published a discussion of what they saw as typical patterns of arousal in their very famous *Human Sexual Response*.[45] They created a four-stage model (see figure 2.5). The stages included the ex-

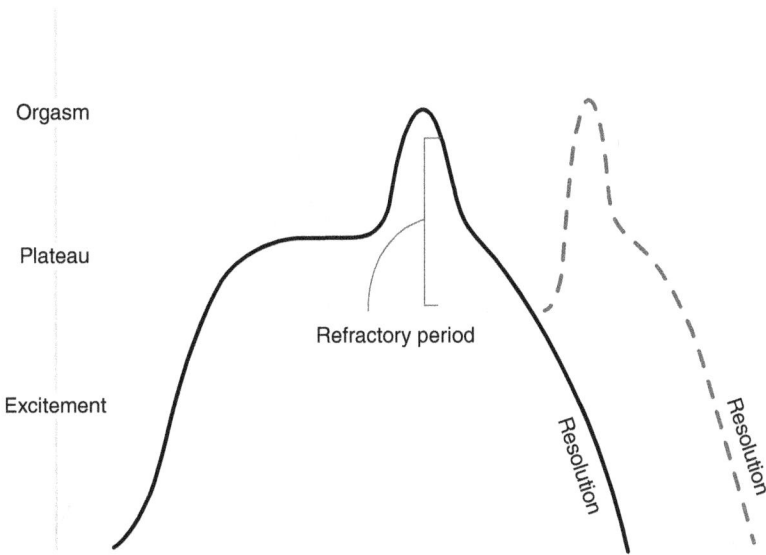

FIGURE 2.5 Masters and Johnson's arousal model

citement phase (arousal), the plateau phase (the period immediately prior to orgasm), orgasm, and the resolution phase (following orgasm). People with a penis have a refractory period following orgasm, during which further ejaculation is impossible. However, people with vaginas do not have a refractory period and can occasionally have one or more additional orgasms after partial resolution phases.

Helen Singer Kaplan endeavored to further the work of Masters and Johnson. She developed her own theory of arousal, which closely mirrored the physiological responses reported by Masters and Johnson but added a psychological dimension. She critiqued Masters and Johnson for their purely physiological theory and argued that thoughts, feelings, and emotions were involved. Responding to the fact that her clients tended to focus on a disinterest in sex, she offered a three-phase model of arousal (see figure 2.6) that added the psychological dimension of desire, which she saw as necessary before arousal and orgasm (Kaplan, 1985): Desire → arousal → orgasm.

Masters and Johnson and Kaplan have been critiqued for the linearity of their models.[46] Although both sets of researchers had studied male and female arousal, their critics argued that the models were more compatible

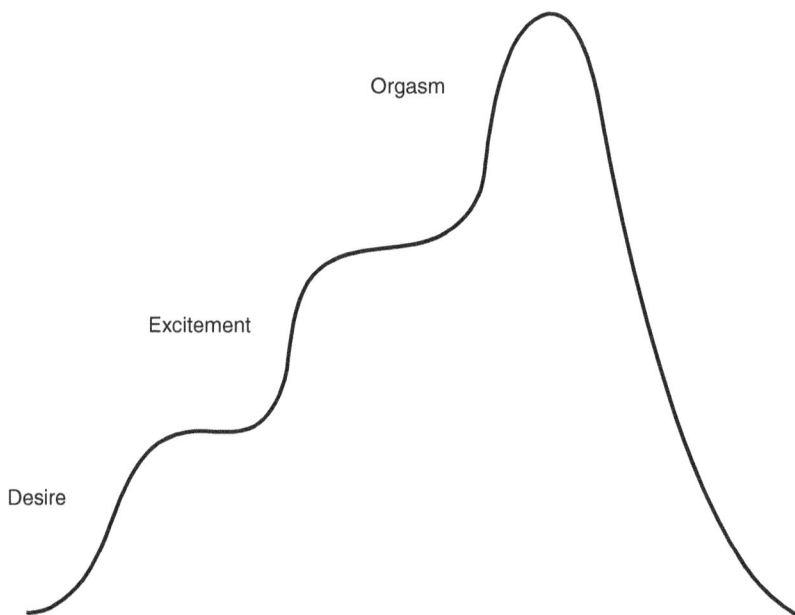

FIGURE 2.6 Kaplan's sexual response model

with the male arousal response than with the female. Beverly Whipple and Karen Brash-McGreer and then Rosemary Basson offered alternative models that were circular rather than linear and focused more specifically on the relationship between desire and arousal in women (see figures 2.7 and 2.8).[47]

As illustrated in figure 2.7, Whipple and Brash-McGreer expanded David Reed's (linear) model but built in the idea that pleasure in one encounter leads to desire for another. In other words, positive sexual encounters are self-reinforcing, while negative sexual encounters diminish desire.[48] The four stages—seduction (including desire), sensations (the excitement and plateau phases), surrender (the orgasm phase), and reflection (the resolution phase)—are circular; positive surrender and reflection experiences reinforce positive sexual feelings and increase the likelihood of more sexual encounters.

Basson developed a new model that was also circular but was not attached to the linear models developed earlier (see figure 2.8).[49] Spontaneous sexual drive sits in the center of the circle, with sexual stimuli, sexual arousal, arousal and sexual desire, emotional and physical satisfaction, and

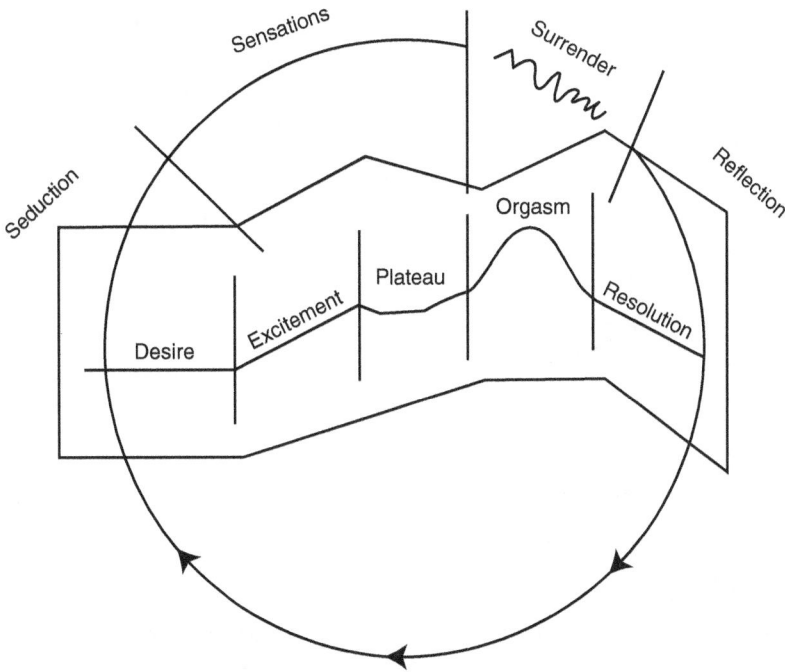

FIGURE 2.7 Whipple and Brash-McGreer's sexual response model

emotional intimacy in separate boxes on the perimeter. There are also bio-logical and psychological factors that influence the feedback loop.

Sandra Leiblum leveled a critique similar to that of Basson and Whipple and McGreer, suggesting that women do not necessarily have spontaneous feelings of sexual desire and that when desire does occur it does not neces-sarily lead to sexual arousal.[50] Like Basson, Leiblum suggested that arousal may come before desire for some people. Basson argued that women do not typically maintain spontaneous sexual desire in long-term relation-ships. Instead, they desire emotional intimacy and relationship satisfaction. She suggested that women desire sex in the service of desire for intimacy instead or in addition to desire for the pleasurable physical experience.[51] Basson also argued that the sexual response happened in context, with cog-nitive factors serving to mediate the response. Positive emotions of trust, love, and happiness amplified positive feelings and the subsequent sexual

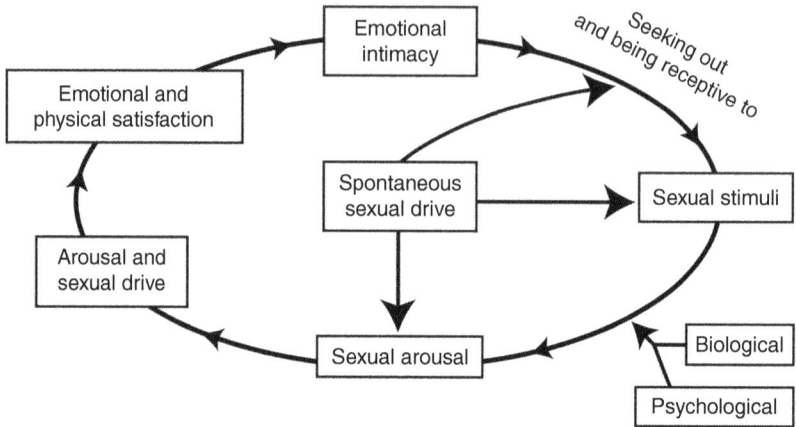

FIGURE 2.8 Basson's 2001 model of arousal response

response. Conversely, negative emotions of anger, fear, and resentment could depress desire and arousal and interrupt the arousal response.

In subsequent years, Basson evolved her model (see figure 2.9) by placing initial sexual desire in the middle, though not necessarily considering it the starting point. Deliberate attention to stimuli runs through biological and psychological factors that process the stimuli and impact the subjective and autonomic nervous system responses. Other features include arousal triggering desire, sexual satisfaction and absence of pain, other rewards such as emotional ones and increased well-being, and multiple motivations. Basson suggested that a woman could cycle through different phases multiple times during one sexual encounter.[52]

All of these sexual response models have common physiological responses to sexual arousal. Initial arousal is accompanied by an increase in heart rate, erection of the penis or clitoris, and vaginal lubrication. The brain (specifically, the hypothalamus) signals the pituitary gland to secrete hormones, which in turn trigger the adrenal glands to release their hormones (adrenaline). Changes in blood flow create vasocongestion, producing the appearance of flushing on the skin and the engorgement of the genitals and breasts. And the increase in heart rate can trigger a feeling of breathlessness. There is also a common experience of myotonia or progressive muscle ten-

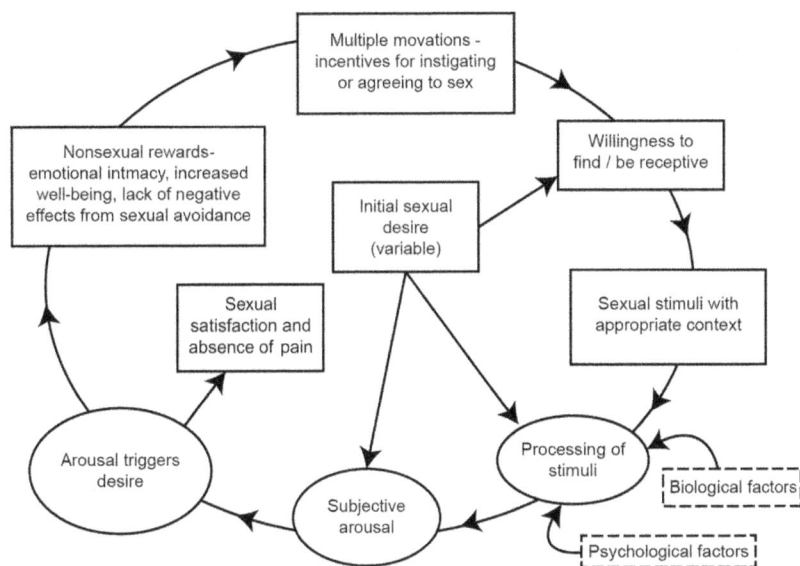

FIGURE 2.9 Basson's 2008 model of arousal response

sion, experienced as a pleasurable sensation and often resolved through orgasm. (Experiences of orgasm are thought to be quite similar across all people—narrative descriptions of orgasm were not identifiable by sex).[53] Orgasm triggers the release of the "cuddle chemicals" (oxytocin in women and vasopressin in men), which increases pleasurable feelings and a sense of attachment.[54]

Current models of sexuality see the achievement of orgasm as success and everything else as failure. Working with clients to shift this expectation can be an important point for intervention. It can be helpful to recommend some of the interventions initiated by Masters and Johnson such as sensate focus, where the initial purpose is to engage in sensual, intimate touch that purposefully avoids the genitals—though it can progress to include the genitals and foreplay—and should not end in climax.

Tantric sex is a spiritual sexual practice that originated in India and is based on the idea that orgasms are the life force and should be conserved. The practice focuses on prolonged mutual intimacy and sensuality that can last several hours, and the purpose of the experience is to achieve spiritual transcendence through sustained sexual arousal. Practicing some of the principles of tantric sex can help some people by using the techniques to enhance sexual intensity and to shift from the "product"-focused orgasm-based sex to the journey-focused sensation and intimacy. Such interventions can be especially helpful in addressing issues of performance anxiety or to bridge gaps in intimacy.

UNPACKING THE ROLE OF THE SENSES IN AROUSAL

Desire and arousal are critical points of intervention, as we will see in chapter 9, but also points of self-learning. Before you read further, jot down five things that arouse you or "turn you on." If you identify as asexual and aren't aroused by anything, then note five things that your clients have identified as arousing or that you have seen represented as a point of arousal in movies.

Now that you have your list, we are going to run through the five senses and look at how they are associated with arousal. Below is an example of a word association list that my students developed in response to my question about arousal, categorized into the five senses. Be aware that items on the list may be triggering for some people, so please take care if that may apply to you.

- Smell—pheromones, sweat, vaginal fluid, semen, cologne (a multi-billion-dollar industry invested in trying to make you smell appealing and "sexy"—from AXE and Old Spice to Chanel and Beyoncé).
- Sound—music (everything from Barry White to The Weeknd), moaning, screaming, "talking dirty," the crack of a whip, the sound of a zipper, the sound of flesh on flesh (some sounds that work less well are a baby crying or the door opening).
- Sight—initial attraction, sexy advertising (another industry that tries to sell clothes, cars, phones, and more based on looks), pornography, gazing into someone's eyes.
- Taste—chocolate, strawberries, champagne, whipped cream, lips, skin, sexual secretions.

- Touch—tickling, slapping, kissing, caressing, cold, heat, hard surfaces, soft surfaces, silk, latex, leather, straps, soft touches, rough touches, being restrained, the brush of a feather.

To what extent can the five things you wrote down at the start of this section fit under the rubric of the senses? Is there a different category of things that turn you on that are unrelated to the senses? When working with clients, helping them understand what turns them on—and what turns them off—is an important function. Part of developing sexual health and satisfaction is the capacity to identify what you want and when and then communicating that information to your partner or partners.

Another crucial concept is that arousal is not static. The things that arouse people may change over time or with different partners or when they are in different moods. It is important to discover all of this information so that your clients can be more fully connected to their sexual potential. We will revisit the senses and arousal in chapter 9, as they are important factors and points of intervention in the treatment of disorders and dysfunctions.

CHAPTER SUMMARY

This chapter provided foundational information on anatomy, physiology, and arousal. It described reproductive characteristics and emphasized how social workers can dispel myths that clients might have absorbed that are related to their bodies. It also recognized the limits of our knowledge and the importance of referring clients to physicians for medical consultation or testing when appropriate.

The chapter urged social workers not to make assumptions related to the anatomy and physiology of clients and their partners and to be careful not to dichotomize language so as to make room for clients who aren't represented by the sex/gender binary, including those who are intersex. The chapter also discussed the evolution of sexual arousal theory, from Masters and Johnson and Kaplan to more recent nonlinear models—including Basson's, which allows desire to occur before or after arousal. This is true for many people, especially cis-women.[55]

DISCUSSION QUESTIONS

1. How do cultural norms about nudity impact our comfort with genitalia?
2. What are some of the topics related to anatomy that clients may present with in practice?
3. Given the power of language, what are the underlying messages in the words we use to describe penises versus vaginas? How, if at all, have you internalized these messages?
4. What are the key similarities in the arousal models presented?
5. What are the key distinctions in the arousal models presented?
6. Choose one of the arousal models presented. How would you strengthen it to present an even more inclusive reflection of arousal?

RESOURCES

American Cancer Society: cancer.org
InterACT Youth Advocacy: www.interactadvocates.org
Organization Intersex International (OIi): oiiinternational.com
SexInfo Online: sexinfoonline.com
Testicular Cancer Awareness Foundation: https://www.testicularcancerawarenessfoundation.org
Testicular Cancer Society: https://www.testicularcancersociety.org

3

TAKING A SEXUAL HISTORY

RELEVANT CSWE COMPETENCIES

Competency 2: Engage Diversity and Difference in Practice
Competency 7: Assess Individuals, Families, Groups, Organizations, and
  Communities

I n the introduction and chapter 1 we set the scene for sex-positive social
  work interactions through using inclusive art in the office, updated website information, responsive and inclusive intake forms, and biopsychosocial assessment questions that address sex and sexuality. All of these form
the context for and support the initial information gathering for work with
a client that includes the sexual dimension as an aspect of practice. This
chapter goes beyond the cursory inclusion of sexuality and discusses how
to take a comprehensive sexual history.

The chapter explores different styles of sexual history assessment, with
approaches ranging from very structured to very unstructured. These approaches are offered as a guide that you can use to develop your own professional style and authentic professional voice that fits your personality, setting, and practice. You may find that you are more comfortable sticking to

a very structured script, especially at first. Conversely, you may discover that you dislike the confines of a structured approach and prefer to keep the questions open and the conversation flowing freely. Your approach may change over time as your practice evolves or your clients or settings change. The key is to experiment so that you can find what style works for you in successfully integrating the taking of sexual histories into your practice.

SETTING THE SCENE

There is no one right way to take a sexual history. But there are ways to ensure that your clients feel comfortable and the dialogue is open and flowing. As noted in chapter 1, it is important to create a sex-positive practice space; to take a nonassumptive, nonjudgmental, sex-positive stance; and to be proactive in asking clients about sex.

Above we discussed some of the cultural factors that affect both social workers' and our clients' comfort in talking about sex. Norms in the United States across races and ethnicities tend to make talking about sex taboo, silencing conversations about sexuality—especially healthy, pleasure-focused sexuality. Children and preteens (or tweens) are taught that sex is especially not appropriate for them to talk about, and these norms often stay with us into adulthood. While often we make a decision by reading a great deal of online information, sex is one of the few areas where we believe that providing less information will help people make better decisions.

In practice, then, one of the first goals of taking a comprehensive sexual history is to break the taboo that most people have been socialized to accept and have an open dialogue. There are significant gender, racial, and ethnic differences to be aware of. Thus, the suggestions here are meant as guides, with the understanding that they are generalizations and each client is unique.

Male sexuality is typically more celebrated and encouraged than female sexuality, but even for men talking about sex is reserved for conversations with friends or perhaps "the talk" with a (usually male) relative.[1] Polite men are not supposed to talk about sex in mixed company. Similarly, women might talk about sex with their friends, but they are not supposed to be promiscuous or to focus on pleasure.[2] If anything, magazines aimed at teens or young women have long focused on "how to please your man." In the past decade this has changed, and a number of empowerment organizations now exist to help young women find their social, political, and sexual voice—including online media sites like Bustle, Demystified, and Feministing. *Teen Vogue* has also been leading the charge with articles such as "Anal Sex: Safety, How Tos, Tips, and More" and "Why Sex Education for Disabled People Is So Important."[3] Yet cultural norms have not changed dramatically, so social workers should expect to have to break through the taboo at least some of the time, especially with older clients.

Does race and culture affect openness in talking about sex? Some Caribbean cultures have a very secretive stance toward sex and, although Latin cultures have a reputation for fiery and romantic personalities, conversations about sexuality are often limited.[4] One study of conversations about sexuality between Latinx mothers and daughters found that mothers could discuss the potential negative consequences of sex but not the positive aspects of sexuality or prevention, like contraception, with their daughters.[5] Mothers attributed their difficulties in having sexual conversations to the culture of silence and the messaging that they received growing up. The study found that while the adolescent girls wanted these conversations with their mothers, they were afraid of being punished for being sexually promiscuous if they raised the issue.[6] Interestingly, despite the expectation that U.S. adults would be reluctant to talk about sex, in their groundbreaking National Health and Social Life Survey, Edward Laumann, John Gagnon, Robert Michael, and Stuart Michaels found that adults were quite willing to talk about sex with lay interviewers who had had a brief training on the subject.[7] A helpful strategy is to model comfort in talking about sex, which will relax clients and give them the opportunity to develop their own comfort.

BREAKING THE ICE

When you start work with a new client, there are strategies you can use to break the ice, make the client comfortable, and develop rapport. The same strategies can be used when you take a sexual history. To acclimate clients to talking about sex, a social worker can rely on something outside the therapeutic relationship to introduce the topic without putting the conversation directly in the context of the client's own sexuality. For example, you might say "Some people find it a little awkward talking about sex—is that true for you?" or "Do you feel comfortable talking about sex with your friends or partners?" Depending on the response you receive, you might follow up by asking, "Is there any one that you feel comfortable talking to about sex?"

Another point of entry is to ask clients about their history of talking about sex at home, at school, or online: "Did anyone talk about sex in your house growing up? If so, who?" "Did you talk to siblings or cousins about sex? Which ones? Were they older or younger than you?" "Are you more comfortable talking about sex online or in a text than in person? If so, why? What makes you feel safer?" In this way you can open the door for real conversations about sex by talking about the idea of it rather than diving right in.

If clients report difficulty in discussing sex, you might ask why. You might also give them something to read or a podcast to listen to, either in a session (if the material is very short) or outside. You can then discuss the article or podcast as a way to explore sex-related content. Again, this technique externalizes the conversation but breaks the ice.

AVOIDING ASSUMPTIONS

It cannot be overemphasized how important it is not to make assumptions or use language that conveys assumptions to your clients. As you take a sexual history, stay curious—especially about what activities your client participates in, with whom, and when. To recap the information in chapter 1: Do not assume a number of partners, sex or gender of partners, specific sexual behaviors, roles of your client or their partners, or their enjoyment or engagement in different behaviors. Do not phrase questions in a way that assumes a partner's gender or the number of partners involved. For example, do not assume that a self-identified gay man is not having sex with women, that lesbians don't have sex with men, or that heterosexuals do not have same-sex experiences or fantasies. Lisa Diamond's work on sexual fluidity in women is a good example of why these kinds of assumptions should be avoided.[8] Likewise, do not assume that because a client had a very devout religious upbringing and still practices that faith that they do not also take part in BDSM (bondage and discipline, dominance and submission, and sadism and masochism), or that a client who is paralyzed and uses a wheelchair does not have an exciting and deeply gratifying sex life.

Use open prompts such as the following: "Are you currently in any intimate relationships? Are they sexual?" "Describe your first positive sexual relationship." "What is your commitment to your partner? What is their commitment to you?" (Again, don't assume that the commitment is equal.) Keep an open, curious, unassuming stance, which gives the client room to express themselves and you room to expand your own notions of sexuality and sexual expression.

There is a difference between adding some sexual health questions to an intake form and conducting a comprehensive sexual history. Sexual health questions included in an intake form often have a particular purpose. For example, your organization may use questions designed from the perspective of a public health concern about HIV and other sexually transmitted diseases, or questions related to pregnancy prevention and reproductive health. Some general umbrella questions about sexual health and well-being may be a way to segue into more specific questions about the extent of clients' sexual activity, their satisfaction with their sexual relationships, and their practices related to safe sex and pregnancy (e.g., "Are you doing anything about STIs [sexually transmitted infections] or HIV or pregnancy prevention?") Again, even with these few specific questions, be careful not to make assumptions and remember that some sexual histories are complicated by abuse and/or violence. For example, asking at what age the client first had sexual intercourse can be a confusing question for people who are very sexually active but have never had intercourse according to the traditional definition. In addition, be aware that some people may have had very bad first experiences with sex that were coercive or violent, which may affect their answers to questions about their sexual history. As you explore the subject with clients, you might ask, "What is an early good memory of sexuality?" and later ask about any bad memories or experiences.

MEDICAL MODEL SEXUAL HISTORY TAKING: THE FIVE Ps

If you work in an agency with a public health or medical background, you may have come across a medical model for taking a sexual history. For example, the Centers for Disease Control and Prevention (CDC) employs an approach based on the five Ps: partners, practices, protection (from sexually transmitted diseases [STDs], past (history of STDs), and prevention (of pregnancy).[9] This model emphasizes risk assessment and disease prevention. Because it's based on sexual health in the medical rather than the holistic sense, it focuses on biological and some social factors.

The five Ps are self-explanatory:

- Partners: The number of past sexual partners and some understanding of who they are in relation to gender, sexuality, relationship, and so on.
- Practices: Types of sexual behaviors the person currently engages in, as well as those they have engaged in in the past. Here you might ask about specific practices such as anal or oral sex, especially if you are practicing in the context of a health center—where the data might be required for reporting.
- Protection: The steps the person takes to protect themselves from infection (or from infecting others) with STIs or STDs, such as condom or dental dam use.
- Past history: Prior exposure to STIs and STDs. This can also be an opportunity to talk about whether the person has made any changes in their practices related to safer sex.
- Prevention: Whether the person is currently taking any steps to prevent pregnancy or has been pregnant. If they are trying to prevent pregnancy, how do they feel about the method they are using, and how consistent are they in using it or completing any necessary follow-up, if relevant? You can

also ask about past pregnancies and, if relevant, more detailed questions such as whether the fetus was healthy, whether it was carried to term, and whether they were in a relationship with the other parent. Again, you can also get a sense of prior sexual behavior and potential changes in that behavior over time.

As you can see, the five Ps model focuses on disease and prevention without attending to the psychological or sociocultural factors that may be affecting your client.[10] The challenge is how to apply it in a sex-positive rather than a sex-punitive way. It is even more important to set a sex-positive scene while using this approach, since you will then be much more likely to get accurate and honest information (which is the point of the approach).

Moving beyond a short sexual history, the next section considers more comprehensive models of sexual history taking, which add the psychological dimension of the biopsychosocial that is missing from the five Ps approach.

SOCIAL WORK VALUES AND SEXUAL HISTORIES

There is little social work literature on taking a sexual history. However, the three long-form approaches outlined here can be applied from a social work perspective and with a social work sensibility, which means honoring the dignity and worth of the person.[11] Social work is distinct from other health professions because of its attention to the whole person and their environment. As discussed in previous chapters, social workers use a holistic assessment strategy that encompasses the biopsychosocial (meaning that it accounts for the biological, psychological, and social environment interactions). We should use the same approach when assessing sexual health and sexual well-being.

A holistic approach honors the social work perspective articulated in the "2015 Educational Policy and Accreditation Standards" of the Council on Social Work Education (CSWE), the social work education accrediting body that states that the purpose of social work is to "promote human and community well-being. . . . [While] guided by a person-in-environment framework, a global perspective, [and] respect for human diversity."[12] Under CSWE's Practice Competency 7—"assess individuals, families, groups, organizations, and communities"—social workers are expected to "apply knowledge of human behavior and the social environment, person-in-environment, and other multidisciplinary theoretical frameworks in interventions with clients and constituencies."[13] Therefore, the approaches described here—while differing in style (more directive versus less directive) and degree of structure (more structured versus less structured)—are all compatible with a biopsychosocial model that includes assessing multiple dimensions of an issue, including the biological, psychological, and social facets of the person-in-environment.

A STRUCTURED APPROACH

In the 2011 edition of the instructor's manual for their textbook, *Human Sexuality*, Robert Crooks and Karla Baur offered a very structured approach to sexual history taking, using twenty-one questions.[14] They stopped using the full set of sexual history questions in later editions of the text. However, I am including here an adaptation I made of their approach (with twenty-three questions), since I think a structured approach can be quite helpful for someone who is just beginning to practice social work and needs a little extra guidance (see box 3.1). The first five of the twenty-three questions move through content on family or household composition, how affection was expressed between family members, how arguments were resolved, and the primary relationship in the household. Since clients may have grown up with extended family members or in different group homes or foster placements, not defaulting to language that assumes a nuclear family is affirming. If you already have background history on your client or know them well, you can insert the appropriate phrasing. These background questions explore the messaging and modeling that clients received regarding relationships, affection, and disagreements that often inform their current functioning. One of the questions also addresses the kinds of cultural and religious messages the client received about sex, the extent to which those messages were restrictive or permissive, and whether they changed over time. Religious and cultural beliefs about sexuality learned in childhood are often deeply engrained and highly influential in current functioning. The question also addresses racial and ethnic messaging about sex and sexuality, since sexual scripts are constructed in relation to race, culture, ethnicity, and gender.[15] For example, stereotypical narratives reinforced by the media and impacting development include the Madonna-whore dichotomy applied to women in general, the Jezebel narrative of promiscuity targeted at African American women, and the dominance of machismo directed at Latin men.

The next six questions refer to adolescence and puberty. Where did clients learn about sex? What kind of sex games did they play as a child, and how did they feel about those? The questions also ask about physical changes during puberty, which can illuminate the client's relationship to their physical self as a sexual person. Exploring this transition can also be informative, since it can be a pivotal point for people whose physical changes were not aligned with their experience of gender. Taking time to explore the physical, social, and emotional aspects of puberty provides critical background information. The questions then ask when the person learned about menstruation and nocturnal emissions and from whom, and about experiences with and messages about masturbation. Normalizing some of the discomfort typically experienced during these conversations or providing the opportunity for a corrective experience has therapeutic value.

Question 12 asks about "upsetting sexual experiences" that happened to the client as a child or to their siblings, as well as exploring whether they disclosed that information at the time and what the reaction was if they did. Here it can be helpful to have some background information on a client, but do not assume that because they have not mentioned any upsetting sexual experiences in treatment so far, they did not have any negative experiences. They may have chosen not to mention the events or felt that they were not relevant. Asking the direct question can serve to provide permission, but understandably it can also be upsetting. Be aware of the timing of your questions, and if you are conducting the sexual history over more than one session, make sure such a potentially triggering question is not raised too close to the end of the session.

Subsequent questions ask about dating history and first sexual experiences, if the person has had any. Physical and emotional reactions to both sexual and nonsexual touch relative to enjoyment and pain are also explored. One question directly addresses fantasies, asking whether clients have had them, whether they share them with anyone, and how they feel about them. Another question asks specifically about same-sex fantasies and exploration.

The final few questions explore clients' experiences of themselves as sexual beings, the importance of sex in their lives, their feelings about affection and commitment, their thoughts on an ideal partner, and the extent to which they can discuss sex with others—including whether they can disclose their sexual likes and dislikes to sexual partner(s). The questions provided here serve as a guide that you can adapt, adjust, and add to as needed or as fits with your professional style. The goal is to create a comprehensive picture of the client's development of a sexual self, as a frame of reference for the sexual person they are today and who they want to be in the future.

Box 3.1
VERY STRUCTURED SEXUAL HISTORY QUESTIONS

1. Describe the makeup of the family or adults you grew up with. Who were the adults, and how many of them were there? Were there siblings, step-siblings, or other children? What were the occupations of the adults? What were the relationships between people like? Who was closest to whom? Who confided in whom?

2. Did the adults show affection to the children? If so, how? Did the children express affection toward each other? In what ways? Were you comfortable with how affection was expressed? Were there any emotions that were not allowed to be expressed?

3. How were arguments resolved? Among the adults, the children, both? Was there any violence during arguments or in general? (Make sure that referrals are available if your setting is not equipped for practice with people who have experienced violence and trauma).

4. How would you describe the adults' relationship? Did they argue often? Did they show affection? Did they enjoy shared interests and activities? Did they enjoy individual interests and activities?

5. What kinds of cultural or religious messages did you receive about sex? How, if at all, did race/ethnicity play a role in that messaging? Was the messaging consistent or did it change over time?

6. How did you first learn about sex and from whom? Looking back, how do you feel about your sex education?

7. What sex games did you play as a child, and with whom? Looking back, how do you feel about those games?

8. Did you masturbate as a child? Was masturbation an accepted activity growing up? How did you know?

9. When did you first notice physical changes in your body related to puberty? Did you feel prepared for them? How did you react?

10. How did you first learn about menstruation and periods? If applicable, when did you have your first period? How did you feel about it then and now? How did the adults react?

11. How did you first learn about erections and nocturnal emissions? If applicable, when did you have your first erection and nocturnal emission? How did you feel about it then and now?

12. Did any upsetting sexual experiences happen to you as a child? To other children in the household/space? If applicable, did you tell anyone? What was their reaction? If applicable, have you received any therapy related to the experiences?

13. Did you date as a child or adolescent? If so, when did you first start dating? What were your first dates like? When did you begin to become sexual during dates? How did you feel about becoming sexual?

14. When/if your relationships became more sexual, did you feel prepared for it? What kinds of activities did you engage in (e.g., oral, anal, penetrative, kinky)? Did you know what you were doing? How did you feel afterwards? How do you feel about it now? If you have not been sexual, how do you feel about that?

Box 3.1   (*continued*)

15. Are there any physical or mental health issues that have impacted your sexuality? Have you ever had pain during sexual activities? Have you ever had issues with becoming or staying aroused? Do you have people you would talk to if you encountered these issues?

16. How do you feel about being touched in a nonsexual way? In a sexual way? What parts of your body are the most responsive when touched? Which parts are the least responsive (or irritated) by touch? Do you enjoy touching yourself? Your sexual partner?

17. How do you feel emotionally during sex? How do you feel about your body during sex?

18. What kind of fantasies do you experience? Have they changed over time? How do you feel about having those fantasies? Have you shared your fantasies with anyone? What were their reactions? Are you ever worried by your fantasies? Do you wish you had more or less fantasies?

19. At what ages, if any, did you have same-sex fantasies? At what ages, if any, did you engage in same-sex exploration? How do you feel about these experiences?

20. Can you discuss sex and sexuality with other people? Your partner(s)? Can you ask for what you like and be clear about your dislikes?

21. What, if anything, do you do in relation to reproductive health? For example, do you use contraception or barriers or get tested? Do you know the symptoms of STIs and what to do about them? Do you know how to recognize STIs in your partner?

22. How important is sex to you? How would you describe yourself as a sexual person? How important is affection? How important is commitment? Would you describe yourself as romantic?

23. Describe your ideal partner. If applicable, how does this compare to the relationship you are in now? What aspects, if any, would you want to change? Do you think those changes are possible?

Source: Adapted from Crooks and Baur, *Our Sexuality*. Republished with permission of Cengage Learning.

You can see that the content of the questions based on Crooks and Baur's original list are very comprehensive. Even though the list is in chronological order, you can find a way to implement it in your own style. And you can certainly skip questions if their content has already been covered or jump ahead to cover a topic that appears later in the list, if it seems appropriate to do so. Many of my students feel comfortable starting out with this very structured format. Other students find the format too artificial and dislike how stilted it made them feel. I am offering different examples in the hope you will find some combination of formats and questions that works for you.

A SEXOLOGICAL ECOSYSTEMS PERSPECTIVE

Stephanie Buehler presents a sexological ecosystemic perspective that fits well with a social work perspective because it is evolved from Bronfenbrenner's ecosystems theory.[16] Ecosystems theory posits that a child develops in response to their relationships with their social environment. Different layers of social context are identified within the theory as impacting development, including the microsystem with which the child is in direct contact, such as family, school, or church; the mesosystem, which represents interactions between institutions in the microsystem or between individuals; the exosystem, which is external to the child and not in direct contact with them but which nevertheless has an influence on them, such as community, society and culture; the macrosystem, which is characterized by laws, cultural values, and social norms in the environment; and finally the chronosystem, which is the system of time and which impacts the child as a part of maturation (such as hormonal changes) or as part of external events (such as a violent incident or war).

The sexological ecosystems approach examines microsystems, mesosystems, exosystems, macrosystems, and chronosystems as they relate to sexuality. In the *Sexological Ecosystemic Questionnaire*, Buehler provides a series of questions that help social workers explore each system with their client.[17] Beginning with the microsystem, this sexual history survey gathers chronological experiences for each major developmental stage, from early childhood to adolescence. Questions relate to the person's experiences of their gender and sexual exploration, education, puberty, and abuse experiences. Buehler's questions from each age range include:

Early Childhood

- Can you remember first knowing that you had a gender? . . .
- Do you remember first recognizing your genitals? . . .

Middle Childhood

- Did your parents [or other adult caregiver] talk to you about sex? . . .
- If your parents [or other adult caregiver] discovered you involved in sex play or self-exploration/masturbation, how did they respond? . . .

Preteen

- What were your feelings about puberty? How did you feel about the changes in your body? . . .
- Was there any sexual teasing or harassment you'd like to talk about?
- Tell me about having crushes or romantic fantasies. . . .

Adolescence

- If you started experimenting sexually during adolescence, was it in the context of a relationship? Was the relationship a healthy one?
- Were early experiences pleasurable, or was there something about any of them that bothered you? . . .
- Were you truthful with yourself and others about sexual knowledge and/or experiences? How did you relate to peers and their sexuality? . . . [18]

Exploring the microsystem incorporates questions about biological or health issues, including psychological issues that may have influenced sexual or social development. It also asks about medications or substances that the person has taken or is taking.

The mesosystem questions focus on relationships in late adolescence and adulthood. The questions include:

- Did you have any relationships lasting more than a few months? Did they include sexual activity, and, if so, was it pleasurable? . . .
- Did you have anyone you could get information from as a teen?
- Was there ever, at any age, an unwanted pregnancy? . . .
- Have you had relationships that included satisfying sex? What made them satisfying? . . .
- Do you have sexual fantasies? Do you enjoy them, or not? Do you share them?
- Do you have any sexual behaviors (e.g., a fetish) that interferes with sexual enjoyment with yourself or a partner? . . .
- Are any of your sexual problems possibly related to stress, like change in job, moving, birth of a child, death of a loved one, and so on?[19]

The sexological exosystem focuses on institutions such as schools, religion, the media, government, and the health care system. These institutions influence a person's development, though not as intimately as family members or peers do. While more indirect, the institutions can still have a powerful effect on sexual development, health, and well-being. Questions exploring the sexological exosystem seek to identify the key institutions that exert or have exerted influence on the person and how those institutions have or have not supported their experiences of sexuality. For example, was the client raised within a religious community? What media were readily available in their household when they were growing up? How have social media influenced their sexuality—positively or negatively? Did they go to a parochial school or a large urban public school? Specific questions outlined by Buehler include:

- If you have a spiritual life, does it or does it not support your exploration of your sexuality?
- Have you left or changed religion because of differences in ideas about sexuality? How has that been for you?

- Does your workplace support work/life balance? How does this affect your sexual expression?
- Tell me about any interactions with health care providers regarding sexual concerns? Did they go well?[20]

The sexological macrosystem refers to broader systems that influence development without a client's necessarily having direct contact with them: culture, social norms, attitudes and beliefs, and laws. The effect that historical laws, norms, and attitudes about sex may have on a person are also included in the macrosystem assessment. For example, the way sex trade is regulated—legal in some places but not in others—or the historical oppression of gays and lesbians are examples of the macrosystem. Questions include:

- Tell me about attitudes toward sex in your culture/culture of your family of origin.
- In what ways was your family more or less permissive?
- What attitudes do you have about how people of any gender are supposed to act in a sexual relationship? For example, are men supposed to be the initiators? . . .
- What are your beliefs about the place of sexuality in a person's life? In a person's relationships? . . . [21]

Buehler notes that it is important not to send the sexological ecosystem questions home with the client, so as not to overwhelm them.[22] That holds true for all of the sexual history approaches discussed in this chapter. While you might ask a client to prepare for a session by thinking about a particular event or issue, being asked to provide answers for all of the questions on the sexual history at once, and without the support of the therapeutic environment, may make the client feel bombarded or overwhelmed, especially if they have any significant negative sexual history.

IASENZA'S GUIDELINES FOR SEXUAL HISTORY TAKING

The third approach to sexual history taking is a very unstructured narrative approach, which covers similar content but in a more organic way. The key difference between the first two approaches and this one is that in this case you have the critical areas to cover in your head but you let the conversation flow and guide the client through an exploration of their sexuality in an ad hoc fashion, until all the major areas of consideration have been addressed. This approach allows you to be less rigid in your pursuit of information and gives you room to delve deeper into specific areas as they arise, if appropriate.

Suzanne Iasenza provides a very queer-friendly, sex-positive lens through which to explore key aspects of sexual history, including the periods of childhood, adolescence, and adulthood, societal influences, and current sexual functioning.[23] For each of the main subheadings, Iasenza offers key areas that the assessment should cover—many of which are similar to those discussed above. For example, under childhood she recommends explorations of the following topics:

> types of relations with family members; parental relationships; gender experience/identity/role; peer relations; first sexual feelings (same and/ or other sex); masturbation; peer sexual play; sex education . . . ; religiosity; race/ethnic/class experiences; messages about sex; how affection was shown; how nudity/body issues were handled; how privacy was managed; how boys and girls were treated; any unpleasant, confusing, embarrassing, or disturbing sexual experiences; medical treatments in self or family members; sexual/physical/verbal/emotional abuse and neglect; substance use.[24]

The list related to adolescence includes "peer relationships; school experience; experience of puberty; body development & image; menstruation; pregnancies or abortions; wet dreams; dating; self-esteem; masturbation (methods and fantasies); sexual behavior and attractions (heterosexual, homosexual, bisexual, pansexual); coming out experiences; first inter-course/sexual experience; substance use."[25] Some of the categories are repeated, since the client's experience of them might have changed depending on developmental stage. For example, peer relations may have shifted from childhood to adolescence, as may the amount and type of substance use or relationship toward and feelings about masturbation.

Topics that Iasenza recommends addressing in the adulthood section include "medical history (including psychiatric treatment and psychotherapy), relationship history; sexual experiences; masturbation; fantasies; dreams; sexual problems (in self or partners); STDs; HIV status and safer sex; birth control; children; menopause; medications; substance use; occupational history; peer/family relations; coming out experiences at home and work."[26]

Iasenza adds two sections that are distinct from some of the other available models. One section considers societal influences, such as the effects of discrimination or bias based on a range of identities including "race, ethnicity, sex, gender identity/role/expression, class, sexual orientation, religion, age, disability, and family form." The other section directly addresses current sexual functioning, including strengths, difficulties, "likes and dislikes about the partner and/or self, monogamy, non-sexual activities (including individually and as a couple), communication about sex, intimacy, and affection."[27]

As you move through the questions presented here with your clients, look for themes that may emerge like guilt, shame, confusion, insecurity, fear, boundary violations, misconceptions, and regret. Explore with your clients how these experiences affect their current sexual functioning and well-being. One further question that can be helpful to add from a strengths perspective is based on Jack Morin's work on sexual fantasy. Morin asked people to describe peak sexual experiences as a way to understand their fantasies and sexual potential.[28] Asking clients to describe a peak sexual experience can provide helpful insights into their sexual functioning and also serves as a platform from which to help them draw on their strengths.

Some beginning practitioners find the narrative format for sexual history taking overwhelming especially at first, feeling that they do not have enough guidance and worrying that they will omit important questions or information. For others, however, the format feels more natural and organic, and they enjoy the lack of structure. As you can see, the three models cover much of the same material, so your task is to find the right lens and level of structure that works for you and your practice style.

THE DOUPE MODEL

So far we have discussed the CDC's medical prevention and risk-assessment approach to sexual history taking and a few comprehensive sexual history assessment techniques that give a social worker room to find their own voice. In this section we will take a brief look at a model that can be applied when a client comes in with a specific sexual issue that they would like to address when your setting does not allow the time or format for a complete sexual history. For example, clients may come to you concerned about their ability to "let go" during sexual activity or because they have a bad relationship with oral sex, a medical illness has changed their enjoyment of sex, they are concerned that they are overusing hook-up apps, or their formerly exciting and connected sex life with their spouse is waning.

In these situations, you would ideally conduct a thorough sexual history assessment like one of those discussed above. However, that is not always possible given practice settings and time constraints. Whether or not you have comprehensive background information about a client, the DOUPE model is a useful tool.[29] DOUPE stands for description, onset, understanding, past (treatment efforts), and expectations. It was developed by Sallie Foley predominantly for use in medical settings, but we can apply it in social service and psychotherapeutic settings, too.[30]

"Description" refers to describing the issue, which gives you a chance to explore with the client how they understand the problem, what troubles them about it, and how they feel in relation to the issue. As the client talks, you may pick up some nonverbal cues from their body language, mannerisms, and tone about how they feel. Do not rush through the description phase assuming you know what the problem is. Instead, give the client time to explore how they understand the issue.

During the onset phase of assessment, you will ask when the issue occurred. You want to know whether it is recent or ongoing, and whether it had sudden onset or it came on gradually. You want to understand whether this is something the client has dealt with in the past or this is the first occurrence.

The understanding phase addresses the client's understanding of the problem. It can be helpful to combine the description phase with the understanding phase, so that the conversation flows more naturally. You can also ask directly: "How do you understand the problem?" "What do you make of it?" or "If you had to guess what this was about, what would some of your thoughts be?" In this way you can test the client's understanding of the issue and have a chance to test some of your own assumptions against that.

The past treatment efforts phase of the assessment provides a chance to ask clients what they have already done to address the issue. Have they already been to a physician for a health screening or medical tests? Have they done online research or read any books on the issue? Have they talked to friends or family members? Is there a family history with the same issue? Is there anything in their health or medication history that might be relevant? What about attempts at self-medication, including the use of herbs, alcohol, or drugs?

The final phase is expectations. What does the client hope the outcome of the treatment will be? Do they hope to improve or find a cure? And what would a successful outcome look like for them? It is important to get a sense of how realistic their expectations are and assess the degree to which they feel hopeless.

CHAPTER SUMMARY

This chapter discussed a variety of approaches to taking a sexual history, including medical, structured and unstructured, and ecosystems approaches.[31] It emphasized the importance of testing different approaches to find which fits most comfortably with your style, setting, and authentic professional voice. There is no one right way. Often, professionals just starting out in their careers or just beginning to add sexual history taking to their professional repertoire feel more comfortable with a structured set of questions that guides what to say and when and how to say it. Others feel constricted by a more rigid set of questions and prefer a looser and more freewheeling narrative approach that allows the client to drive the conversation. In practice, social workers tend to end up somewhere between these two approaches.

Whichever approach you use, become familiar with the questions and content beforehand so you can build naturally on the dialogue in your session. Try different approaches and see which fits organically with your practice setting, client population, and personal style and the length of your relationship with the client. Interestingly, even if the style of questioning (narrative versus prescriptive, for example) differs, the content is quite consistent and the arc of the questions is often similar across approaches.

The chapter also provided examples of two shorter sexual history assessments. The CDC's five Ps approach was developed from a public health perspective but is applicable in a range of settings when applied from a sex-positive perspective.[32] The DOUPE model is designed to assess specific sexual concerns presented by a client.[33] All of the questions are focused on understanding the specific presenting problem and what efforts have been made to address it. The chapter presented a variety of tools to use in assessing your client's history with and current experiences of sexuality. Your task is to find your authentic professional voice and use these tools to explore more fully the sexual dimension of your client's well-being.

DISCUSSION QUESTIONS

1. Compare and contrast the three in-depth sexual history models. What do you see as the strengths and weaknesses of each?
2. Which of the sexual history models (or what combination of them) do you think you would feel most comfortable using in practice? Why?
3. How would you adapt the CDC's five Ps sexual history assessment to have a sex-positive social work lens?

RESOURCES

Buehler Institute: https://thebuehlerinstitute.com/forms/

Centers for Disease Control and Prevention, *A Guide to Taking a Sexual History*: : https://www.cdc.gov/std/treatment/sexualhistory.pdf

"Sexual History—the Right Way!" (still not a great way): https://www.youtube.com/watch?v=jNfhiWUhtaA

"Sexual History—the Wrong Way": https://www.youtube.com/watch?v=MKuTXMLC-fY

Sexuality Information and Education Council of the United States (SIECUS), "Taking a Sexual History" (adapted from the CDC resource above): https://siecus.org/wp-content/uploads/2018/07/1.7-Taking-A-Sexual-History.pdf

4

SEXUAL IDENTITY

RELEVANT CSWE COMPETENCIES

Competency 1: Demonstrate Ethical and Professional Behavior

Competency 2: Engage Diversity and Difference in Practice

Competency 3: Advance Human Rights and Social, Economic,
and Environmental Justice

WHAT IS IDENTITY?

Before you read any further, write down the first five of your identities that
pop into your head. There are no right or wrong answers to this one. Just
capture whichever five traits pop into your head first.

Take a look at the five you wrote down and see what aspects of your life
they reflect. You may have written student, social worker, husband, daughter,
son, immigrant, queer, woman, teacher, Christian, African American, activist, trans, liberal, conservative, Jew, or any number of other identities.
Some of these you inherited, while you have adopted others along the way.

Some are static and stay constant over time, while others are dynamic and change—sometimes frequently.

Look at your list. Do the identities convey you in relation to others, like wife, daughter, son, husband, boss, parent, child? Do they convey what you do, like writer, coach, scientist, yoga teacher, massage therapist, student, painter, artist, activist, actor, singer, or engineer? Or do they convey which groups you belong to (perhaps those related to your cultural identity, racial identity or ethnicity), like Puerto Rican, Columbian, British, Latin, African, black, Jewish or Irish? Do some of them relate to your sexuality, like heterosexual, queer, pansexual, asexual, or gay? Or your gender, like female, male, cis-female, transmasculine, nonbinary, or male? Are they identities that you have given yourself or have they been assigned to you? Now think about what identities you would have written down if you had done this exercise five or ten years ago. How have your identities changed over time?

Identity can be defined as "parts of a self[,] composed of the meanings that (people) attach to the multiple roles they typically play," or can be applied to a group or social movement.[1] Social identity theory purports that it is self-categorization—how an individual "categorizes, classifies, and names the self"—that forms the identity.[2] So sexual identity, along with gender identity (which we'll discuss in chapter 5), forms a part of one's overall identity. This means how you view your own sexual identity, as well as how you identify your sexuality to the world.

SEXUAL IDENTITY, ATTRACTION, AND BEHAVIOR

Sexual identity first emerged out of Sigmund Freud's work on the psychosexual stages of development.[3] Freud proposed that moving through and completing the stages of oral, anal, and genital fixation represented normal identity development. He proposed that everyone started as bisexual and progressed eventually to opposite-sex attraction. In this way, he believed same-sex attraction was an arrested fixation at an early stage of development. While Freud's theory has been widely criticized because of its development from a male, phallocentric perspective and its pathologiza-tion of a range of typical sexual behaviors, it did encourage the study of psychosexual development.

Subsequently, Erik Erikson proposed a linear eight-stage model of de-velopment based predominantly on his clinical observations of children and adolescents.[4] The fifth stage in Erikson's model is named identity versus role confusion. This chronological model assigned the task of resolving conflict related to role confusion and establishing a stable sense of identity to the periods of adolescence and young adulthood. Role confusion is character-ized by the following questions: Who am I? Who does society expect me to be? Working through role confusion can involve boundary testing, ex-ploration, and acting out. While some criticize Erikson's stages for their linearity, which is not reflective of the often iterative process of develop-ment, it's true that adolescence and young adulthood are prominent times for the exploration of sexual identity.

So if identity is your understanding of who you are and the roles you play, that means sexual identity is the way in which you define yourself rela-tive to your sexuality. Do you identify as heterosexual, gay, lesbian, bisex-ual, pansexual, asexual, demisexual, queer, aromantic, something else, or none of these at all? While some identities are assigned by society, it is important that sexual identity be self-defined.

In some ways, sexual identity has become synonymous with (and limited to) lesbian, gay, bisexual, queer, and questioning identities—which fit to-gether under the umbrella of LGBTQ. But today we are witnessing an ever-growing array of possible sexual identities (see box 4.1). Many people have discovered that the available labels do not capture their experiences, so they search for descriptors that fit them more comfortably. Given this dynamic nature of sexual identity language and identification, I recommend staying abreast of current trends by paying attention to social media; keeping up with professional literature; and, perhaps most importantly, asking your cli-ents how they understand and label their identities.

It is especially important to discover what an identity means to your cli-ents, so that you and they aren't working from different understandings of the same label. For example, if your client identifies as queer, ask what that identity means to them.

Sexual identity is not necessarily sexual orientation. While some researchers use the term "sexual orientation" to refer specifically to sexual attraction, most argue that it represents an amalgam of your attractions, behavior, and self-identified sexual identity.[5] According to this definition, sexual attraction refers to the genders of those to whom you are sexually attracted—which could be all people, just men, just women, both men and women, or neither. Orientation concerns those who create sexual arousal within you, while sexual behavior refers to the people with whom you have sex.

As we will discuss, your choices of sexual partners may be stable or fluid, changing frequently or occasionally over time. For this reason, questionnaires about sexual behavior often include questions about prior partners and behaviors. This can help you avoid making assumptions about your client's past behavior simply based on their current behavior.

Imagine yourself in this scenario. Your client, Jonathon, comes to you because he recently broke up with his girlfriend of three years. You know that Jonathon has started dating again, but you have not spent very much time exploring that. By asking Jonathon about his dating experiences and the partners he's exploring, you discover that Jonathon is dating men and women. Had you made assumptions based on his recent breakup, you would have missed the fact that Jonathon identifies himself as bisexual and chooses partners based on perceived fit and attraction rather than gender.

When sexual attraction, behavior, and identity are aligned, your sexuality is said to be concordant. A cisgender male who finds himself attracted to men, is sexually engaged with men, and identifies himself as gay is concordant. So is a cisgender female who is attracted to men, is sexually engaged with men, and identifies herself as heterosexual. Conversely, a cisgender male who is attracted to men but has sex with women and identifies himself as heterosexual is discordant. When discussing sexual orientation and identity with clients, be sure to explore all three aspects of attraction, behavior, and identity to uncover the extent of their concordance or discordance. You may also want to explore the degree to which their differences in attraction, behavior, and identity are simply representative of changes over time. Perhaps the three dimensions are out of sync temporarily or during a transition or a period of sexual fluidity, and do not indicate permanent discordance.

EXPANDING NOTIONS OF SEXUAL IDENTITY

At some point during the sexual identity class I teach, I ask students to list as many different sexual identities as they can. As with the vagina and penis exercise discussed in chapter 2, I challenge them to come up with identities that I have not yet heard of. When I began teaching human sexuality in 1999, the list was quite short: homosexual, lesbian, gay, bisexual, and heterosexual. Occasionally someone would add asexual as well. Now the list is extensive and evolving, a reflection of our increasingly nuanced understanding of attraction, behavior, and sexual identity. The following is a list with definitions from a recent class. It is not exhaustive, but it does provide a range of identities you might encounter. As mentioned in chapter 1, language is dynamic and evolving, and it is possible that meanings assigned in this list will become outdated, so keep checking that your understanding of a term matches that of your clients.

Box 4.1
SEXUAL IDENTITIES

- Heterosexual. An attraction to those of the "opposite" gender identity. For instance, a cisgender male attracted to a cisgender female, a masculine-identified person attracted to a feminine-identified person, or a transgender female attracted to a cisgender male.
- Bisexual. An attraction to both male- and female-identified people, including cisgender and transgender individuals.
- Lesbian. A cisgender or transgender female who is attracted to other cisgender or transgender females.
- Gay. A cisgender or transgender male who is attracted to cisgender or transgender males. This term is also used as an alternative to homosexual, which includes both lesbian women and gay men. Thus, a gay woman is attracted to other women or female-identified people.
- Asexual. No sexual attraction.

> *Box 4.1* *(continued)*
>
> - Gray ace. A person who is not sexually attracted to most people but may occasionally experience sexual attraction.
> - Pansexual. A person who is attracted to people across a range of gender identities and expressions. This is an alternative to bisexual, without reinforcing the gender binary implied by that term.
> - Omnisexual. A person who is attracted to all people, regardless of gender.
> - Aromantic. A person who is not romantically attracted to people.
> - Grayromantic. A person who occasionally experiences romantic attraction.
> - Romantic. Someone who experiences romantic but not sexual attraction.
> - Queer. People who do not conform to the dominant heterosexual (and heteronormative) paradigm.
> - Demisexual. People who rarely experience sexual attraction to others but may do so if they have a strong connection to someone first (for example, as friends).
> - Polyamorous. A person who is sexually or romantically involved with more than one other person at a time.
> - Dom/Sub. This stands for dominatrix/submissive identities, subpopulations of the BDSM (bondage and discipline, dominance and submission, and sadism and masochism) or kink community. Dom/Subs derive sexual identity and pleasure from dominant and/or submissive roles that can be either sexual or nonsexual, in the context of BDSM relationships.

SEXUAL IDENTITY RESEARCH, HISTORY, AND ADVANCES

One of the most pivotal characters in sexual identity research is Alfred Kinsey, a twentieth-century American biologist who became the first major sexologist. Along with his team, Kinsey studied the sexual behaviors and identities of eighteen thousand people.[6] Based on this work, he developed the now famous Kinsey Scale, which places a person's sexual attraction on a scale ranging from 0 (exclusively opposite-sex attraction) to 6 (exclusively same-sex attraction). The points in between represent gradations of attraction between these two poles. As we have discussed previously and will explore more fully in chapter 5, the notion of opposite-sex attraction versus same-sex attraction is limited by its definitions of gender. But the research and scale were both groundbreaking, and they may represent the first scientific recognition of the fact that a significant number of people who identified themselves as heterosexual had had same-sex attraction or experiences. In fact, 37 percent of the men interviewed reported some same-sex experience, as did a smaller proportion of females (13 percent). Kinsey's work established variation in sexual attraction and behavior regardless of identity, revealing that there was much more of a gray area than had previously been thought.

Several pivotal moments in lesbian, gay, and (to a lesser extent) bisexual history saw members of sexual minority groups become more visible in the fight against discrimination. The gay rights movement began in earnest with the 1969 Stonewall Riots, when patrons of the Stonewall Inn, a gay bar in Greenwich Village, in New York City, resisted arrest during a police raid. To mark the anniversary, the New York LGBTQ community instituted an annual gay pride parade.

In the 1950s, being gay was considered pathological, and homosexuality was included in the American Psychiatric Association's *Diagnostic and Statistical Manual of Mental Disorders* (*DSM*) as a paraphilia (an abnormal sexual desire; see chapters 8 and 9 for more in-depth discussions of paraphilias and their depathologization).[7] This changed only when Evelyn Hooker published powerful research showing comparable rates of mental health issues in both heterosexual and homosexual men.[8] This research, along with the rising gay rights movement sparked by Stonewall, pushed the *DSM* to change the category of homosexuality to a "sexual orientation disturbance."[9] *DSM*'s third edition shifted this to "ego-dystonic homosexuality."[10] Only in the revised third edition, released in 1987, was that categorization removed.[11]

In 1977, when pride parades and gay activism were taking root across the country, Harvey Milk was elected to the San Francisco Board of Supervisors. An outspoken, charismatic advocate and pivotal figure within the gay pride movement in the 1970s, he was murdered by a fellow board member in 1978. Still, it seemed that the work of Stonewall and Milk was accelerating the acceptance of gay men and women in America. That changed with the arrival of the HIV/AIDS epidemic that decimated the gay male community in the early 1980s.

Human immunosuppression virus (HIV), which progresses into autoimmune deficiency syndrome (AIDS), was first called GRID (gay-related immune disorder) because it disproportionately affected gay men. Fear of the virus spread rapidly across the world, and ignorance about the means of its transmission meant that those with the disease were often quarantined and shunned.[12] The conservative and religious right took the opportunity to blame the disease on what they referred to as God's wrath toward people who committed the sin of homosexuality, and progress toward LGBTQ rights stalled and was even reversed. Outspoken advocates like Larry Kramer, a founding member of the AIDS Coalition to Unleash Power (ACT UP), tried tirelessly to draw attention to AIDS as a public health crisis. President Ronald Reagan ignored the epidemic until 1985. It was only when people considered to be deserving of help (like hemophiliacs) began contracting the disease that public attention and resources became available.[13] It is no accident that the largest funding for HIV/AIDS treatment to this day is funded through the Ryan White Comprehensive AIDS Resources Emergency Act of 1990, named after a young hemophiliac who contracted the disease from a blood transfusion.

The pendulum for gay rights legislation swung back in the late 1990s and 2000s. First, the implementation of the "don't ask, don't tell" policy allowed gay people to serve in the military (with the proviso that they not disclose their sexual identity). Then came the decriminalization of sodomy laws in *Lawrence v. Texas* in 2003, and finally certain states began to recognize same-sex marriage—starting with Massachusetts in 2004.

However, even as LGBTQ rights seemed to be expanding, anti-LGBTQ groups worked against them—most notably to prevent federal or state legalization of same-sex marriage and with legislation like the Defense of Marriage Act of 1996, which defined marriage as a union between one man and one woman and was signed into law by President Bill Clinton. In 2013, the pendulum swung again, and Edie Windsor won her case in the Supreme Court, overturning section 3 of the Defense of Marriage Act as unconstitutional. This paved the way for *Obergefell v. Hodges*, in which the Supreme Court legalized same-sex marriage federally in 2015, immediately overturning any state prohibitions.

But homophobia has not been stamped out in America. During 2016, six antigay measures were passed in Florida, Kansas, Mississippi, and Tennessee. More were passed in Texas, South Dakota, and Alabama during 2017. The number of hate crimes toward LGBTQ people is also still incredibly high—twenty-eight people were killed in 2016 (not counting the forty-nine killed at the Pulse nightclub in Orlando, Florida), and isolated incidents continued to increase in 2017, with fifty-two LGBT people being killed—perhaps related to the current political climate.[14] And although the school climate survey conducted biannually by the Gay Lesbian Sexuality Education Network (GLSEN) has shown some improvement in recent years, the rate of that improvement seems to be slowing.[15] The statistics on harassment and discrimination in schools is still startling: 70.1 percent of young people reported verbal harassment based on their sexual orientation and 59.1 percent reported such harassment based on gender expression, while 48.7 percent reported electronic harassment and 28.9 percent reported physical harassment.[16] This harassment hurts school performance and increases dropout rates, which puts LGBT youth at greater risk of poverty.[17]

Perhaps as a result of the still-hostile environment, LGBTQ people (especially youth) are at a higher risk of substance use, depression, anxiety, and post-traumatic stress disorder.[18] They also have far more elevated risk of suicide, with 31 percent of LGBT youth in one study reporting having attempted suicide, compared to 4.1 percent of the general population.[19] Refer to the resources section at the end of the chapter for tools from GLSEN and True Colors United (formerly the True Colors Fund), which help create affirming environments in school and agency settings, and the Trevor Project, which provides support for individuals at risk of suicide.

The omission of sexual and gender identity from the census makes it nearly impossible to determine how many members of sexual minority groups live in America. The Williams Institute estimates that 11.3 million adults identify themselves as LGBT, of which approximately 1.4 million are transgender.[20] Census data suggest that there are approximately 935, 229 same-sex couples in the United States.[21] In a synthesis of LGBT population data in the United States, Karen Fredriksen-Goldsen and Hyun-Jun Kim estimate that there are approximately 2.7 million LGBT individuals over the age of fifty (or 2.4 percent of the population) in the country.[22] The authors also identified health disparities as a serious area of concern for older LGBT adults, who were at greater risk for nine out of twelve chronic health conditions—including a weakened immune system, neck pain, and lower-back pain.[23]

As social workers practicing with sexual minority clients, we must understand that while conditions have certainly improved dramatically, especially in cities, members of sexual minority groups are still the targets of significant stigma and discrimination. Exploring current or past experiences of discrimination and harassment with your clients can provide powerful insights into their experience of the world and feelings of safety and belonging. Often members of these groups have to work hard to develop personal resilience and a social safety net to protect themselves from the negative messaging in society at large. Given social work's ethical imperative to honor the dignity and worth of all people and to address social injustice, advocating for the rights of clients in these groups is key to the social worker's role.[24]

COMING OUT AS GAY

Vivienne Cass has presented the most widely known early coming-out model.[25] This model identifies a six-stage linear process, according to which people move through stages from identity confusion to identity synthesis (see box 4.2). During the first stage, identity confusion, people question who they are with respect to their sexuality in relation to their world and acknowledge that they are different in some way from their heterosexual peers. In the next stage, identity comparison, they begin to recognize that they might be different because they are gay. During the third stage, identity tolerance, they recognize that they are probably gay. In the fourth stage, identity acceptance, they acknowledge that they are gay and become more comfortable with that idea. During the fifth stage, identity pride, they openly express their gay identity and take pride in and find connection through that identity. In the final stage, identity synthesis, they integrate their gay identity into notions of their fuller self, and their gayness becomes a positive aspect of who they are.

Cass's model highlights the need for the individual to work through the cognitive dissonance of two conflicting ideas: "I'm gay, but (or and) being gay is bad." The social worker's role is to support the client as they resolve that conflict, helping them understand that they are not bad, and to work from a social justice perspective to end discrimination and stigma based on nonheterosexual identity.

Box 4.2
COMING-OUT MODEL

Identity confusion: Who am I? Am I different?
Identity comparison: Maybe I am gay.
Identity tolerance: I may be gay.
Identity acceptance: I am gay.
Identity pride: I am proud to be gay!
Identity synthesis: Being gay is one positive aspect of who I am.

Some have critiqued Cass's model and pointed out that the coming-out process is often iterative rather than linear.[26] People may proceed through the process at different speeds and in a different order. It is possible that someone is out about their gay identity with friends and at work but not with their family. In addition, the idea that someone can focus on these developmental tasks comes from a privileged position. It is much harder to attend to sexual identity if you're preoccupied with finding food and shelter. From a person-in-environment perspective, try to understand how hard it can be to work through these developmental stages in the context of a hostile sociopolitical environment, in which an LGBT identity is constantly marginalized or erased. Despite these criticisms, looking at potential developmental milestones of integrating an understanding of sexual identity can help us work with clients.

One key caution is never to assume that those clients who are younger and are coming out at a time when same-sex marriage is federally recognized are subject to less stigma and discrimination. While the climate has changed, LGBT acceptance is uneven in America. In the LGBT healthy aging study, Fredriksen-Goldsen found that those in the invisible generation (who lived through the Great Depression and World War II) and the silenced generation (who lived through the McCarthy era) experienced less discrimination and stigmatization than those in the pride (who lived through the Stonewall Riots and the late 1960s and early 1970s) or baby-boomer generation. She posits that this is because those in the last generation were less closeted and thus more visible targets for violence.[27]

Although in discussions of sexuality, emphasis is often placed on gay and lesbian identities, the following section explores asexuality, bisexuality, and polyamory in more depth. This is an effort to reveal the existence of these sexual identities and raise their visibility.

ASEXUALITY

While there has been very little social work research on asexuality, some scholarship has begun to emerge. Lori Brotto and Morag Yule conducted a literature review to determine whether asexuality met the criteria for a psychiatric syndrome (or a symptom of one), a paraphilia, an independent sexual orientation, or none of the above.[28] The authors concluded that there was not sufficient evidence to define asexuality as a psychiatric condition or a paraphilia (though they recognized that some people who identify as asexual also have a paraphilia), but they concluded that "asexuality is a heterogeneous entity that likely meets conditions for a sexual orientation, and that researchers should further explore evidence for such a categorization."[29] Cranney also argued that asexuality meets the criteria for a sexual orientation.[30]

Asexuals are becoming more visible.[31] The number of people who identify themselves as asexual remains small: They are estimated to make up 0.5–1.5 percent of the population.[32] However, Anthony Bogaert argues that the rates are likely similar to those who identify as gay or lesbian, with much less media and political attention making asexual people hesitant to come out.[33] It is important to note that while asexual people do not experience sexual attraction, they may experience romantic attachment and intimacy.[34] Nuanced identities that include gray ace, demisexual, or aromantic (see box 4.1) have evolved out of the inadequacy of the label "asexual" to capture some of the variety of ways in which people experience sexuality, intimacy, and romantic attachment. We can sometimes differentiate between people with low desire and people who are, in fact, asexual by discussing sexual fantasies and masturbation. Research suggests that those who identify as asexual have far fewer sexual fantasies, and 40 percent report never having had a sexual fantasy.[35] Those who identified as asexual also masturbated significantly less frequently than those who did not.[36]

Nicolette Robbins, Kathryn Graff Low, and Anna Query proposed a coming-out model for asexuality that bears some similarities to Cass's model.[37] While the authors acknowledge that for some asexuals there is no practical value to coming out, it can help others locate potential romantic partners and a community. This model was built on themes that emerged from the authors' qualitative study on the experiences of asexuals in coming out that included "skepticism from family and friends, lack of acceptance and misunderstanding, non-disclosure of the asexual identity, relief upon discovering the asexual community, and the role of the internet in asexual discovery and expression."[38] The six stages in their model are outlined in box 4.3.

Box 4.3
ASEXUAL COMING-OUT MODEL

Identity confusion: having a sense of being different or "broken"[39]

Discovery of terminology: identity discovery through the internet

Exploration and education: internet learning

Identity acceptance and salience negotiation: recognizing asexuality as "valid"and exploring the meaning of the asexual label for oneself

Coming out: deciding to acknowledge one's asexual identity to others

Identity integration: self-acceptance and pride in one's asexual identity, regardless of whether one comes out to others

---

The authors note that the identity confusion stage may feel quite different for people who identify as asexual compared to lesbians, gays, or bisexuals because there is such limited information about asexuality—few people have even heard of it. The invisibility and silence around asexuality in the common lexicon makes stage two (discovery of terminology) critically important to give individuals language for their experience. In stage three (exploration and education), the internet has played a crucial role in creating access to both information and community. Stage four (identity acceptance and salience negotiation) is a point of departure from other coming-out models. While identity acceptance is a consistent stage, salience negotiation is not. Coming out as asexual may not have any particular purpose for an individual who is uninterested in developing relationships or finding a partner. While not all asexual people are in relationships, those who are may be in relationships with other asexual people or with sexual people who choose to be nonsexual or who navigate occasional sexual relationships with their partner. For those who chose to navigate stage 5 (coming out), the experience was an expression of a key part of their identity, educating others, and a "strategy for coping with sexual-normative expectations."[40] Stage 6 (identity integration) is developing an internalized sense of pride and self-acceptance around their asexual identity and can be experienced whether or not they chose to come out. Thus, stage 6 can occur regardless of whether or to what extent stage 5 occurs. The prevalence of information about asexuality both in the academic literature and on the internet is increasing. The Asexual Visibility and Education Network (https://www.asexuality.org/) is an important online resource that has created a space for both community building and education related to asexuality. Helping your clients locate information and develop a community are important steps to reducing feelings of isolation. However, as with other sexual orientations and identities, never assume the client is distressed or wants to explore their sexuality unless they express such concerns in session. Avoiding pathologizing sexual-minority status is part of an affirming practice.

NONMONOSEXUALITY: BISEXUALITY, PANSEXUALITY, AND OMNISEXUALITY

The invisibility of bisexuality in the social work literature mirrors the felt experience of many bisexual people who don't feel that they belong or are welcomed by the heterosexual or gay communities.[41] Pepper Schwartz and Martha Kempner start their myth section with "Poor bisexuals! No one wants to believe in them."[42] An important part of the therapeutic relationship is to make the client's bisexual identity feel visible and not anticipate that this is a phase en route to a fully gay identity.

While bisexuality emerged in the 1970s, it has not been embraced and expanded in the way that may have been anticipated. Fewer people are claiming the label "bisexual," compared to more expansive and less stigmatized terms like "pansexual," "omnisexual," and "queer."[43] In a study of nonmonosexuals (people attracted to individuals of more than one sex), only 13.5 percent identified as bisexual, with the remainder claiming one of twenty-one other identities—including "queer" and "pansexual." Interestingly, 57 percent had identified as bisexual at some point but no longer did, which speaks to the evolving nature of identity and the limitations of a binary identity. In addition, 13.5 percent preferred not to attach any label to their sexual identity. The label "queer", though more expansive, was used selectively by some participants who felt uncomfortable with its roots in academia and the implied connection to white privilege, but who found it helpful in some situations.

Why not choose a bisexual label? The key reasons participants gave were the stigma of it and transgender awareness. Rather than recognizing bisexuality as having a particular sexual attraction, people often see it as specific to sexual behavior and equate it with promiscuity.[44] This myth has created a distrust of bisexuality and of bisexuals as people who have multiple partners, are more likely to cheat, and are more likely to transmit sexually transmitted infections—especially HIV.[45]

Another limitation of the bisexual label is that it reinforces the gender binary and so feels limiting and transphobic.[46] In this way, the term "bisexual" implies that there are only two sexes, leaving no room for transgender or nonbinary identities or attractions. So for those who acknowledge being attracted to all people or who have nonbinary gender identities, "bisexual" does not fit. These individuals prefer the more inclusive "pansexual," "omnisexual," or "queer."

For clients who explore or embrace a bisexual identity, we must affirm that identity, never minimizing or erasing it. Supporting and connecting clients to networks and online resources (see the resources section at the end of the chapter) helps them develop a community—which they report is more difficult for them than for members of other sexual minority groups.[47] Those who have a partner with a different gender presentation than their own are often read as heterosexual, while those with a partner who appears to be of the same gender are often read as gay. In both situations, their bisexual identity is erased. Bisexuals with a same-sex partner often report feeling welcomed by the gay and lesbian community, only to be rejected when they take a partner with a different gender presentation.

Given this social context, the coming-out process is different for bisexuals than for members of other sexual minority groups. Mary Bradford proposed a four-stage identity-development model that includes questioning reality (when the individual recognizes their attraction to both sexes but does not have modeling for that as a reality); inventing identity (when the individual acknowledges their attractions and begins to seek a fitting label for their reality); maintaining identity (when the individual exerts their bisexual identity despite a social context of marginalization, stigma, and erasure); and transforming action, an additional stage that not all people move to (when the individual works to create a community or take on a leadership role in the bisexual community).[48]

Bisexuals in relationships are faced with the choice of when to come out—on an online profile, on a first date, or at some further point that feels appropriate.[49] Such situations and disclosures can cause anxiety, as people may fear being rejected by a potential partner just on the basis of their identity.

Research suggests that the marginalization, stigmatization, and invisibility of bisexual identity has taken its toll. Bisexuals report worse mental health and higher substance use than heterosexuals, lesbians, or gays.[50] In their summary of the literature on bisexual health behaviors and outcomes, Greta Bauer and David Brennan acknowledged that bisexuals reported more anxiety and mood disorders, interpersonal violence, suicidal ideation, drug use during sex, and unmet service needs.[51] They also reported that bisexual men were at greater sexual health risk, and bisexual women were at increased risk of depression and sexually transmitted infections. Providing clients with a sex-positive, safe, affirming, and open space to explore their sexual identity may be a step toward reducing these disparities. We must avoid pathologization, but we must also not ignore the potential issues. As Weber points out, "it is vital that social workers do not assume that all bisexual people share similar experiences, relationships, and sexual practices."[52]

Geordana makes important recommendations for social work practice with bisexual individuals. Some have already been covered, such as not making assumptions about a client's orientation or gender identity or assuming that their presenting problem stems from their bisexual identity. Weber's other suggestions are worth reinforcing as well—such as developing your own self-awareness and understanding your own feelings related to the dominant norm of heterosexuality and to bisexuals. Acknowledge your own homophobia, biphobia, and transphobia by exploring the ways in which you "propogat(e) institutionalized and socialized oppression."[53] And "model bi-affirming behavior" in couples and family treatment.[54]

POLYAMORY

Sexual identities that fall under the umbrella of polyamorous or consensually nonmonogamous, as well as what Jeffrey Parsons and coauthors call "monogamish," will be explored fully in chapter 8.[55] Here, however, we will briefly review these as part of our coverage of sexual identities.

Elisabeth Sheff defined polyamory as "consensual, openly conducted, multiple-partner relationships," while Christian Klesse acknowledges its use as an "umbrella term and synonym for consensual nonmonogamy."[56] It is important to mention it here as another sexual identity that has suffered from invisibility, marginalization, and stigmatization.[57] This invisibility makes it difficult to estimate the prevalence of polyamory. Sheff shows how estimates from internet polyamory sites differ dramatically, from 1.2 million to 9.8 million.[58]

Regardless of how many people practice polyamory, you can operate from the position that polyamory is a viable relationship option for clients. Some people claim a polyamorous sexual identity that does not relate to the gender identity of their partner, while others claim polyamorous and other identities, like queer polyamorous or lesbian polyamorous. The last two identities refer to practicing consensual nonmonogamy in the context of relationships exclusively with individuals with a variety of gender identities (polyamorous pansexual) or exclusively with women (lesbian polyamorous). Williams and Prior highlighted the dearth of knowledge about polyamory within social work. They urge you to explore your own biases related to monogamy and nonmonogamy and expand your understanding by reviewing both the professional and the popular literature.[59] Chapter 8 provides concrete resources to guide this process.

FLUID VERSUS STATIC IDENTITY

Some research has suggested that cisgendered women's sexual attraction and behavior is more fluid over time and that cisgendered men's is more static.[60] Meredith Chivers and coauthors conducted studies of physical and subjective sexual arousal using vaginal pulse amplitude and penile plethysmography to measure engorgement in the genitals as a result of observing images.[61] Men who had sex with men were aroused by images of men, and men who had sex with women were aroused by images of women. However, women were aroused by images of both men and women, whether or not they identified as heterosexual or gay. There is some question about whether these findings still hold, with some researchers suggesting that male sexuality may also be quite fluid.[62] And obviously there can be sexually fluid males and sexually static females. But in general, females are more likely to vary who they are sexually and romantically involved with. Thus, it is vital not to assume anything about sexual identity and behavior. An open, nonjudgmental stance provides the client with the space to share their experiences without preconceived expectations limiting their comfort.

Imagine that you are in practice. Gail, a divorced forty-six-year-old cisgender female with two children in college, comes to you because she is having difficulty talking to her children about her new relationship. You avoid making assumptions and instead lead with an open-ended question: "Tell me about your current relationship." It turns out that her new relationship is with a woman, and she is nervous that her two sons will react badly. When you ask Gail about her relationship history, you learn that she grew up in the South and felt compelled to get married to a man and have children because that was what was expected. Although she loves her former husband and sons very much, she wanted a chance to live authentically. As much as she feels ready to explore this aspect of her identity, she is also terrified. You provide a safe space for her to explore her feelings and affirm her efforts to express her authentic self. Had you made assumptions about Gail's current relationship, your interaction could have been very different—perhaps making Gail feel uncomfortable and even turning her away from treatment. Remaining open and curious creates room for clients to share their experiences with you.

ONLINE COMMUNITIES AND SEXUAL IDENTITY

Evidence suggests that the expansion in the numbers of sexual identities has been facilitated by the increased availability of online communities. The ability to search for, find information about, and connect with others whose experiences resonate with our own is increasing. Online communities expand our ability to meet people with similar and compatible identities, reduce our feelings of isolation, and provide both comfort and information.[63] Understanding the potential for online communities to be a source of both education and community for clients in sexual minority groups can provide an important resource as they explore their identity and test out appropriateness of fit.

IDENTITY-AFFIRMING PRACTICE

Unfortunately, the harm of a hostile social, political, or family environment means that people who do not identify as heterosexual suffer. As a result, those who identify as lesbian, gay, bisexual, pansexual, or queer are more likely to have higher rates of substance use, mental health issues, suicide attempts, and homelessness.[64] While 4–5 percent of the population is thought to identify as LGB, approximately 30 percent of homeless youth are thought to be LGBT.[65] A disproportionate number of these are young people of color.[66] Research suggests that hostile home environments contribute significantly to these numbers.[67] These experiences of discrimination emanate from homophobia, which has been defined as the "fear and/or hatred of gays, lesbians, and same-sex closeness."[68] It represents micro- and individual-level oppression based on sexual identity that is demonstrated through people's attitudes and behaviors.[69] Growing up in a society where homophobia or heterosexism is prevalent can lead people to internalize those attitudes.

Social workers have an opportunity to work on behalf of LGBTQ young people to combat homophobia and heterosexism, as well as to work with their families to expand understanding. One helpful resource is the

Family Acceptance Project (https://familyproject.sfsu.edu), spearheaded by Caitlin Ryan, which works to foster family acceptance of LGBTQ young people from various religious, cultural, and geographic backgrounds. The organization tries to find even a small shift in acceptance and common ground and works to maintain family connections whenever feasible and safe. Just as you may work with individuals to help them come out in relation to their specific sexual or gender identities, you may also help families with their own tasks of coming out over time.

Imagine that you are working with Tim, a fourteen-year-old cisgender male who attends the local public high school. Tim's parents reached out to get support for Tim, as the transition to high school seems to have been particularly hard for him. Usually happy-go-lucky and socially engaged, Tim has become quiet, even sullen. His parents worry that something is going on, but he won't talk to them. You spend a few sessions developing rapport and trust and let him sit for long periods of silence when he chooses to do so. Eventually, Tim opens up and tells you that he feels different. He isn't into girls, even though he tries hard to be. He is scared that he might be gay.

You first create a space for Tim to explore his fears about what being gay means to him. Then, when appropriate, you give him a chance to identify possible allies—people he might confide in so he does not feel so alone. Then you help him identify positive resources both in person and online, such as the school's gay-straight alliance. Identifying allies and resources, along with role-playing conversations, provides Tim with enough support to feel comfortable with his realization and identity for now. By providing unconditional positive regard and a space free of judgment, you allow Tim to work through his ambivalence and fear and also recognize his strengths and resilience. From a sex-positive perspective, you make sure that Tim knows he is allowed to have sexual desires and deserves to develop his full sexual self. When he is ready, and if appropriate, you can connect Tim's family to the Family Acceptance Project. You remind Tim that you remain available as a resource for him and his parents as he continues to explore his sexuality. This example of affirming practice is in stark contrast to reparative or conversion therapy.

Considerable work has been done to dispel the legitimacy and outline the significant dangers associated with reparative therapy, aimed at "converting" people who identity as gay, lesbian, or bisexual to a heterosexual orientation. Be sure to explore with your clients whether they have been exposed to reparative therapy techniques, as research suggests they may have very damaging results—with former clients describing feelings of "suppression, disconnection, and a sense of inauthenticity."[70]

Given that heterosexism still expects and assumes dominance of heterosexuality and considers sexual minority identities to be "other" or nonnormative, social workers should be aware of the potential for gay-affirming or sexual minority–affirming therapy as a way to combat stigma and generate resilience. The theme again is to provide a nonjudgmental space for your clients to explore their identity or issues related to sexuality through the lens of their identity without having a static, patriarchal, heteronormative expectation imposed upon them. Simply providing an affirming space can make a critical difference in reducing the risk for suicide, depression, substance use, and other potentially negative outcomes.

CHAPTER SUMMARY

This chapter explored sexual identity and the role of social workers in affirming nonheterosexual and nonmonosexual identities, providing clients with support and resources to identify and create a community when appropriate. The chapter also reinforced the ways in which identity labels evolve to meet the changing social and political landscape. It covered models for coming out as lesbian, gay, asexual, and bisexual as reference frames, while noting that everyone's unique experiences with sexuality should be recognized and affirmed. Finally, simply because a client presents as lesbian, bisexual, aromantic or any other sexual identity does not mean that this should necessarily be the focus of treatment. It may be just one identifying contextual factor for whatever is going on. Sex-positive social work can make people with marginalized sexual identities feel seen and supported—not pathologized.

DISCUSSION QUESTIONS

1. As suggested at the beginning of the chapter, jot down five identities that come to your mind. What categories do they represent (for example, relational, action or occupation, social group, or cultural or religious affiliation)? How have these changed or stayed the same from five years ago?

2. Discuss the impact of sexual minority status on adolescent development. How might a hostile social context impact development, both positively and negatively?

3. What do you consider to be some of the main factors in sexual identity–affirming practice?

4. Review the coming-out models presented for gay, lesbian, and asexual people. In what ways are the models similar and different? How, if at all, would you revise the models to be more reflective of the experiences you have seen?

RESOURCES

Asexual Visibility and Education Network: https://www.asexuality.org
American Institute of Bisexuality: http://www.americaninstituteofbisexuality.org
Bisexual Resource Center: https://biresource.org
Family Acceptance Project: https://familyproject.sfsu.edu
Gay Lesbian Sexuality Education Network (GLSEN): https://www.glsen.org (for resources and tool kits aimed at creating a more affirming school climate)
Trevor Project: http://www.thetrevorproject.org/ (for resources and a lifeline aimed at preventing LGBTQ suicide)
True Colors United: https://truecolorsunited.org (for resources to help create more inclusive and affirming agency settings, such as the True Inclusion Toolkit [https://www.missionbox.com/article/667/true-colors-fund-true-inclusion-toolkit])

5

GENDER IDENTITY

RELEVANT CSWE COMPETENCIES

Competency 1: Demonstrate Ethical and Professional Behavior

Competency 2: Engage Diversity and Difference in Practice

Competency 3: Advance Human Rights and Social, Economic, and Environmental Justice

When I hand out my syllabus at the beginning of each course, I often ask my students why they think there is a single session on gender identity when the course is about human sexuality. You may be wondering the same thing about this chapter. My students guess a host of reasons, many of which are right. Here I will focus on two main ones: First, regular use of the acronym LGBTQ (lesbian, gay, bisexual, transgender, and queer or questioning) has caused some confusion, and many people conflate sexual identity and gender identity and think that "transgender" is a sexual identity. As we saw in chapter 4, all people have a sexual identity that is separate from their gender identity, whether they are cisgender, nonbinary, transgender, or any other gender identity. A transgender female may identify as heterosexual, lesbian, queer, or asexual. None of these identifications changes their sense of gender identity. This is because there is a distinction between gender identity (how we feel about and present our gender to the world) and sexual identity (our sexual attractions and behaviors).

Second, I include gender identity in the course and in this book because it is rarely covered elsewhere in the social work curriculum. When it is covered, it is often pathologized and discussed in reference to the inclusion of gender dysphoria in the fifth edition of the American Psychiatric Association's *Diagnostic and Statistical Manual of Mental Disorders* (*DSM*).[1] Discussing gender identity in a factual, affirming, and nonpathologizing way better prepares social workers for the realities of gender identity in practice.

DISTINGUISHING BETWEEN SEX AND GENDER

As we saw in chapter 4, identity is how we define who we are and how others define us. Gender identity is how we understand ourselves in relation to gender and gender expression regardless of our anatomy, which until recently was rigidly expressed by the binary of male (or masculine) and female (or feminine). While many people conflate sex and gender, they are in fact distinct. Your sex is your biological, genetic, and chromosomal attributes and your anatomy, whereas your gender is how you experience, present, and perform your masculinity, femininity, both, or neither. For example, in chapter 2 we discussed intersex individuals who are born with some combination of typically male or female genitalia and chromosome patterns. Though they're intersex, their gender depends entirely on how they feel and choose to express themselves to the world.

In the excellent video introduction to transgender identity created by the New York City LGBT Center, the social worker Carrie Davis notes that people often have an irrational fear of gender differences.[2] I challenge you to contemplate your relationship to gender and gender roles, and why gender difference might feel scary for you. What conscious or unconscious biases do you have about sex and gender roles? I also encourage you to consider exactly what feels scary about it, as a way to unpack any underlying transphobia—fear or dislike of or prejudice against transgender people or people who do not perform typical masculine or feminine gender roles. In many ways, we use gender markers as a quick way to categorize people and understand how we should relate to them. For example, if you know you're talking to a five-year-old boy, you may think you should talk about sports or *Star Wars*, whereas with a five-year-old girl you might discuss dancing or baking. This is an ingrained generalization that we mistakenly use for comfort. Or you may find yourself complimenting girls on their appearance (their hair, shoes, or clothes), while you compliment boys on their achievements (their grades or sports trophies).

Our need to identify gender as a way of understanding and relating to someone is illustrated in how we treat people who are expecting a baby. Often the first thing we ask someone who is pregnant or becoming a parent is "What is the sex?" or "Is it a boy or a girl?" We do this so we can understand who we think they are and what we may expect of them. These days many people even throw "gender reveal" parties, where the sex of the baby is disclosed to family members and friends before the birth. People who throw these parties often divide clothes into pink or blue and toys into dolls or trucks, indicating the expected presentation and activities for boys and girls—active and nurturing, respectively. Such practices are widespread. If you think about when and how you first learned about gender, you might be tempted to reply, "I just knew." But if you look more closely, most likely social expectations were reinforced through cultural or religious norms in your home, and in other major institutions, especially schools and media.

Gender roles and the things associated with them, such as clothes and activities, are culturally defined. For example, while pink is currently thought to be a very feminine color, in medieval England it was a masculine color, and girls wore blue. Similarly, in the United States only girls and women are expected to wear skirts, but in Scotland men proudly wear kilts. Gender roles and expression differ across cultures, but in the United States boys are discouraged from expressing emotions and taught not to cry, while girls are encouraged to express a full range of emotions, even with tears.[3] Americans are suspicious of androgyny, which is unfortunate because everything might be simpler if we created universal access to bathrooms, for example, or pronouns that are universally applicable. Yet we are more comfortable maintaining the patriarchal systems to which we have become accustomed. In fact, in the Vanatinai language of Papua New Guinea there are no masculine and feminine pronouns, which results in a very egalitarian society.[4] Certainly, if our goal is equality, then there is no need for distinction.[5]

The theoretical explanation for how we enact our gender (and sexuality) is called heteronormativity. Part of the context of patriarchy, heteronormativity is the social expectation that there are two (and only two) distinct genders, with each having distinct roles.[6] Related to these distinct gender roles is the cultural assumption that "heterosexuality is normative and that nonheterosexuality is deviant and intrinsically less desirable."[7] This sets up the social expectations attached to those roles: women are nurturers, fragile, and in need of protection; while men are leaders, providers, and protectors. There is no room for those who do not fit neatly within these roles, so they are stigmatized, discriminated against, and oppressed. A large percentage of the school-based violence noted in the Gay Lesbian Sexuality Education Network survey discussed in chapter 4 was in response to transgression of gender roles, norms, and behavior. In fact, 94 percent of LGBTQ students in the survey had heard negative comments based on their gender expression, related to their not being masculine or feminine enough.[8]

With rigid gender roles come expectations of sexual behavior. The defined gender roles of passive versus active play out in sexuality: male-identified people are taught and expected to initiate sexual activity, and female-identified people are taught to be passive, receptive, and hard to get. This can create anxiety for men who are expected to always initiate sex and for women who learn that they should set firm boundaries around sexual activity, which become difficult to transcend within a sexual experience to be fully free, present, and engaged.

While the media visibility of transgender individuals and celebrities has increased as transgender celebrities like Laverne Cox and Caitlin Jenner have shared their stories publicly (see figure 5.1), people who fall under the transgender umbrella are still at much greater risk for violence, housing and job discrimination, and harassment at school. They also do not have the federal protection that they need to ensure their safety and equality. In 2018, twenty-nine transgender people were murdered, the highest number ever

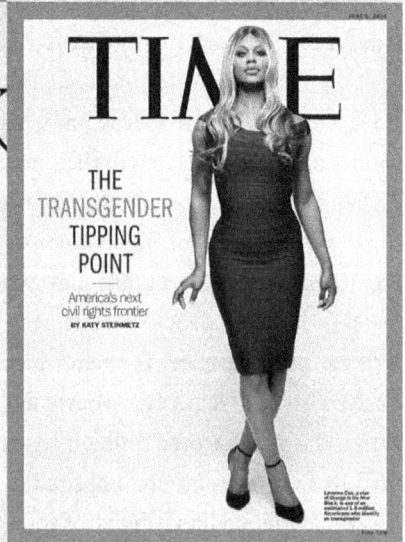

FIGURE 5.1 National magazine covers representing transgender people

recorded, and most of them were transgender women of color—the most vulnerable targets of violence and discrimination.[9] These women are at much greater risk for suicide attempts and dying by suicide.[10] In fact, in the United States Transgender Survey of more than 27,000 people, 82 percent had had suicidal thoughts, and 40 percent had attempted suicide.[11] These are devastating statistics. Technicalities in data collection and underreporting mean that the figures are likely to be underestimates. As with LGBQ individuals, transgender students are more likely to drop out of school because of bullying and victimization, which means they are less likely to graduate—which in turn affects their college attendance and earning potential.[12] This also robs society of important intellectual and creative social capital. We lose their potential contributions, and the economy as a whole suffers.[13]

LANGUAGE IS DYNAMIC

We saw in chapter 4 (on sexual identity) that language is dynamic, ever changing, and evolving to capture the nuances of our experiences. Language reinforces the norms of the dominant culture, so it can enforce the gender binary and transphobia. In this way, language is a powerful tool through which we can communicate our understanding, affirmation, and support. However, because language is always evolving, it is important to stay abreast of current terminology. Resources like True Colors United, and Gender Spectrum offer terminology and language guidelines (see box 5.1 for some definitions). It is also important to have a dialogue with your clients so you use language that feels affirming and not disparaging to them. For example, some people use the term "gender nonconforming." However, others feel that is punitive, positioning those who do not uphold traditional gender roles as gender outlaws. For this reason they may prefer the term "gender nonbinary," which captures the fact that their gender transcends the traditional binary. Others may embrace their role as gender outlaws or may prefer to use no term at all. As always, maintain open communication with your clients so you affirm their understanding of their identity and use language that feels supportive and inclusive.

An example of the quickly changing terminology can be found in the term "cisgender." Recently, cisgender has come into common usage to represent someone whose biological sex is congruent with their gender identity. The term has been embraced as a counterbalance to the term "transgender." Juxtaposing "transgender female" and "female" supposes that only the transgender person's gender needs a qualification, indicating that female is the norm and transgender is aberrant. However, using "transgender female" along with "cisgender female" qualifies both terms, and they are treated equally.

Despite this logic, which emanated from Dana Defosse in the field of biology and was subsequently embraced first by transgender activists and later by academics, it is not beyond critique. Anne Enke points out that if we believe that gender is not permanent and immutable but rather socially constructed, as Butler and other queer and feminist scholars have asserted, then the use of "cis" "arrives to affirm not only that it is possible for one to *stay* 'a woman' but also that one *is* 'born a woman' after all."[14] In this way, "cis" and "trans" become yet another binary. There is also an implication that use of the term "cisgender," embraced within academia, comes with an undertone of educational, race, and class privilege that is not available to everyone. This shows how language is dynamic and can be personally interpreted. So again, check with your clients about their preferred terminology and how they understand it. For example, you can ask your clients, "How do you identify your gender?"

Box 5.1

DEFINITIONS

KEY TERM	DEFINITION
Cisgender	A term used to describe a person whose assigned sex at birth corresponds with their gender identity.
Cisgenderism	An ideology that delegitimizes people's own knowledge of their genders and their bodies;[15] the assumption that all people are cisgender, the belief system that underlies transphobia.[16]

Cisnormativity	The belief that people will live out the experience of their gender in the sex they were assigned at birth, similar to the way in which heteronormativity sets up two binary genders with specific expectations around gender role behavior;[17] presumes that man and woman are the only viable gender categories.
Gender expansive	A term used to encompass the range of gender identities and expressions under the transgender umbrella; preferred over the commonly used term "gender nonconforming," which implies there is a norm to which individuals should conform.
Genderqueer	An identity label used by people whose gender identity and/or expression differs from the man-woman binary and/or who do not ascribe to traditional gender roles.[18]
Nonbinary	A term used by individuals to describe their experience of gender as outside of or somewhere between the binary categories of man and woman.
Transgender	An umbrella term referring to a person whose gender differs from societal expectations of their assigned sex at birth or who defy traditional gender categories in some way.[19]
Transphobia	"Intense dislike of or prejudice against transgender people or irrational fear, anger, hatred, disgust, for and/or discomfort with individuals who do not conform to society's gender expectations."[20] Transphobia typically refers to individual interpersonal actions and attitudes, whereas cisgenderism broadens the analysis to the structural level.

Source: From J. Shelton, and SJ Dodd, "Beyond the Binary: Addressing Cisnormativity in the Social Work Classroom," *Journal of Social Work Education,* table 1, 56, no. 1 (2020): 179–185. Reprinted by permission of the Publisher Taylor and Francis.

AVOIDING THE GENDER BINARY
AND ITS ASSUMPTIONS

Implicit within the chapter so far has been the notion that the gender binary is socially constructed, narrow, and confining. It can also be damaging for people who feel unable to perform or conform to strictly held gender standards. So as with all of the topics we have discussed so far, avoid assumptions.

Don't assume that you understand a person's experience of their gender, how they identify, or whether they have always presented and identified themselves the way they currently do. This also holds for partners, friends, or family members of clients.

Consider Sharon, a fifty-four-year-old cisgender female. She has been your client for just over a month. She came to you because she has been suffering chronic lower back pain for the past six months, and it has pushed her into a depression. One day, Sharon is very upset about a report in the news that three transgender youth were assaulted at a bus stop near her home. You begin to explore Sharon's reaction to the events and try to get an understanding of what aspects of the event are particularly upsetting for her. After a little while she says, "My dad transitioned to female when I was thirty-five, so I find this very upsetting. What if she had been visiting me?" Although you had explored Sharon's childhood and her family relationships, you had used the gender-neutral language of "parent" in your exchanges, which left room for her to describe her family for you. You created a sex- and gender-positive environment in which Sharon felt comfortable to disclose that she has a parent who identifies as transgender, which can inform how you explore the violent event with her.

As this example indicates, you should avoid making assumptions about not only your clients' sexual and gender identity, but also about the sexual and gender identity of their loved ones, friends, and partners. As discussed in the next section, sometimes our assumptions are revealed by our reflexive use of pronouns.

A WORD ON PRONOUNS

Pronouns such as he, his, or him and she, her, or hers are used routinely and almost subconsciously assigned to people, whether we know them or not and regardless of whether we have asked them for their pronouns. If we do not know them, we usually make an assumption about their pronouns based on the extent their appearance can be read as male or female. While there is some disagreement within the transgender community about requesting disclosure of pronouns, a universal approach to asking everyone for their pronouns offers an opportunity for everyone to claim the pronouns of their choice. Some people find the practice of requesting a pronoun insulting—for example, Laverne Cox says, "I think what I'm going for is obvious"—while others feel uncomfortable and "outed" by the process. Jen Manion and Dean Spade have eloquently presented the pros and cons of asking pronouns, illustrating disagreement within the transgender and gender nonbinary community. Perhaps it's best to avoid sex-assigned pronouns altogether, as in the Vanatinai example, since they are unnecessary in language or in life.[21] Assigning sex to pronouns simply reinforces a patriarchal hierarchy and reinforces gender roles. In fact, the gender-neutral pronoun "they" has been accepted for singular usage by the American Psychological Association style guide, and was awarded 2019 "word of the year" by Merriam-Webster's Dictionary.[22]

Importantly, if you ask someone for their pronouns, you should then use them. To do otherwise is called misgendering, and though it happens all the time, it can cause significant distress. It is particularly damaging in the therapeutic setting, where misgendering signals to the client that you do not see them as they wish to be seen or as who they truly are. If you are talking to family members or other providers about a client, be sure to use the correct name and pronoun and correct others who do not. If you accidentally misgender a client, acknowledging your error gives you the opportunity to repair the therapeutic relationship.

PATHOLOGIZING GENDER

In chapter 4, we discussed changes in homosexuality's inclusion in various editions of the *DSM* and its eventual removal. The categorization of issues related to gender identity has also changed through the different editions. In the third edition of the *DSM*, gender identity disorder was listed under psychosexual disorders and defined as "incongruence between anatomic sex and gender identity."[23] In the fourth edition, it was listed under sexual and gender identity disorders, with the definition shifting slightly: "strong and persistent cross-gender identification accompanied by persistent discomfort with one's assigned sex."[24] Importantly, in the fifth edition it has its own chapter and is listed as gender dysphoria.[25] While maintaining a diagnosis at all is problematic, since it is unnecessarily pathologizing and stigmatizing, the shift at least decouples gender identity from sexual dysfunctions and paraphilias; focuses on dysphoria to indicate that having a transgender or nonbinary identity itself is not problematic (rather, it is the distress created by that lived experience that warrants diagnosis); and acknowledges that a "strictly binary gender identity concept is no longer in line with the spectrum of gender identity variations."[26] In all editions, there are separate listings for children and for adolescents and adults. Separating children from adolescents and adults appears warranted, because there seems to be a distinction between whether a child feels they "want" to be or "identify with" a different gender (for example, a biological girl wanting to be a boy) and whether they "are" a different gender (for example, a biological girl believing themselves to be a boy). Those who feel that they are a different gender tend to maintain the feeling through adolescence into adulthood, while those who feel they want to be or identify with a different gender may grow out of those feelings.[27] Importantly, those who grow out of the feelings may still present in a gender fluid way as adults.

For example, imagine you are working with parents of a four-year-old boy who has always felt herself to be a girl. Though it took them some time to adjust, her parents have shifted to using feminine pronouns and her preferred name, Natalie. Natalie's parents have found support through online communities for parents with queer or gender-expansive kids but want more concrete support as they face the transition to the local elementary school. You are able to provide support and affirm the choices they have made to support Natalie in her gender expression, including dressing up as Rainbow Dash for Halloween and wearing dresses to preschool. You give the parents space to explore their fears about the transition from the friendly and familiar preschool setting to which they have all become accustomed to the bigger and less personal public school. You especially give them room to explore their concerns about Natalie being made fun of and picked on.

You are also able to help them think through how they want to approach the principal and teachers at the new school and give them an opportunity to role-play conversations with people from the school as well as with Natalie. You offer to be in touch with the school on their behalf, so that they do not have to do all of the work themselves. You then connect them to the social worker for the school district. The school social worker suggests that the district provide some professional development related to gender inclusiveness to provide concrete strategies for the teachers to use in the classroom. Some examples include not saying "boys and girls line up" but instead referring to "kindergarteners," "friends," or "students"—terms that are not gendered. The training would also emphasize the importance of honoring pronouns and names and being sure to make changes on class lists before saying names out loud to the class. The school social worker also offers to serve as a liaison between the parents and the school if needed. In this case, Natalie has been clear from an early age that she is a girl, and you support her parents in honoring her experience, trying to create a transition and school experience that is as positive as possible.

As gender-variant children approach adolescence, parents have questions. What, they wonder, is the right course of action? The onset of puberty especially can cause significant distress for transgender adolescents, as this is a time when they may feel alienated from their own body. Shifts in social expectations of gendered behavior in adolescence can also create a crisis.[28] In these circumstances, adolescents may take drastic measures to avoid acknowledging their body, including self-harming or skipping showers.[29] Medications known as pubertal blockers or puberty inhibitors can suppress the release of luteinizing and follicle-stimulating hormones and therefore prevent the release of testosterone and estrogen, arresting the physical changes of puberty. This suppression also makes the administration of hormones such as testosterone and estrogen more effective.

Young people who take pubertal blockers avoid having to counteract the physical changes of puberty: the enlarging of the penis and testicles, pronouncement of the Adam's apple, and deepening voice or the development of the breasts and hips. Early access to gender-affirming services and treatment, especially before adolescence, can reduce the trauma of these physical changes that run counter to a person's sense of themselves.[30] While advocates argue that this avoids unnecessary distress and makes physical transition and "passing" (not being read as transgender) easier, others argue that the age at which the medication must be started (ten or eleven) is far too young for a person to know whether they are transgender and could lead to irreversible physical changes and damage that they may later regret. We don't yet know whether such lasting damage actually occurs or whether puberty resumes after a person stops taking the medication. However, awareness of the availability of these types of medications is important. Reviewing available, up-to-date medical information to facilitate understanding some of the pros and cons will help you support clients as they make the choices that are right for them and/or their family members in consultation with the child's medical provider.

The shift in language and diagnostic definitions from gender identity disorder to gender dysphoria means that now to receive a diagnosis, not only must a person feel very uncomfortable with their biological gender, but also that discomfort must cause significant distress that lasts at least six months.[31] However, as Kayley Whalen (writing for the National LGBTQ Task Force) points out, there is a strong feeling that gender dysphoria should be removed from the *DSM* entirely because "gender variance is not a psychiatric disease."[32] Placing transgender identities within a disease framework makes transgender people even more vulnerable to oppression and discrimination within education, employment, housing, child custody, and so on. The diagnosis debate is complicated by the fact that a diagnosis is currently the mechanism with which a person obtains insurance coverage for related gender affirming medications and surgeries. However, such coverage could be provided without a pathologizing diagnosis as with other medical conditions, such as diabetes. For social workers, the takeaway lesson is that we must not pathologize gender variance in and of itself. Some people do experience distress, but we should not assume that is the case. Similarly, if you are approached by a prospective client who is transgender, do not assume that gender is a part of the presenting problem. It may not be.

OPPRESSION, DISCRIMINATION, AND CISSEXISM

Davis suggests that "many, if not most, transgender people struggle consciously or unconsciously as children with the understanding that their gender identities are considered socially and parentally inappropriate or deviant."[33] Davis goes on to suggest that this experience can disrupt their bonds of attachment with parents and caregivers. Given that most children's gender identity is established by age three, our heterocentric and cissexist culture poses a challenge for transgender children.[34] Many trans children experience early trauma as a result. Internalizing negative messages and stereotypes about people who transgress gender roles can create internalized transphobia, in which negative messaging is directed to the self. Transgressing social norms can contribute to mental health strain: transgender individuals suffer significantly higher rates of depression, anxiety, substance use, violence, and HIV compared to the general population.[35] Cultural and social norms related to gender and gender roles contribute to the especially high rates of family rejection among transgender youth, and a disproportionate number of them are homeless or unstably housed.[36] This rejection, compounded by educational and employment discrimination, leads to high rates of participation in the sex trades, including survival sex (that is, exchanging sex for shelter, goods, or money). Survival sex in turn puts people at risk of violence or HIV. Social workers must not only work on the individual level to support transgender individuals but also work to dismantle gendered and cissexist social norms and policies. An example is the controversy around public restrooms. However, there are many other systems that need intervention, including health care and health insurance practices, interpersonal violence services, shelter systems, and incarceration practices—all of which currently put transgender people in jeopardy.

SUPPORTING AUTHENTIC GENDER EXPRESSION AT ANY AGE

While transgender individuals will often say that they knew they were transgender from a very early age, others realize it later in life. Arlene Istar Lev proposed a six-stage model of transgender identity development—which she dubbed "transgender emergence" (see box 5.2)—with distinct needs that may warrant attention at each stage.[37] The stages identified are awareness; seeking information or reaching out; disclosure to significant others; exploration 1 (identity and self-labeling); exploration 2 (transition issues or possible body modification); and, integration (acceptance and post-transition issues). The model is linear, meaning that one stage must be resolved before progressing to the next, but it can also be iterative. A person may circle back and revisit prior stages to achieve fuller resolution and integration.

The initial stage of awareness of Lev's model acknowledges that many gender-variant people experience great distress as they realize their transgression of gender norms.[38] While not everyone experiences great distress, our cisnormative and heteronormative sociopolitical structure ensures that gender variance will generate at least some distress for most non-cis people. At this stage, your social work job is to normalize the experiences that the person may encounter as a result of emerging as transgender or nonbinary.

The second stage is gathering information and reaching out for support. As mentioned in chapter 4 in the context of asexual coming-out experiences, the internet is a treasure trove of information and communities that can alleviate feelings of isolation. The representation of transgender characters and story lines in the media has also helped. As a social worker, you can provide links to key resources and guidance about the quality of information, and you can connect your client to in-person groups.

Stage three is navigating how to disclose a transgender identity to an inner circle of friends and family members. You can provide support and opportunities for the person to explore their fears about identity disclosure. You can also role-play different scenarios with them, so they can explore disclosure strategies that feel authentic to them.

Stage four is the exploration of transgender identities and labels. You can help your client settle into their new identity, exploring different manifestations of gender expression and finding where they feel comfortable.

Stage five is the second level of exploration: transition issues, which often include changes in presentation, hormone treatment, and possibly surgery. You can provide support and information on—and serve as a sounding board for discussions of—issues of transition medication and surgery, especially exploring their risks and effects. You can also provide concrete support for the legal transition, which involves adjusting identification and documentation. Consistent with a sex-positive approach, do not forget to explore the implications of any decisions related to the transition on the person's sexuality and sexual expression. For example, it is important to explore with clients the potential impact of hormone medication and possible side effects on libido. Similarly, discussing ways in which genital sensation may change as a result of hormone treatment or surgical intervention should be addressed, not avoided.

The sixth and final stage of Lev's model is integration—acceptance and posttransition issues. Here your job is simply to support the client.[39] Transition issues will arise, often unexpectedly, along the way. Your client may be frustrated while trying to get their name changed on their college transcript so their application to graduate school is consistent. Or your client may want to explore navigating their high school reunion, which they anticipate will be both an exciting and a nerve-racking opportunity.

Box 5.2
TRANSGENDER EMERGENCE MODEL

- Awareness. Gender-variant individuals are often in significant distress. The need focuses on normalization of experiences involved in emerging as transgender.
- Seeking information or reaching out. A time of seeking education and support. Needs include links to resources and other transgender people
- Disclosure to significant others. This stage represents the struggle over how to disclose a transgender identity to family members and friends. The need focuses on support for the process of integration into the family or friend system.
- Exploration: identity and self-labeling. This stage represents exploration of a range of transgender identities. The need is for support in the articulation of their new identity and to foster comfort with their gender.

Box 5.2 (*continued*)

- Exploration: transition issues or possible body modification. During this stage the individual explores options for transition related to identity, presentation, and possibly physical modifications. The need is for support related to the resolution of decision making and advocacy toward their manifestation.
- Integration: acceptance and posttransition issues. This stage represents the integration and synthesis of transgender identity. The need is for support in adaptation to any transition-related issues.

Source: Lev, *Transgender Emergence.*

Through the application of Lev's model, you can provide critically important sex-positive, gender-affirming interventions and support to clients who are exploring their gender identity and help them address their hopes, ambivalence, and fears.[40]

CHAPTER SUMMARY

This chapter explored the distinction between gender identity and sexual identity. It also examined how according to social learning theory, social and cultural norms that emerge out of a heteronormative, cissexist system and its expectations that dictate gender-appropriate activities and behaviors are passed along. The negative impact of these deeply ingrained gender roles and expectations make transgender and nonbinary individuals targets of violence and discrimination and susceptible to family rejection and homelessness. Structural stigma and oppression lead to high rates of health and mental health issues for transgender and nonbinary people. Social workers can be advocates here, fighting against transgender discrimination and oppression. The chapter discussed the need for further advocacy relative to the pathologizing of gender dysphoria in the fifth edition of the *DSM*.[41] It also explored the dynamic nature of language and how to keep up with shifting terminology and definitions, always checking with clients for their understanding of terms. It covered the importance of honoring a person's pronoun choice and advocating for others' acceptance of that choice. Finally, it reviewed Lev's identity development model of transgender emergence, highlighting potential points of intervention for social workers and the importance of creating a gender-affirming, sex-positive therapeutic space.[42]

DISCUSSION QUESTIONS

1. When and how did you first learn about gender?
2. What conscious (or unconscious) biases do you have about gender?
3. What are some of the ways in which the heteronormative and cissexist social context may impact a person's psychosocial development?
4. What are the potential pros and cons of someone taking puberty blockers? What are your feelings about someone taking puberty blockers?

RESOURCES

Gender Identity Project: https://www.youtube.com/watch?v=UXI9woPbBXY ("Transgender Basics")

Gender Spectrum: www.genderspectrum.org

Human Rights Campaign: www.hrc.org

National Center for Transgender Equality: www.TransEquality.org

Sylvia Rivera Law Project: www.srlp.org

Trevor Project: www.thetrevorproject.org (for a twenty-four-hour suicide hotline)

True Colors United: https://truecolorsunited.org/our-work/training-education/network/

6

SEX ACROSS THE LIFE SPAN:
A VERY BRIEF SCAN

RELEVANT CSWE COMPETENCIES

Competency 2: Engage Diversity and Difference in Practice
Competency 3: Advance Human Rights and Social, Economic,
    and Environmental Justice
Competency 6: Engage with Individuals, Families, Groups,
    Organizations, and Communities
Competency 8: Intervene with Individuals, Families, Groups,
    Organizations, and Communities

Sexuality related to childhood, adolescence, adulthood, and older adulthood has been mentioned at different points throughout the first five chapters of this book. This chapter offers a cursory chronological look at sexuality across different stages of the life span.

During social work education, you are required to study reporting requirements related to child physical and sexual abuse. This chapter does not replace training on suspected child abuse and neglect, although it will review some red flags you might encounter in a treatment setting. Each of these life stages could warrant a chapter or even a full course. The purpose here is to introduce some key issues related to positive sexuality that may be relevant at each stage in the life course.

KIDS HAVE NO INHIBITIONS: AGES 0–2

Cultural taboos about sexuality begin to be instilled at birth. Taboos and sociocultural norms related to child behavior, including sexual behavior, are defined by adults.[1] Adults also dominate the discourses about childhood sexuality, which include the beliefs that children are innocent and asexual and must be regulated and that childhood sexuality is dangerous and morally problematic—or, conversely, that childhood sexuality is normal and important for full health and development.[2] The majority of these scripts suggest that sexuality is something "from which children need protection."[3]

While not necessarily sexual in nature, penises become erect in the womb, and vaginal lubrication occurs within approximately twenty-four hours of birth.[4] Babies require affection to thrive, including hugging and kissing from caregivers. In Harry Harlow's well-known but controversial study,[5] infant monkeys that spent more time with a cloth-covered surrogate mother were more likely to thrive than those that spent more time with a wire surrogate.

Babies often spend time exploring and touching their genitals out of curiosity or in relation to self-soothing (see box 6.1 for sexual developmental markers in childhood). Adults sometimes panic if their child is interested in exploring their genitals, especially if it is a common habit, but unless it is causing significant physical harm, self-soothing is well within the realm of expected behaviors.[6] Several organizations offer checklists of behaviors that are common and those that are rare and may be cause for concern.[7] Often, the marker for concern is if the behavior continues despite negative personal consequences, such as rubbing oneself raw. There is certainly a wide variation in the range of behaviors that can be consider typical.

Infants will often try to explore their genitals in the moments they are without a diaper. To them, exploring their genitals is no different than exploring their ears, elbows, or nose. They are curious about all of their body parts. Infants also tend to show no inhibitions about nudity, since the social and cultural messaging that it is taboo has not yet been absorbed at this early age.

Box 6.1
CHILDHOOD SEXUALITY DEVELOPMENT

AGE	EXPECTED BEHAVIORS
0–2	No inhibitions about nudity Curiosity about bodies or genitals Occasional touching of genitals or masturbating in private and public
3–5	No inhibitions about nudity Curiosity about bodies or genitals of the self and others Occasional touching of genitals or masturbating for self-soothing in private and public Consensual "sexual" play—e.g., playing doctor
6–9	Beginning of inhibitions about nudity in public Deeper awareness of gender roles Curiosity about bodies or genitals of the self and others Touching of genitals or masturbating for self-soothing, more in private Consensual "sexual" play with children of all genders
10–12	Curiosity about adult bodies or genitals (looking for media) Masturbating in private Interest in romantic relationships
13–18	Masturbating in private Sexual feelings Sexual attractions Sexual fantasies

Source: Based on National Sexual Violence Resource Center; E. D. Hutchinson, *Dimensions of Human Behavior: The Changing Life Course* (Thousand Oaks, CA: SAGE Publications, 2015); LeVay, Baldwin, and Baldwin, *Discovering Human Sexuality.*

LOTS OF CURIOSITY: PRESCHOOL
STAGE, AGES 3–5

During the preschool years, children simultaneously become more verbal and more social. They are increasingly curious about exploring the world around them. And that means they are curious about their own genitals and the genitals of others.[8] This is consistent with their general interest in their bodies, what they can do, and how they work. However, as Elizabeth Hutchinson notes, "the genitals seem to hold a special interest as the child learns through experimentation that the genitals can be a source of pleasure"[9] and self-soothing.

Children at this age may also "have some worries about genital difference."[10] For example, someone born with a vagina may wonder, "What happened to my penis? Where did it go? How did I lose it?" In contrast, someone born with a penis may worry that they could lose it or that it may disappear for some reason. At this age, "masturbation is used both for self-soothing and for pleasure."[11] This tends to be the age when children play doctor and desire to see and touch the genitals of their playmates. Hence, we hear the familiar playground phrase, "I'll show you mine if you show me yours." The function of this play is for children to compare themselves to others and allay fears that one's own genitals are somehow different or abnormal.

Adults often worry about children expressing interest in nudity, genitals, and touching, but curiosity in this realm is to be expected. The American Academy of Pediatrics has guidelines for normal behavior in this age group that are similar to those for infants: few to no inhibitions about nudity, interest in the nudity of peers and adults, touching of genitals in public and private, and little sense of personal space—hence, sitting too close to others.[12] Again, adults should investigate behaviors that seem to cause physical or emotional distress, involve coercion, or involve children who are much older or much younger (four or more years apart). Adults should also note if the child is not easily distracted from their behaviors or displays anger when someone tries to stop them.

For children, the main red flags occur when the behavior continues despite repeated requests to stop. This may indicate a compulsive drive.

Take, for example, Paula and Debbie, who are the parents of Brian, a four-year-old cisgender male. They see you because of concerns over Brian's preoccupation with butts. Not just fascinated by his own butt, he is also very interested in other people's butts. He has recently been caught on more than one occasion putting his finger in the anus of other children his age, mostly girls. His parents are especially concerned because the girls have said that they did not want him to do this and have asked him to stop, to no avail. His parents have also told him to stop, but his behavior has not changed.

You recognize that the concern is that Brian has been unable to stop despite repeated requests by peers and adults. Your work is to help Brian explore his feelings around this activity, while helping him identify important boundaries. It is critical not just to shut down the behavior but to help him develop positive sexual feelings within appropriate boundaries. Perhaps you can help him to recognize that he enjoys the sensation when he touches his own anus, but that others may not feel the same way about their anus—and even if they do like the sensation, they may not want him to touch them. Helping Brian identify his own pleasure while also reinforcing boundaries can prevent the whole activity of anal play becoming a taboo and will allow him to explore this aspect of his sexuality more in the future.

Adults may also raise concerns when there is a degree of coercion or bribery or if there is a large age gap. This can often be the case with older siblings or close relatives, such as cousins. When an older child engages in sexual exploration with a younger child, there may be cause for concern. However, curiosity and exploration without coercion or a power differential is typical and serves an important formative function in expanding a child's understanding of their own and others' bodies. It's an opportunity for children to discern which types of touch feel pleasurable and which do not.

To make room for a sex-positive approach to childhood sexuality, understanding the limits and areas for potential concern gives you some freedom to let children explore and express their sexuality without judgment. Box 6.2 outlines key areas for concern and gives parents, guardians, caregivers, and professionals a range of activities and behaviors that fall within the realm of typical. Providing parents and caregivers with this information can relieve their anxieties, as they're unlikely to encounter information about normal childhood sexuality on their own.

While there are very few role models for talking about sex with clients in general, this is especially true for parents and caregivers who want to talk to children. As a social worker, you can model these conversations and provide an opportunity for caregivers to practice through role-playing so that they can find language that works for them. As we discussed in chapter 2, using the correct language for body parts—such as vulva and penis—from an early age can help children form positive relationships with these body parts and clear up the mystery or confusion created by euphemisms. You can also encourage parents and caregivers to determine how much information to provide, remembering that too much information can be overwhelming and too little can signal a need for secrecy about sex.[13]

Box 6.2

POTENTIAL CAUSE FOR CONCERN IN CHILDHOOD SEXUAL BEHAVIORS

- If the child is unable to stop after repeatedly being asked to do so (i.e., there is some level of compulsion).
- If there is some level of self-harm to their activity (physical or emotional).
- If the child persistently makes requests to other children whom they do not know or who are clearly uninterested.
- If there is some level of coercion.
- If there is an age difference (of four or more years), with one or more children being much older than the other or others.

Source: Adapted from American Academy of Pediatrics, *Promoting Healthy Sexual Development and Sexuality in Bright Futures*, 217–227, Preventing Sexual Violence Toolkit.

POTTY JOKES: LATENCY STAGE, AGES 6–9

The stage from six to nine years of age is often called the latency phase, the time when sexuality goes underground. But anyone who has spent time on an elementary school playground can see lots of relationship experimentation, such as games of chase. This might also include learning the difference between positive touch and nonpositive touch, as well as bathroom jokes—*lots* of bathroom jokes.

This sort of experimentation is critical to the development of sex-positive healthy relationships and lays the foundation for positive consent, the development of trust, the fostering of agency, and how to understand boundaries. While this stage is not often recognized as important to sexual development, there are still red flags to look out for that mirror the concerns in box 6.2.

AND SO IT BEGINS: LATE CHILDHOOD, AGES 10–12

The age for the onset of puberty in the United States is moving earlier and earlier. Girls start their periods sometimes as young as nine and often by the age of eleven or twelve.[14] Levels of the sex hormone dehydroepiandrosterone (DHEA) peak between ages ten and twelve.[15] Through this stage, there is a gradual shift toward interest in romantic relationships, though there remains massive variation among individuals. Curiosity about sex and sexuality also peaks, often accompanied by information-seeking behaviors—which have been made considerably easier by the internet.

In the absence of comprehensive sex education at home, church, or school, this is also a time of misinformation. Older relatives, such as siblings or cousins, may pass down information that is then translated on the playground and often morphed or misconstrued. While the internet has made accurate information more available, it has done the same for pornography and graphically violent sexual imagery (we'll discuss the realities and effects of porn in the next section). Filtering this information through a prepubescent developmental lens can lead to confusion, misunderstanding, and even fear of sex.

These trends bolster the need for comprehensive age-appropriate sex education throughout the school years. Increased interest in masturbation also emerges during this period, but it is accompanied by a new awareness of privacy.

HORMONES! ADOLESCENCE, AGES 13–17

When I discuss adolescent sexuality in class, I always ask my students to come up with words relating to adolescence. They yell out things like "stubborn," "puberty," "awkward," "hormonal," "egocentric," "exploration," "curiosity," "drugs," "first relationships," "emotional," "impulsive," "pimples," "menstruation," "angst," "conformity," "the closet," "rebellion," "cliques," and—inevitably—"sex" and "porn." Sex and sexual images are central in the world of many adolescents. In fact, of the students in high school who responded to the Youth Risk Behavior Survey, 39.5 percent said that they had had sex, and 28.7 percent were currently sexually active.[16]

In my class, once we have established the sexual themes that emerge for adolescents, we discuss the major developmental tasks of adolescence. One of these is identity versus role confusion, from Erik Erikson's eight-stage developmental model.[17] In this model, adolescents are tasked with discovering who they are. In attempting this, adolescents try on different roles and selves to see what feels comfortable and what does not. At the same time, they must contend with the physical, emotional, and social changes that are occurring, which may make it difficult to feel comfortable in their skin or congruent with their identity.

In chapters 4 and 5 we discussed why this developmental stage can be especially difficult for those whose gender identity or sexual identity does not adhere strictly to heteronormative sex roles, gender presentation, or monogamous heterosexual identity. But even for adolescents who have cisgender and heterosexual privilege, the landscape can feel hostile.

Another task during this phase is risk taking (such as taking drugs). Of the respondents to the Youth Risk Behavior Survey,[18] 18.8 percent said that they had used alcohol or drugs prior to their last sexual encounter. Other tasks are to create an identity in relation to friends, attraction, sense of self, individuation, and sometimes the emergence of a political self.

Conversations between adults and adolescents at home or in school tend to focus on preventing pregnancy and disease. The focus on pregnancy prevention has been so great that adolescent girls are reportedly having anal sex to maintain their virginity—with devastating consequences in relation to HIV transmission.[19] And while the majority of teenagers engage in masturbation, it is often accompanied by feelings of shame and guilt, especially for those within religious families or communities.[20]

For the most part, adults are not teaching adolescents about desire or pleasure.[21] Instead, they are teaching them to fear sex and focus on abstinence at all cost. This means withholding information that would help adolescents make successful decisions for themselves and their relationships.

Often an adolescent's only reference to pleasure is porn, which is typically created from a male gaze for male gratification—thus setting up very gendered expectations about pleasure.[22] Although a wider range of feminist and queer porn is now available, the majority of free porn is still male dominated. Male-created and quickly produced porn dismisses and even dehumanizes women. After I ask my students about their associations with adolescent sexuality, I ask my male identified students to compare their list to the lists of the female identified ones. They always look quite different. The male identified students' lists contain more words about permission and conquest, while the female identified students' lists have words about prohibition and protection. For example, consider how virginity is said to be taken from girls, rather than given by them.

I've done these exercises for a long time, and I notice that what's missing from all of these descriptions is the notion of communication. By communication I mean identifying needs, feeling agency, making decisions, negotiating, and establishing consent. When these are omitted from sex education, we are giving adolescents only half of the map and expecting them to arrive safely.

School-based sex education has an opportunity to change this narrative by including communication, decision making, consent, and desire in the curriculum. Some curricula have already done this successfully, such as Our Whole Lives curricula for kindergarten and first grade; grades 4–6, 7–9, and 10–12; young adults, and adults, which focus on the topics of boosting self-esteem and self-acceptance, making better decisions, resolving conflicts, understanding your physical body, and not being afraid of differences.[23]

Social workers have a critical role to play in advocating for inclusive, sex-positive sex education. This does not mean promoting sexual activity; rather, it means promoting sexual and emotional intelligence. With this intelligence, young people can develop the skills they need to navigate safe, consensual, and fulfilling sexual and intimate relationships. In fact, research shows that teens exposed to comprehensive sex education do not engage in sexual behaviors earlier but are more likely to practice safe sex when they do.[24]

Josie Crolley-Simic, Elizabeth Vonk, and William Ellsworth provide a case study of a social worker who worked to create a meaningful sexual education program for the middle school where he worked, in the middle of the country.[25] The authors highlight the many skills, both micro (for example, group facilitation) and macro (for example, coalition building), that he used in his efforts. They also provide a meaningful critique of his actions and possible alternative strategies. Their work is a wonderful illustration of the potential social workers have as advocates and brokers of understanding between parents, teachers, administrators, community groups, and (missing from this example) students.

Social workers can advocate for comprehensive and inclusive sex education in schools so that young people have the information they need to understand the physiological and emotional changes related to sexuality that occur in adolescence. Social workers can provide information, education, and support to parents and caregivers to facilitate healthy and honest dialogues in the home about sex. Social workers can encourage parents and caregivers to foster good decision making, helping their teen make healthy choices that feel right for them. Parents and caregivers can support teens in asserting themselves and developing agency around activities that they do and do not want to participate in and can support them in accessing reproductive health services, when appropriate.

Supporting parents as they support their teen is an important function of the social worker, whether this means getting appropriate medical screenings such as testicular exams, breast exams, and pap smears, and testing for sexually transmitted infections (STIs, including HIV) or any other part of developing a lifelong healthy relationship to sex and sexuality.

SEXUAL FREEDOM: YOUNG ADULTHOOD, AGES 18–35

In some ways our culture perceives young adulthood as the freest time for sex and sexuality. In my classroom, students usually shout out word associations like "easily accessible," "single," "know what you are doing," "not committed," "often," "a lot," "prime," "not as awkward," and "hot." They also refer to dating and hook-up apps like Tinder and Grindr.

When words about all the age ranges are up on the board, my students often joke that the young adult column looks the most appealing. But as we dig below the surface, several students acknowledge that there was a feeling of emptiness to some of their experiences and a feeling of pressure that they were supposed to be having a lot of great sex. (The majority of the students fall in this age range, while others reflect back on their young adult experiences.)

These expectations are burdensome for people who feel that they have to be sexual at times when they would prefer not to be. Many students also mention significant concern about avoiding pregnancy and STIs, though they do not always make decisions that support prevention. Some also note that the sex feels free and exciting in some ways but empty in others—perhaps because there is less familiarity, commitment, or intimacy than they desire.

If early young adulthood is often characterized by trying to avoid pregnancy, later young adulthood is often focused on getting pregnant, having children, and creating families. This expectation places a different burden on sex and sexuality, changing sex from a fun outlet and a way of connecting to a loaded activity with a significant outcome attached. Different feelings about whether to start a family or the inability to get pregnant can put significant strain on relationships.

Of course, young adults have a range of sexual experiences. They may feel significant pressure to have an active and engaged sex life that may not fit what they feel or want. Despite continued insecurities and feelings of pressure, most of my students report feeling more confident about their sexual selves by this age and say that they have more enjoyable and satisfying sex in their early thirties, at the end of their young adulthood. Partly this is because there is an opportunity to learn and unlearn at this stage. Individuals have agency to seek out information relevant to their sexual lives from partners, online resources, and professionals. The information shared by peers is also more accurate at this age, so shared learning is more helpful than at younger phases. Feelings of guilt, fear, and shame that can accompany adolescent sex, especially for women, begin to fade as social norms around premarital sex shift from abstinence to an expectation of exploration and pleasure.

Sometimes people need help to move through their feelings of guilt and shame and to develop a more sex-positive feeling of sexual agency. For example, Sandra is a twenty-six-year-old cisgender Latinx female who has been sexually active since she was seventeen years old. She had sex with her high school boyfriend after they had been dating for eight months. She felt lucky that her first sexual experience was in the context of a significant relationship and that she and her boyfriend had similar expectations about their physical relationship.

Despite this positive first experience, Sandra struggled to integrate her sexual self and her experience with the abstinence messages she received at school and home. She had strong support from her peer network, but she also had a negative internal dialogue about sex before marriage. This struggle continued to affect her sexual relationships during college and has resulted in her feeling "frozen" sexually. She feels especially frustrated because this time in her life is supposed to be one of sexual exploration. From a sex-positive social work perspective, you can help Sandra uncouple her actual experience from the messaging she received growing up. You can provide a sounding board for the guilt and shame she experiences as a result of being sexual before marriage. Finally, you can support her as she develops a sense of her own values and how these align with her sexual self.

Helping clients break through negative messaging around sex can facilitate their capacity for intimacy. According to Erikson's developmental stages, the task of young adulthood is intimacy versus isolation.[26] As young adulthood progresses, people develop their capacity for healthy relationships and their interest in intimacy.[27] Removing barriers to intimacy created by shame and guilt related to sex and sexuality can be a positive step. The number of young adults who develop committed romantic relationships or begin to cohabitate with a romantic partner or partners is evidence of this increased capacity for intimacy.

STAGNANT OR FULFILLING?
ADULTHOOD, AGES 36–64

Adulthood is marked by generativity, a focus on producing at work and at home. This may include building one's business, growing one's spiritual life, committing to one's partner, or building a family.

Adulthood marks the onset of physical and emotional shifts, including the loss of reproductive capacity and the physical changes of perimenopause, menopause, and andropause (see chapter 2 for a discussion of the physiological changes associated with these milestones). These days, some women choose to stay unmarried and delay childbearing longer than in the past.[28] With the assistance of reproductive technologies, women can safely have children much later than was previously possible, and 7 percent of women now have their first child after age thirty-five. Thus, some of the developmental tasks of young adulthood and their impact on sexuality have been pushed into adulthood.

Magazines for adult readers frequently include tips on reigniting your sex life or keeping the flame alive. But often people find committed sexuality more fulfilling than the less intimate and less committed sex associated with early adulthood.[29] Toward the end of adulthood, a slow decline in physical health and hormonal changes may decrease interest in sex. These are often coupled with sexual issues like vaginal dryness or erectile dysfunction. Often these symptoms can be managed with the use of lubrication or adjustments in arousal techniques or positioning. While myth would have it that women's sexual drive is lower than men's, research suggests that men and women in partnered relationships are similar in terms of sexual frequency.[30] However, women do have lower frequency of sex when studied as individuals, perhaps because more women than men are widowed.[31]

In general, whether in committed relationships, dating, or single, adults are actively engaged sexual beings. This acceptance can alleviate some of the guilt and shame associated with earlier sexual exploration—as in Sandra's case—but may still affect activities that are more heavily stigmatized, such as same-sex behaviors, anal sex, masturbation, and certain fetishes.

Cultural or religious norms related to sex outside of marriage may still affect a person's capacity for sexual enjoyment at this age. Helping clients identify cultural norms and taboos that may still be causing them problems and exploring their own sexual values can move them toward even greater sexual well-being and growth.

STILL GOING: OLDER ADULTHOOD, AGES 65 AND OLDER

As you can imagine, when my (mainly young adult) students are asked to think about words describing the sexuality of older adults, they often come up with a very dire looking list: "dry," "shriveled," "none," "impotent," "nonexistent," "Viagra," "gross," "boring," and "fragile." They also share some potentially positive words like "slow" or "intimate," but most of the students have a negative opinion of the sexuality of older adults (despite the protest of older students in the room).

However, research suggests that sexual desire and interest are sustained into older adulthood and even late older adulthood for a high proportion of the population.[32] Even TV and other media have begun to portray older adults' capacity for sexuality more openly and realistically, as in documentaries like *69: Sex, Love, Senior* and popular shows like *Grace and Frankie*. In one study of people aged sixty and over, 61 percent reported that their sex life was just as or more physically satisfying than it was in their forties.[33] Increased sexual satisfaction may be attributable to the freedom of not worrying about pregnancy, being alone in the house again after the children have grown, knowing a long-term partner's sexual pleasures, or better communication.

And the American Sexual Health Association study found that far from being asexual, people ages 40–74 had sex on average five times a month—and wanted to have even more sex. Men reported wanting to have sex ten times a month, while for women it was eight times. The researchers found that 71 percent of men and 51 percent of women in their sixties reported being sexually active. The proportions were 57 percent of men and 30 percent of women in their seventies and 25 percent of men and 20 percent of women in their eighties.[34]

In a Swedish study, 46 percent of men ages 70–80 reported having an orgasm at least monthly.[35] Don't make assumptions has been a common theme in this book, and it certainly applies to older adults' sexuality. Specifically, don't assume their sexual identity, gender identity, number of partners, or level of commitment.

People who have been in happy, long-term, committed heterosexual relationships and lose their partner may begin to explore same-sex relationships. It is not uncommon for someone later in life to begin to explore their sexual identity after a major milestone, such as divorce or the death of a spouse. Similarly, someone who has lived as cisgender may feel unable to do so any longer and may transition in older adulthood. And a seventy-seven-year-old living alone may have an active social life with several sexual partners.

From a sex-positive, strengths-based perspective, social workers can focus on helping clients maintain their sexual well-being as one dimension of their overall well-being. In the trailer for the documentary *69: Sex, Love, Senior*, one of the interviewees dismisses the idea that sex in older adulthood is in any way inferior: He describes it as "full blown sexuality."[36] Working with clients to develop their own full-blown sexuality, whatever that might look like, is a sex-positive goal at any age.

Baby boomers in particular are upending this notion of a sexless older adulthood. Not only do they expect to have a fulfilling sex life, but they also share their joy with anyone who will listen. The availability of products like Viagra and Cialis to achieve and sustain an erection have contributed to the increase in sexual activity into older adulthood. Some argue that they have also changed the face of older adult sexuality, not necessarily positively, by increasing the coital imperative.[37]

Social workers seem to find older adults the most difficult of all age groups with whom to talk about sex, perhaps because of cultural norms related to respect, and perhaps because our culture typically portrays older adults as asexual.[38] Our society often associates sex with procreation for the young and fertile[39] or maintains that physical attractiveness and youth are essential for desire.[40] Here, once again, you may have to go beyond your comfort zone, pretending to be comfortable if necessary until you are.

For example, a cisgender Caucasian woman named Frances, age seventy-two, comes to see you. She was married to her husband, Michael, for fifty-one years and had had limited sexual experience before her marriage. Michael died two years ago, and Frances has been seeing you for the past year to get support in coping with her grief. She is beginning to express that she is lonely and wants some companionship and what she describes as "closeness."

You work with Frances to explore how she feels about having any type of intimate relationship with someone who isn't Michael. Frances does not want to betray her relationship with Michael but also knows that he would want her to be happy. Over the course of the next few months of your work together, Frances shares that while it feels strange to be moving on from Michael, she is both excited and terrified at the idea of being sexual with someone else. You give Frances the space to explore who she is as a sexual person, which until now has been defined in relationship to Michael. Giving Frances room to explore aspects of her sexual self separate from Michael helps her realize that she is a distinct sexual being and there are aspects of sexuality in which she is still interested. You help Frances explore what she knows about sex, what she likes, and the ways in which she feels unprepared to begin dating. When she expresses interest in and confusion about online dating, you sit with her to explore more traditional online dating sites, like OkCupid or Match.com and even dating apps. Sitting with Frances gives you not only the opportunity to help her navigate the technology involved in online dating but also a platform to use in exploring her ambivalence, excitement, and fears as they come up. You role-play different response scenarios with her, and she begins to feel that dating could be a real possibility. While she is still nervous and occasionally struggles with feelings of betraying Michael, she can also recognize her unique sexuality and is becoming excited at the possibility of exploring a new dimension of her sexual self.

If you are working in a setting where adult children or a caregiver accompany the older adult to an appointment, be sure to create some privacy so you can talk to the older adult about their sexual health and concerns without their child or caregiver present. You also want to make sure to leave sufficient time for conversations about sexual health, since older adults "tend not to feel comfortable if they do not perceive there to be time."[41]

Health care professionals' failure to talk about sex with older adults has led to some significant public health problems. Although older adults come in contact with health professionals more regularly than any other age group does, they are asked very infrequently about their sexual health, well-being, and safety. This silence has led to increased risk and rates of HIV and STIs in older adults. In 2017, 17 percent of new HIV infections were in people fifty and older, 42 percent of whom identified as black or African American and 18 percent as Latinx.[42] Complicating matters is the fact that symptoms of HIV can look similar to those of other medical issues common in older adults, and older adults are less likely to be tested for HIV. Medical providers could talk to older adults about using pre-exposure prophylaxis, especially in the cases of women or gay men who don't want to ask their partner to use a condom. (Only 10 percent of people over sixty-five in New York City reported using a condom the last time they had sex.)[43] Older adults are also susceptible to other STIs. In fact, from 2017 to 2018, syphilis rates increased by 21 percent for those ages 55–64 and by 29 percent for those over 65.[44]

Using the permission, limited information, specific suggestions, and intensive therapy (PLISSIT) model[45] can ease direct work with older adults having sexual problems. First, you may want to use permission giving, which is about giving permission both to have a conversation about sex and to want and expect to have a fulfilling sex life. It is also about giving people permission not to participate in sexual activities they are uncomfortable with as well. Some people are apologetic or feel undeserving of sexual satisfaction. They may say that their questions or desires are "silly," "frivolous," or "icing on the cake." During the permission phase, help clients understand that they have a right to sexual health and well-being. In fact, an article posted on the website of the American Sexual Health Association acknowledges the importance of "sexual rights for seniors," which positions intimacy as a human right.[46]

The limited information stage of the PLISSIT model allows you to filter available information for your clients. For this stage, the social worker's role is related to psychological education. The information available on the internet can be overwhelming for anyone, but it can be especially so for older adults who may have reduced facility with computers, diminishing cognitive capacity, or deteriorating eyesight. Social workers can sit with a client and walk them through relevant information, as well as protecting them from unnecessarily scary information.

Social workers can tailor suggestions to the specific needs of the client, taking into account any physical limitations. It can be helpful to encourage clients to be creative, perhaps reframing their expectations about sexual intimacy and pleasure or shifting the focus away from orgasm to sensory pleasure and arousal. You may include recommendations for positioning, lubrication, communication, and shifting focus or expectations.

As with clients of any age, the intensive therapy stage typically involves a referral to a sex therapist who can provide more specialized therapy. Ideally, the referral should be to a therapist who specializes in working with older adults.

CHAPTER SUMMARY

This chapter discussed ways in which social workers can support positive sexual development throughout the life span, as well as the importance of addressing sexuality at all ages and all stages. The chapter summarized key age-based milestones and the sexual development for that age.

Key recommendations for childhood were the inclusion of sex-positive conversations, correctly identifying body parts, understanding boundaries and personal space, practicing clear communication, understanding consent, and practicing decision making. For adolescence recommendations included providing accurate information about sexual health and wellness, the importance of fostering communication skills and role-playing possible dialogues to help create confidence within relationships, and the reminder that acknowledging the importance of pleasure and desire (for all parties involved) helps create a sex-positive foundation,

The chapter discussed how in young adulthood and adulthood, social workers may need to help clients relearn or unlearn some things about sex and sexuality, supporting clients as they explore negative, mixed, or inaccurate messaging from their youth. The chapter also covered how social workers may help clients to navigate reproductive health issues, including pregnancy prevention and pregnancy planning. Providing a sounding board as well as clear, accurate, and nonjudgmental information, the social worker can be a valuable resource for people pursuing sex-positive adulthood.

Importantly, the chapter acknowledged the sexual dimension of older adulthood as critical for overall health and well-being. It reinforced that the social worker should engage older adult clients in conversations about relationships and sexuality and discussed stark statistics related to STIs (including HIV) for this age group. The chapter illustrated how social workers can be an invaluable resource to support sex-positive development throughout the life span.

DISCUSSION QUESTIONS

1. What are some of the common themes that occur in the "cause for concern" category of childhood sexuality?
2. What are some of the roles that social workers can play in relation to sex education?

3. What does sex-positive, affirming, and inclusive sex education look like?

4. How can you support a young adult to increase their sense of sexual health and well-being?

5. What are some reasons why rates of STIs (including HIV) are increasing in older adults? How can social workers intervene to address this issue?

RESOURCES

Ageisnotacondom.org: www.ageisnotacondom.org
American Academy of Pediatrics: www.AAP.org
National Sexual Violence Resource Center: www.nsvrc.org
Planned Parenthood: www.plannedparenthood.org
SIECUS: Sex Ed for Social Change: www.siecus.org

7

COMMUNICATING ABOUT
LOVE AND INTIMACY

RELEVANT CSWE COMPETENCIES

Competency 2: Engage Diversity and Difference in Practice
Competency 6: Engage with Individuals, Families, Groups,
    Organizations, and Communities
Competency 8: Intervene with Individuals, Families, Groups,
    Organizations, and Communities

Social workers tend to be more comfortable working with clients on issues of love, intimacy, and communication than they are working on issues of sex. While love, intimacy, and clear communication certainly can make some people uncomfortable, there are far fewer cultural taboos associated with them.

This chapter explores several proposed answers to the question, "What is love?" It also addresses aspects of intimacy and ways to support clients as they develop their capacity for intimate relationships. Finally, it explores communication skills that are essential to developing sexual satisfaction and a sex-positive sense of self. As we've already discussed, supporting clients as they navigate relationships, intimacy, and sexual communication from a sex-positive perspective can contribute to overall well-being, since increased sexual activity is related to a longer life span and higher self-esteem.[1]

WHAT IS LOVE?

Before we begin, grab a piece of paper and jot down your answer to the question, "What is love?" If you can't come up with a definition, then think of some words that you associate with the concept of love.

You may have found it quite hard to come up with a neat definition of love, since love is a nebulous concept. Love also has a complicated relationship with sex. Some people see love as a necessary precursor to sex, while others see the two as separate—one physiological and one psychological.

Social workers can help clients understand their perspective on the relationship between love and sex and how this affects their potential for a sex-positive sense of self. One helpful exercise is to ask clients, either alone or with a partner, to divide a page in half from top to bottom. On one side they should write down what love means to them. On the other side they should write what sex means to them. (Using the prompts "Love is . . ." and "Sex is . . ." at the top of the page can be helpful.) Compare the meanings they attach to each. In this way, you can tease out how their ideas of the two are similar or different. The exercise can help the client make connections with their feelings about each concept. It is also a window into relationships, a way for them to understand their feelings about love and sex and how these may influence their needs and expectations related to sex. You can also try replacing the word "love" with "intimacy" in the exercise and see whether this yields a slightly different perspective that may be more appropriate for your clients.

Consider Stella (a twenty-six-year-old Asian cis-woman) and her partner, Damon (a twenty-eight-year-old African American cis-man), who completed this exercise in your office. Stella wrote that love is "enduring, rare, special, precious, elusive, and the ultimate." For sex, she wrote "intense, deep, intimate, hot, connecting, passionate, sensual, and steamy." For her, both love and sex evoked intense emotions and a feeling of deep connection. But Damon wrote that love is "elusive, intense, lasting, special, and demanding," while sex is "physical, fun, a release, frivolous, hot, and lighthearted." For him, love is intense and challenging, whereas sex is a fun release.

With this insight, you help Stella and Damon discuss what sex means for them individually and help them understand that Stella attaches deep meaning to their physical relationship, while Damon sees it as—and wants it to be—lighthearted and playful. You help them communicate their needs more clearly to each other. In time, Damon begins to recognize when Stella needs sex to be sensual, intense, and romantic. Similarly, Stella begins to recognize when Damon wants sex to be silly and more physical than emotional. The exercise and your intervention helped them read each other's cues and find a balance.

Robert Sternberg[2] tried to answer the question of what love is. He proposed a triangle, with each side representing a different dimension: intimacy, passion, and commitment (see figure 7.1). When a relationship has high levels of intimacy but no passion or commitment, then it is a friendship. If a relationship has high levels of commitment but no intimacy or passion, then it is what Sternberg called "empty love."[3]

Romantic relationships tend to represent some combination of the three components in differing amounts. For example, Sternberg posited that when relationships begin, in the infatuation stage that is sometimes called limerance, passion is high but intimacy and commitment are lower. He called this "infatuated love" or "passionate love."[4] In passionate love, the physical connection overpowers commitment and intimacy. This type of love causes an actual physiological arousal, like having butterflies in your stomach, a faster heart rate, sweaty palms, and flushed cheeks. Serotonin levels, which usually help manage anxiety and obsessive thinking, decrease, allowing you to focus narrowly on the new person.[5] In this early stage of a relationship, you do not yet know exactly who the other person is, so you can project traits and feelings onto them. Marla Reese-Weber refers to this as the "honeymoon stage" in her three-phase model of relationships.[6] You may overlook annoyances and avoid conflicts, creating an idealized version of the person in your head and leaving room for unencumbered physical connection.

But as Sternberg notes, the more you know someone, the more you become aware of their faults, or the ways they do not live up to your idealized standard. Over time, passion tends to diminish. The newness wears off, and

Liking

Intimacy

Intimacy + Passion

Romantic love

Intimacy + Passion + Commitment

Consummate love

Intimacy + Commitment

Companionate love

Passion

Infatuation

Passion + Commitment

Fatuous love

Commitment

Empty love

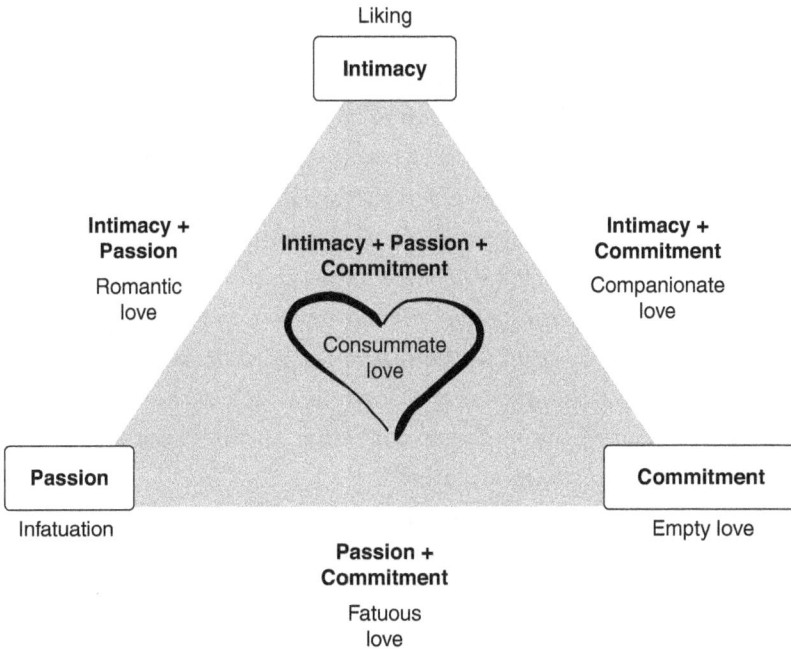

FIGURE 7.1 Sternberg's love triangle

serotonin and dopamine levels return to normal—so feelings of ecstasy, excitement, and stress diminish.[7] Typically, people see this shift as a warning sign that love is fading. They may end the relationship at this point. However, this transition may instead signal a shift to what Sternberg calls "companionate love."[8]

Companionate love represents a shift toward the side of the triangle where intimacy and commitment meet. Companionate love may have less physical intensity, but it has deeper emotional familiarity and attachment. In fact, oxytocin and vasopressin, strongly associated with attachment and pair-bonding, are the dominant hormones during this phase.[9] Robert Crooks and Karla Baur describe this type of love as a "thoughtful appreciation" of your partner.[10] With companionate love, you are aware of your partner's shortcomings, but you can tolerate them. Typically, during this phase you also develop the capacity to communicate about sex, deepen trust related to sexual activity, and are more willing to take sexual risks. The relationship and sex are not necessarily as passionate as in the initial phases of the relationship (though some people report that they are), but they can be more satisfying, since people are more familiar with what their partner likes and have a secure foundation from which to take sexual risks.[11]

When exploring issues about relationships with your clients, it can be helpful to assess each partner's experience of Sternberg's three dimensions. Where would they place their relationship within the triangle? Do they place themselves on the left side, with lots of passion and some intimacy, or on the right side, with a lot of intimacy and commitment but not much passion? Are they close on the bottom of the triangle, with passion and commitment but lacking intimacy? Or are they right in the center, enjoying high levels of intimacy, passion, and commitment—experiencing what Sternberg called "consummate love"?[12]

Not only is it important to understand where your client is on the triangle but also the location(s) of their partner(s). If you are working with a couple or "throuple" (three people in a committed relationship with each other), do they place their relationship in different places on the triangle? If so, how does the difference reflect the power dynamics within the relationship? Relationship compatibility increases when partners experience equal passion, intimacy, and commitment. As relationships develop, the better matched the partners are in their feelings of intimacy and commitment, the more likely the relationship will thrive. If there is a significant mismatch—perhaps when one person feels deeply committed but the other does not—then feelings of security and expectations become unbalanced. Helping clients explore these dimensions can illuminate the dynamics of the relationship and provide a shared language to use in communicating.

ATTACHMENT THEORY, CONNECTIONS, AND NEUROSCIENCE

The fields of neuroscience and brain chemistry have begun to contribute significantly to our understanding of love, attachment, and how we engage in relationships. As we saw in chapter 3, where we discussed taking a sexual history, a person's childhood experiences and attachments set the foundation for their adult relationships. The ways in which love, affection, commitment, attraction, and jealousy were expressed by caregivers during childhood can determine how a person navigates relationships, connection, and intimacy later in life.[13] Models of relationship satisfaction and longevity can inform our current relationship tendencies. Even though we usually want to avoid repeating past mistakes or improve on the relationships of their childhoods, we are often subconsciously drawn to people who are "dauntingly similar—warts and all, and especially the warts—to the caretakers who reared us."[14] Given this tendency to pick partners who resemble parents or guardians, we often try to have reparative experiences with people who are not equipped to provide them.

Many current views build upon the work of the early attachment theorists John Bowlby and Mary Ainsworth and her colleagues.[15] Attachment represents our "ability to form emotional bonds with other people."[16] It is a critical survival mechanism during childhood that ensures that we are nurtured and protected. Positive attachment creates a psychological connection that allows people to feel pleasure and self-soothe. Bowlby also posited that people who did not create secure attachments were more prone to negative developmental outcomes and higher levels of depression, aggression, and delinquency.[17]

Building on Bowlby's work, Ainsworth and colleagues studied how children responded in different scenarios, specifically when in a room with their mother, with a stranger and their mother, or with only a stranger.[18] They distilled the children's responses into three different attachment types, which they labeled secure, anxious-ambivalent, and avoidant (see box 7.1). From the perspective of Ainsworth and colleagues, secure attachment is preferable to the other two types, since the child is not anxious about exploring a new environment and is easily comforted by their mother after distress.[19]

Writing about experiences from his private practice, Stan Tatkin[20] takes the three attachment types of Ainsworth and colleagues and translates them into ways of relating in adult primary relationships. He dubs them anchors (secure), waves (anxious-ambivalent), and islands (avoidant) (see box 7.1). Though these are similar to the traits that Ainsworth and colleagues highlighted,[21] Tatkin does not elevate one attachment type over another, although he does acknowledge that in sustained and fulfilling relationships people tend to develop anchor traits.[22] He argues that we all have traits of all three types, and that some people emphasize more traits of one type at any given time. He also argues, optimistically, that all attachment types can be used to form strong loving relationships under the right conditions, when the person's partner understands them and responds according to their needs at a particular moment.

Box 7.1
CHARACTERISTICS OF DIFFERENT ATTACHMENT STYLES

ATTACHMENT TYPE

AINSWORTH

Secure	Anxious-ambivalent	Avoidant

TATKIN

Anchor	Wave	Island
Secure as people	Generous or giving	Independent
Comfortable with closeness to others	Want to be close but don't believe others want to be close to them	Uncomfortable being close to others
Willing and able to commit	Focus on caring for others	Self-reliant
Typically happy	Can see all sides of an issue	Look after themselves
Adapt easily	Happy when around others	Productive and creative (especially when given space)
		Low maintenance
Don't fear abandonment	Fear partner does not love them and so may leave (abandonment)	Believe partner will inevitably leave, as love is transitory
	Tendency to want to merge with partner	Worry about too much dependence

Source: Adapted from Ainsworth et al., *Patterns of Attachment*; Tatkin, *Wired for Love*; Crooks and Baur, *Our Sexuality*.

Tatkin emphasizes the neuroscience behind attraction and attachment in his books, including *Wired for Love, Your Brain on Love, and Wired for Dating*.[23] Neuroscientists have begun to unpack that passionate, obsessed feeling that occurs at the beginning of a relationship, known in polyamorous communities as new relationship energy. The natural high associated with this energy comes from the body's chemical reactions, especially increases in norepinephrine, dopamine, and phenylethylamine. Some have likened this high to that provided by amphetamines.[24] Much of this elation is created by activation of the dopamine reward system.[25] At the same time, serotonin is decreased. Since serotonin usually intervenes to prevent feelings of anxiety and obsession, its absence means that you can become intensely focused on the person of interest, and feelings of anxiety and obsession can become overpowering.[26]

Neuroscientists suggest that these chemical reactions at the beginning of relationships make us lose our judgment and change the way we perceive things.[27] There are two reasons for this. One is that as we evolved, our species focused on procreation, not long-term relationships. For this reason, we make bad choices for a long-term perspective. The other is that altered brain chemistry—including increased dopamine, vasopressin, and norepinephrine and decreased serotonin—means that "people who are in love are not able to honestly judge their lover's character."[28] In the early stages of a relationship, the chemical reactions create a "fog of love,"[29] which impairs our capacity to make judgments and compromises our ability to analyze the extent to which someone is a good match for us. Tatkin recommends using family members or friends to evaluate partners and relationships, since they are likely to have a more realistic view of who the new partner is and how well you are matched.[30]

Infatuation does not last indefinitely. The body cannot maintain the high demand for the neurotransmitters, so it begins to recalibrate production to prior levels. Initial feelings of obsession and giddiness subside. Research suggests that although neurotransmitter production settles as relationships shift toward companionate or consummate love, endorphin production increases, which creates a feeling of "security, euphoria, tranquility, and peace."[31] This accounts for the feelings of safety and security of people in long-term relationships, but it can also account for a decrease in sexual desire.

SUCCESSFUL VERBAL AND NONVERBAL COMMUNICATION

In previous chapters, we've discussed why talking about sex can be difficult. Now we are going to look at how those difficulties specifically impact communication about sexual performance and relationship. One barrier is that language—especially positive language—is often not available. As we saw in chapter 2, words for vagina are often loaded and negative, and the medical names can seem clinical and awkward when used as part of a sexual experience. But finding a language that you and your partner(s) can use to communicate about body parts, activities, or likes and dislikes is critically important to your comfort and sexual satisfaction. One study found that increased sexual communication was related to increased sexual satisfaction.[32] Another found that people who had playful names for their (and their partner's) genitals improved sexual problems.[33] During sex you need to be able to communicate with your partner(s) about what does and doesn't feel good, as well as what you would like them to change or add and whether to keep doing what they are doing. Having the language to efficiently and effectively communicate those needs without pulling you out of arousal is key. Nicknames are one way to communicate clearly without adding embarrassment or making something seem clinical and unsexy.

Another factor that complicates communication about sex is that this topic is often loaded because of the risk to a person's ego. You can help your clients understand that when receiving feedback, our natural tendency is to focus on the negatives and interpret any suggestion as "you did something wrong" or "that was bad," even if someone mentioned two hundred good things and only one thing that was ever so slightly off. This can help clients understand why their gentle suggestion may be misinterpreted as criticism. I sometimes joke in class that when driving, people are reluctant to stop and ask for directions, even if they are really lost—so what hope do we have that they will ask for help about sex? But I also point out that the best tennis players in the world, like Serena Williams and Roger Federer, still have a coach, because there is always something that can get even better. You can encourage your clients to approach sexuality the same way, with an openness to learning, discovering, and improving.

You can also recommend your clients not to debrief immediately after sex, except to focus on the positives and how close they feel (if appropriate) to their partner(s). The period immediately following sexual activity can be a physically and emotionally vulnerable time. The chemical reactions involved in sexual arousal and orgasm can create a vulnerable emotional state, which can make it difficult to process feedback and again leaves one likely to focus on the negatives far more than the positives. It's very hard to hear constructive feedback, and that can immediately create distance in the intimacy (which may be a subconscious goal—something to explore). Your client may have good intentions in saying, "That was really, really good, but I prefer it when you are a little firmer with your touch." But this could erase feelings of closeness and create a barrier between them and their partner(s). Instead, suggest that they take the pressure off by finding a more neutral time when they don't feel as open or vulnerable to have a conversation that provides feedback.

When they do provide feedback, make sure that it focuses on "I" statements, such as "I really like it when you nibble my ear and kiss my neck," rather than "You never nibble my ear or kiss my neck!" One feels like an invitation, while the other feels like a complaint. When John Gottman researched divorce prediction, he looked at how couples had difficult conversations and resolve conflicts.[34] The first predictor of a negative outcome for the conversation and the relationship is a "harsh setup." If the conversation starts with criticism, then the outcome is likely to be negative. When we feel criticized or attacked, our adrenaline kicks in, and we instinctively want to defend ourselves. This applies to giving feedback about sex to a partner. So help your client focus on the positives and what they would like their experience to be, not on what is bad or missing. (We will discuss focusing on the positive further in the following section.)

Allowing complaints or resentments to accumulate can also be harmful.[35] The habit of avoiding conflict may ease the situation in the moment, but it can lead to unresolved issues that fester and create larger problems later. If left unaddressed, annoyances can increase in significance. Direct and compassionate communication can clear the air and allow the relationship to move forward without an undercurrent of unresolved issues.

Perhaps the final factor that impedes sexual communication is that many people do not actually know what they like or what feels good to them, so they can't effectively communicate that information to their sexual partners. The sociocultural context hinders the development of a sex-positive outlook and inhibits sexual agency, especially for women. This context means that many people have not had an opportunity to learn what they like, and they feel reluctant or even ashamed to explore or verbalize sexual desires and preferences.

Help clients analyze their sexual relationships and learn from their past positive experiences. Jack Morin asked people about their peak sexual experiences in an attempt to uncover what was arousing, significant, and special about those circumstances.[36] Encouraging your client to think about past positive experiences and really try to understand what factors made those interactions feel so good can be a step toward self-learning. Helping clients permit themselves to explore their sexual likes and needs and gain confidence in expressing them is an important role for social workers.

A favorite resource for clients to explore likes and dislikes with a partner is the yes/no/maybe list. Box 7.2 provides one example of such a list, but several versions are available online, and you can customize your own. Sometimes people complete the lists separately and compare notes; other times they talk through a list together. Filling out the list can be an opportunity to discover new things, since sometimes there are items on it with which one or more partners are not familiar. Often partners are surprised at what receives a yes, a no, or a maybe, and this surprise can spark positive conversations and open doors to greater sexual variety. If you recommend completing the list to clients, help them take a nonjudgmental stance with their partner. You don't want to create the opposite effect: a shocked or negative reaction that shuts down sexual communication.

Box 7.2

A SHORTENED VERSION OF A YES/NO/MAYBE LIST

This list can be completed individually and shared or completed together. Note the things that are a definite yes, no, or maybe.

ACTIVITY	YES	NO	MAYBE
Skinny-dipping			
Sexting			
Making videos			
Anal play			
Watching porn			
Blindfolds or gags			
Cock rings			
Spanking			
Wooden paddles			
Whips			
Handcuffs			
Food play			
Ice play			
Oral sex			
Lingerie			
Foot play			
Outdoor sex			
Group sex			

FOCUSING ON THE POSITIVES

Positive communication sets the tone for positive relationships. As Jennifer Rosier and James Tyler point out, "frequent, loving communication in romantic relationships is important."[37] Negative communication has a damaging effect and can destroy a relationship. Gottman studied couples' communication patterns to predict the extent to which relationships would last and which would not.[38] One of the key characteristics he identified in couples with relationship longevity was a certain ratio: five positive statements to every negative statement.

If you are working with two people who tend to be negative and focus on the faults of their partner, work with them to identify this pattern, explore how they feel about giving and receiving negative statements, and then work with them to shift their focus to the positive. Often, people think positive thoughts but do not voice them, while they're quick to voice negative thoughts.

Eric (age thirty-one) and Jamal (age thirty-five) visit you at your office. They have been dating for eighteen months and recently moved in together. The initial excitement of living together has faded more quickly than either of them expected, and they are stuck in a negative spiral. Neither of them lived with a partner before, and both have unrealistic expectations about how they will cohabit. Listening to them address each other, you can quickly identify the negative pattern in their interactions. They are focused on the habits that annoy each other, which include leaving smelly shoes in the living room, not emptying the trash, "tidying" things away so they can't be found, and being so focused on television or video games that they don't respond to the other's questions or requests. When they visited each other's apartments, they could overlook minor annoyances because they were temporary and it was the other person's space. Now that they share a space, there is nowhere to go to escape. Symbolically, moving in together may also add a dimension of pressure to the relationship and feelings that it has to succeed.

Understanding these different dimensions and using Gottman's predictors of longevity in relationships,[39] you can help Eric and Jamal get back in touch with each other's positive attributes and the positive aspects of their relationship that made them make this commitment. You might also encourage them to change the tone of their interactions and monitor their ratio of criticisms to affirmations. For example, Jamal's shifting from complaining about Eric's towel being on the floor to saying how much he appreciates Eric's smile or how excited he is to wake up with him every day can help them put their relationship back on track. Their improved communication should increase feelings of closeness and intimacy.

Along with Gottman's positive statements, there are other ways to stabilize and secure relationships. Tatkin recommends answering security questions immediately, with no pause at all.[40] For example, if a partner asks, "Do you love me?" the answer should be a quick and emphatic "Yes! Absolutely!" Or if a partner asks, "Will you love me forever?" The answer should come without a moment of hesitation: "I will, I can't wait."

Now you might be thinking, "I can't possibly know if I will love you forever, so how can I answer that?" This is true. But the question is really about your intention: "Do you intend to love me forever? Do you want to love me forever? Can you imagine loving me forever?" If you pause or hesitate in your answer even for a moment, you allow a touch of doubt to creep in. This can destabilize a relationship, especially over time. So if your intention is to love the person forever, say so immediately and emphatically.

ACTIVE LISTENING

There are many qualities important to strong communication: active listening, maintaining eye contact, providing positive feedback, supporting the partner's efforts to communicate, and maintaining unconditional positive regard. As you can see, the good news is that effective sexual communication mirrors good social work skills, especially listening skills. For example, some techniques include nodding your head to communicate agreement and attunement, providing appropriate facial expressions that demonstrate engagement and attention, and providing empathy. So you should be able to pass along guidance about good communication skills to your clients. For example, you can ask your clients to restate what they think the other person is saying, which ensures that they understand. Neuroscience research has begun to show that when you sustain eye contact with someone there is a synchronizing of brain activity, which makes you feel more in sync and connected.[41] Therefore, maintaining eye contact during the conversation can synchronize your brain activity with that of the other person, creating more attunement and deepening your connection. Thus, the lessons you have already learned in social work school about active listening and body language can be applied to sexual communication and passed along to your clients. In chapter 3, we discussed how clients can break the ice first by talking about talking about sex. The same is true as you help them navigate talking about their sexual relationships. You may recommend that your clients read something that has sexual content and then talk about it with their partner(s). Or you might suggest they watch something with sexual content (perhaps a movie, a documentary, or pornography) and then discuss it. The idea is for the conversation to start outside of themselves and their relationship. They are not talking about their sex life. Rather, they are talking about something with sexual content, becoming more comfortable in doing so, and finding language in a low-stakes situation. You can also encourage them to share all or parts of their sexual histories with each other as a way to talk about prior experiences without making the conversation about the present and the current relationship.

Another technique that can help clients communicate more effectively is to encourage the use of open-ended questions. Such questions allow people to express themselves without putting limits on them. Consider starting with a few close-ended questions to put the topic on the table, and then transition into more open-ended questions to allow for more nuance in the conversation. The idea is to help the person be expressive—and as you know from your social work training, open-ended questions facilitate that more effectively.

Finally, when possible encourage clients to communicate face-to-face. There is a greater potential for miscommunication when texting or messaging. Electronic communication excludes verbal and nonverbal cues like tone, which help us interpret the meaning of what someone says to us.[42] In person, you can put a hand on your partner's leg, maintain eye contact, smile, or use a soft tone to help communicate your feelings and offer reassurance. None of these are possible in electronic communication. For this reason, it may be better to encourage your clients to save important conversations until they can take place in person, or at least on the phone, so that they can add an extra dimension to their communication.

TALKING ABOUT JEALOUSY

Jealousy is a common plague in relationships that often presents in practice. As we have discussed, relationships that generate safe and secure feelings create peace and contentment. If other relationships or interests threaten those feelings of safety and security, then instability and distress can occur. Jealousy is one reaction to these threats. The tendency toward jealousy can be higher in people with low self-esteem, so working with clients on self-esteem and self-worth can build resilience to jealousy. It is helpful to provide clients with support when dealing with jealous feelings to normalize the experience and try to unpack what underlying fears are creating the feelings. Anita Wagner of Practical Polyamory has created a useful resource that you can use to help support your clients as they work through jealous feelings and come to a deeper understanding of them.[43] While the resource is aimed at people in polyamorous relationship, the key points are relevant to anyone, regardless of relationship status. Wagner identifies six types of fear that may be underlying jealous feelings. They are the fears of the unknown, change, losing power and control, scarcity, loss, and abandonment. Helping clients explore which of these fears underlies their jealousy can facilitate individual understanding and positive communication.

TECHNOLOGY AND RELATIONSHIPS

Technology has significantly shifted how we interact in romantic relationships. As Emily Campbell and Christine Murray note, technology is "ultimately changing the process for initiating, maintaining, and terminating intimate relationships."[44] Many people use dating sites like OkCupid, Bumble, or Hinge to find potential long-term partners. Others use hook-up apps like Grindr and Tinder to find instant sexual partners. Researchers have attributed the shorter durations of relationships in general and the unwillingness to work on current relationships to the increased access to alternative partners, since another potential partner is only a swipe away.[45] And while technology and social networking sites have increased access to potential partners, they have also contributed to relationship issues. Internet infidelity (emotional or sexual communication that may or may not transition to in-person contact) is leading to increasing rates of relationship dissolution and divorce.[46]

Positive aspects of technology include the ability for partners to stay in regular contact with each other throughout the day, even when they are in meetings or other situations where they would not have been able to communicate in the past. People in long-distance relationships also benefit from improved technology with visual platforms such as FaceTime and WhatsApp, which make it easier to stay connected and increase intimacy from a distance.

Texting and messaging create a private platform for partners to communicate secretly about their affection, love, and desire. Some people find it easier to flirt or send erotic messages via text, so the platform creates a new dimension for their relationship. One study of Mayan youth from Zinacatan (in Chiapas, Mexico) revealed that they had actually created language where none previously existed for romantic communication specifically geared toward texting.[47] The youth created this genre of communication away from the elders, giving them privacy for self-expression.

But online communication can also lead to confusion and misunderstanding. In the absence of any tone of voice or nonverbal cues, communication can be hard to decipher. One person may think the other is angry or upset when they are not. Trying to find ways to add context to the messages or using emojis or gifs to communicate feelings can clarify communication. And of course sensitive topics should be discussed only face-to-face.

Sometimes a person may feel neglected when their partner is focused on their phone or computer rather than on them. One study discovered that we have a more negative impression of our partners' smartphone use than of our own: Yair Amichai-Hamburger and Shir Etgar found that people identified their own cell phone multitasking as situational but their partners' multitasking as an intentional behavioral pattern. As a result, in contrast to their own scores, "partners' smartphone multitasking scores were negatively related to ratings of romantic intimacy."[48]

CHAPTER SUMMARY

This chapter explored Sternberg's triangle of love (passion, intimacy, and commitment) and the different levels of each within relationships.[49] It also discussed the chemical reactions that occur during the early stages of a relationship that make new relationships seductive, driving obsession and impairing judgment. In addition, it discussed the three dominant styles of attachment and the ways in which they may affect our relationships. Throughout, it clarified that positive communication is a critical component in successful relationships. It highlighted the fact that sharing the key social work skills of active listening with clients can help them enhance their own communication capacity. Finally, it explored the potential positives and negatives associated with technology and relationships.

DISCUSSION QUESTIONS

1. What were the components of Sternberg's love triangle?
2. Think of a relationship you are familiar with and consider where in the triangle you would put the people in that relationship. As far as you are aware, have their positions changed over time?
3. What are some ways in which you can use Sternberg's love triangle to facilitate communications about relationships?
4. Discuss key aspects of the three dominant attachment styles. What are some of the important factors of each for clients to consider when developing relationships?
5. Discuss ways in which active listening skills from social work practice can be modeled for or used with clients.

RESOURCES

Gottman Institute: www.gottman.com
Practical Polyamory: http://www.practicalpolyamory.com

8

ALT SEX

RELEVANT CSWE COMPETENCIES

Competency 2: Engage Diversity and Difference in Practice

Competency 3: Advance Human Rights and Social, Economic, and Environmental Justice

Competency 6: Engage with Individuals, Families, Groups, Organizations, and Communities

Competency 8: Intervene with Individuals, Families, Groups, Organizations, and Communities

In this chapter we will address some of the practices that fall under the category of alternative or alt sex, which Peggy Kleinplatz calls "extraordinary sex."[1] This is in contrast to "vanilla" or plain sex, or "normative sexualities (those that are procreative, heterosexual, monogamous and genitally focused)."[2] The alt sex movement has worked to destigmatize and depathologize sexual activities that previously may have been considered atypical but that are enjoyed by a range of consenting adults alone or together without causing harm.

This chapter might challenge you. It may push the boundaries of what you expect to encounter when discussing sex with clients. However, given our emphasis on nonjudgmental, strengths-based, sex-positive practice, we can provide a framework for engaging with clients to address a range of activities that may be unfamiliar to us.

PARAPHILIAS AND FETISHES

Paraphilia is sexual arousal that occurs in relation to "objects, events, or people outside what is considered the norm."[3] A critical point of distinction between the activities discussed in this chapter and those discussed in the next chapter on disorders and dysfunctions is that the activities here are noncoercive. They are engaged in freely, with active consent, and without explicit or implicit coercion by adults. As we will see in the next chapter, coercive paraphilias involve an unwilling participant, sometimes a minor, and can cause harm. Some examples are exhibitionism and frotterism.

Noncoercive paraphilias, on the other hand, are engaged in alone or with adults who have given active and clear consent and who are not coerced by any power dynamic. Paraphilias range from the more common (such as

---

Box 8.1

EXAMPLES OF NONCOERCIVE PARAPHILIAS

Coprophilia: feces (may be called scatalogia or scat)

Klismaphilia: receiving or administering enemas

Plushophilia: stuffed toys

Podophilia: feet

Trichophilia: hair

Urophilia: urine (also known as water sports or golden showers)

---

arousal in response to shoes, leather, lace, feet, and underwear) to the rare (such as arousal in response to a roller coaster or couch). These noncoercive paraphilias are included in the American Psychiatric Association's *Diagnostic and Statistical Manual of Mental Disorders*, 5th ed.,[4] but are diagnosed only if the behavior causes significant distress or impairment (see box 8.1 for examples of typical noncoercive paraphilias).

The close association between coercive and noncoercive paraphilia can sometimes bias mental health professionals against all paraphilic activity. This association—and the dominant paradigm of heteronormativity that strongly centralizes heterosexual vanilla sex—can also lead to clients internalizing shame related to their fetishes, paraphilias, and sexual behaviors. A sex-positive social worker must provide a space for the client to explore their feelings regarding social norms about sexuality without judgment. The social worker should also work with the client to identify and expunge internalized shame. Connecting clients to in-person and online communities such as FetLife or apps such as Feeld (for kink and poly people) can reduce feelings of isolation and provide a sense of community to counterbalance societal narratives about difference.

Adjacent to paraphilias are fetishes. Fetishes represent arousal in response to an inanimate object or body part. But they are different from paraphilias because a fetish, either live or in fantasy, is the singular focus for sexual arousal. In other words, they are objects of sexual fixation, and arousal cannot be achieved without them.[5]

A sex-positive social worker does not assume that a noncoercive fetish is problematic. It only becomes problematic if it causes the client emotional distress or significant physical harm.

It may be hard for you to imagine how paraphilias or fetishes may present in practice. Imagine that Michelle, a thirty-eight-year-old Latinx gender queer, comes to you because they are hitting a roadblock in their relationship with Claire, a thirty-two year-old African American cisgender female. The two have been dating for about eight months and have had an exciting and free-flowing sexual connection. But Michelle has been holding back a key aspect of their sexuality: their love of being spanked. While Michelle has successfully navigated conversations about spanking and other mild BDSM (bondage and discipline, dominance and submission, and sadism and masochism) behaviors like blindfolding with prior sexual partners, they are reluctant to do so with Claire, who is more conservative than their previous partners. Michelle feels that Claire is the real deal and doesn't want to do anything that would jeopardize their relationship.

You can provide an affirming space for Michelle to explore their fears and role-play what a conversation with Claire might be like. You can help them explore their hopes and fears about Claire's possible reactions. You might also connect Michelle to online resources, including the National Coalition for Sexual Freedom (NCSF), and print resources. These resources on thriving BDSM communities may help Michelle feel less alone and give them hope.

After role-playing several more times, Michelle realizes that they cannot be fully happy unless Claire at least knows about this aspect of their sexual identity. They resolve that they will be all right if Claire is not into it, but they won't if they don't "come clean." They hate having a secret between them and Claire and want a chance for their intimacy to grow even deeper. Before Michelle discloses their desires to Claire, you could work with them on how to manage Claire's potential reactions, including the possibility that she will feel as if she is not fulfilling Michelle's sexual desires and even the unlikely possibility that Claire will react with horror and judgment. Michelle becomes optimistic that their relationship can survive the disclosure and prepares to talk to Claire.

BEYOND *50 SHADES OF GREY*

The popular book *50 Shades of Grey*, by E. L. James (and its sequels and the subsequent movie series), catapulted one version of BDSM into the mainstream. BDSM is also known as kinky sex or simply kink (see box 8.2 for a fuller definition of BDSM). BDSM practitioners have largely criticized the portrayal of BDSM represented by Christian Grey in the books and movies as coercive and not representative of most BDSM practitioners. However, the series did bring BDSM more clearly into the public sphere and destigmatized some aspects of kink, such as blindfolding or using soft restraints. The series of books and movies—along with other movies, like the 2002 film *Secretary*—have led to conversations about BDSM both publicly and between partners.

Box 8.2
BDSM DEFINITIONS

Bondage: The use of physical restraints, such as handcuffs, ropes, and scarves.

Discipline: The use of power dynamics to physically or psychologically restrain or "punish" another person.

Dominance: Inflicting intense physical or psychological stimuli or pain on another person, often for the purpose of sexual arousal for the self and/or partner(s).

Dominant, dominatrix, or dom: A person who inflicts physical stimuli or pain or psychological stimuli or commands on another person, often for the purpose of sexual arousal for the self and/or partner(s).

Fetish: An inanimate object or body part that is necessary and crucial for sexual arousal.

Masochism: Deriving sexual pleasure or arousal from receiving physical or psychological stimuli or pain from another person.

Paraphilia: Sexual arousal created by an inanimate object or body part that is not necessary or crucial for arousal (arousal can be achieved in other ways).

Submission: Receiving physical or psychological stimuli, pain, commands, or humiliation, often for the purpose of sexual arousal for the self and/or partner(s).

Submissive or sub: A person who receives physical or psychological stimuli, pain, commands or humiliation, often for the purpose of sexual arousal for the self and/or partner(s).

> Switch: A person who sometimes takes the role of dominant and some-times that of submissive.
>
> Sadism: Deriving sexual pleasure and arousal from inflicting physical or psychological stimuli or pain on another person.

WHAT IS BDSM?

Although BDSM is more visible than ever, there is still some confusion about its nature. Megan Yost and L. E. Hunter[6] describe BDSM as a "sexual identity and a set of sexual practices characterized by explicit, negotiated power differentials, with a 'top' or 'dominant' person guiding interaction and a 'bottom' or 'submissive' individual following instructions or receiving sensation from the dominant. For most, but not all, practitioners, BDSM has an erotic appeal and takes place within a sexualized encounter."[7]

Engagement in some level of BDSM activity is common, with 14 percent of men and 11 percent of women reporting some kind of BDSM experience.[8] In their survey of 1,516 adults, Christian Joyal, Amelie Cossette, and Vanessa Lapierre found that a large percentage of people also fantasize about being sexually dominated (65 percent of women and 53 percent of men) or dominating (47 percent of women and 60 percent of men).[9] Specifically, 51 percent of the women acknowledged having fantasies of being tied up, 36.3 percent had had fantasies of being spanked or whipped, and 28.9 percent had fantasized about being forced to have sex. The numbers for men were similar: 46.2 percent, 28.5 percent, and 30.7 percent, respectively.

There is a wide range of intensity of BDSM practice, from occasionally teasing a partner with a feather all the way to a 24/7 submission/dominance relationship, in which practitioners engage in their submissive and dominant roles all the time, usually while living together. Throughout a BDSM encounter, participants negotiate boundaries about the type, intensity, duration, and context for the play or "scene." Clear communication is critical before the scene (to set it up) and during it (to ensure that everyone remains

comfortable with what is happening). Setting the boundaries for participation and recognizing potential safety hazards is known as risk-aware
consensual kink (RACK). We will explore the idea of consent within this
practice in the next section.

CONSENT WITHIN BDSM PRACTICE

As we have emphasized throughout this chapter, the most basic distinctions between healthy, sex-positive exploration of paraphilias and those
that are cause for concern is that the latter includes coercion and the involvement of minors. From a sex-positive perspective, consent is the foundation of healthy sexuality. Empowering women and marginalized people
to develop sexual agency is a critical human rights issue.[10] Within BDSM
communities, consent is carefully negotiated, articulated, and communi-
cated to ensure that appropriate boundaries are in place for the sexual experience. Practitioners establish in advance what activities are permissible
and impermissible. Here are some examples: hand restraints may be okay,
but not leg restraints; spanking with a paddle may be okay, but not with a
whip and not to draw blood. Participants also choose a safe word (such as
"blue" or "chair") to signal when the scene should be stopped. Safe words
are used rather than words like "stop" or "no" because the practice may
include humiliation that purposefully involves the dom refusing to heed
the sub's requests for them to stop.

As the BDSM community evolved, the notion of safe, sane, and consensual play emerged, making it clear that although dangerous activities
may be participated in (for example, play with needles, heat, or restraints),
they should be engaged in safely, sanely, and consensually. This meant
that the practitioners would negotiate the boundaries of the scene ahead
of time, obtain active consent, establish a safe word, and take care to
practice in a way that did not harm participants. Over time, however, the
notion of "safe" came to seem antithetical to many of the tenets of BDSM,
where feeling unsafe may be part of the appeal. Pressing against the edges

of safety (known as edge play) may be a purposeful part of the activity, creating adrenaline and arousal and fostering a deep connection and trust between participants. Evolving away from the idea of safe and sane, the community embraced RACK in the spirit of BDSM practice.[11] RACK acknowledges that practice is not always safe, but that the risks of the activity are engaged in knowingly. Consent, however, remains central to the philosophy.

Yost and Hunter asked people what attracted them to BDSM and received two distinct answers: "(1) BDSM interests are an intrinsic part of the self and (2) BDSM interests developed because of external influences."[12] So for some people a BDSM identity and practice felt like an innate part of who they were as a person. It was there, inside, waiting to be explored and exposed. For others, a distinct external event or events catalyzed their interest and exploration. Given that BDSM has largely been pathologized through the *Diagnostic and Statistical Manual of Mental Disorders*, the researchers anticipated that practitioners would feel a need to "construct narratives to explain and provide justification for [their] interests."[13] Eva Jozifkova found that 40 percent had recognized their interest in BDSM before age eighteen.[14] This is relevant not just for people working with adults but also for those working with adolescents.

BECOMING A KINK-AWARE SOCIAL WORKER

As a sex-positive social worker, you can help clients explore, understand, and establish the fantasies, behaviors, and boundaries that work for them. You can provide an affirming environment in which to explore fantasies or hopes for future activities alone or with partners and to process experiences they may already have had. You may also be called upon to help people navigate discrepancies in their kink-related desires relative to those of a partner or partners, as was the case with Michelle and Claire.

You might direct clients to resources such as Jack Morin's *The Erotic Mind*[15] or discuss with them their sexual fantasies and peak experiences.

Clients may identify with aspects of the narratives described or discover that their interests and fantasies—even dark ones, like rape fantasies—are actually quite common. To provide an affirming therapeutic space, it is important to check your own biases. As Jonathan Powls and Jason Davies note, "Clinicians need to be mindful of the evidence here that the majority of SM practitioners represent a nondeviant, well-adjusted, and well-functioning majority."[16]

Since people with a BDSM identity experience more stigmatization and discrimination than none practitioners, you can also provide a nonjudgmental counter to social pressures.[17] Providing an affirming space and allowing clients to explore their feelings, such as anger or hurt as a result of experiences of discrimination, can help them avoid internalizing shame.

Beuhler suggested that a kink-aware therapist "is one who does not assume that a paraphilia is problematic; that many forms of sexual expression are acceptable if they do no harm; and that the therapist needs to acknowledge that he or she [they], too, may have fantasies or have acted on behaviors that might be considered outside the norm, even if they are mild, in order to engender compassion for the client who is kinky."[18] As with all social work practice, you should meet the client where they are with their BDSM practice. Affirm the client's experiences with kink and work with them to integrate that aspect of themselves into their overall positive sense of identity. Also, be sensitive to their experiences of discrimination and feelings of stigmatization.

CONSENSUAL NONMONOGAMY

Nonmonogamy is a term usually applied to sexual encounters that occur beyond the bounds of a couple's relationship, whether they are married, cohabiting, or simply have an agreement of fidelity. While nonmonogamy in general can be either open or secret, consensual nonmonogamy (CNM) is transparent and known by all parties involved.[19] This is an umbrella term used to describe a range of CNM practices including polyamory, swinging, and group sex (see box 8.3 for definitions).

CNM runs counter to current Western norms, which privilege monogamy, coupleism, and familialism.[20] The dominant narrative dictates that a person will meet someone of the opposite sex, fall in love, marry, and build a family, remaining committed and faithful throughout. We tend to ascribe positive traits to those people who adhere to this life course.

Just as heteronormativity assumes and privileges being heterosexual and cisnormativity assumes and privileges being cisgendered, mononormativity is the assumption and privileging of monogamous couple relationships. Despite cultural shifts in Europe and the United States away from a heterosexual requirement for marriage, parenting, and adoption, the imperatives of monogamy and coupleism remain.[21] As with heteronormativity and cisnormativity, you must interrogate your own biases to strengthen your sex-positive approach (see the section on cornerstones of CNM as well as box 8.4 for some suggestions as to how to do this). While nonmonogamy is often pathologized, research suggests that there are no mental health differences between those who participate in CNM and those who do not, and relationship quality is reportedly similar.[22] And while we have at least one gene (related to vasopressin) that codes for monogamy, scientists have suggested that "humans are more similar to nonmonogamous species than monogamous species."[23]

Box 8.3
CONSENSUAL NONMONOGAMY (CNM) DEFINITIONS

CNM or ethical nonmonogamy: Engaging in emotional and sexual relationships with multiple people simultaneously with the full knowledge and consent of each participating person. People may be involved together (e.g., creating a triad or triangle, in which all people are in the relationship together) or separately (e.g., people have separate relationships with the same or multiple partners but not with each other).

Box 8.3 *(continued)*

Group sex: Sexual encounters involving a number of people at the same time who do not necessarily have an emotional or commitment-based connection to one another.

Monogamish: Couple relationships that occasionally include additional sexual partners, either with both members of the couple or just one of them.

Partnered nonmonogamy: Occurs when a "primary" couple agrees to engage in consensual sexual relationships beyond the couple—which may involve both members of the couple or just one of them.

Polyamory: Sheff defined polyamory as "consensual, openly conducted, multiple-partner relationships."[24] Christian Klesse acknowledged that it is sometimes an "umbrella term and synonym for consensual non-monogamy."[25]

Polyfidelity: A relationship involving three or more people who are emotionally and/or sexually committed to each other exclusively.

Polygamy: The illegal practice of being married to more than one person simultaneously.

Swinging: Having consensual sexual experiences with other people in the context of a primary relationship and usually in a specific location. Also known as "the lifestyle."

One form of CNM, known as polyamory, tends to be stigmatized partly because it is often confused with polygamy. But polyamory and polygamy are very different. Polygamy is an illegal practice in which one person (typically male) marries multiple other people (typically female) concurrently. It is often associated with religious or cultural practices and may involve coercion, especially the coercion of young women into marriage at a very early age.

As we discussed in chapter 4, polyamory (often referred to as poly or polyam) is a sexual identity associated with simultaneous, transparent relationships with multiple partners. In their article drawing attention to how little social workers understood diverse sexualities, especially polyamory, D. J. Williams and Emily Prior defined it as the "preference of loving or being romantically involved with more than one person at a time with all people involved knowing about each other (thus, it is not 'cheating')."[26] Similar to the case with noncoercive paraphilias, the relationship structure here is also voluntary and noncoercive and does not include minors.

Polyamory has been heteronormalized by pornography in which representations of multiple-partnered sex usually include two women focused on pleasuring one man. This association with pornography has also led to the dominant narrative about polyamory: that it focuses on sexual centrality and excess, rather than on intense emotional connections. The heteronormative paradigm and dominance of the belief that monogamy and fidelity are necessary for happiness and fulfillment sets up an underlying fear of nonmonogamy, which leads to mistrust, stigmatization, and oppression.[27] However, polyamorous relationships are often characterized by emotional attunement, honesty, communication, and trust.[28]

HOW PREVALENT IS CNM?

In chapter 4 we learned that it is difficult to estimate how many people identify as consensually nonmonogamous or polyamorous because the identity is invisible, marginalized, and stigmatized.[29] Nevertheless, rough estimates suggest that 4–5 percent of adults in the United States engage in some type of CNM.[30] Ethan Levine and coauthors noted that in the 2012 National Survey of Sexual Health and Behavior, 4 percent of the respondents reported being in open relationships.[31]. The authors found no differences in age, race, ethnicity, or socioeconomic status, but they did find a higher likelihood of engaging in CNM among males and people who identified themselves as lesbian, gay, or bisexual (LGB).

Two national samples of single people drawn from similar pools of participants found a much higher rate of participation in CNM: approximately 21 percent.[32] Specifically, M. L. Haupert and coauthors studied data from the annual Singles in America study, looking at two distinct samples of adults from two separate years (2013 and 2014).[33] The authors found that 21.2 percent of respondents in the first study and 21.9 percent in the second study reported having engaged in CNM. Similar to the work of Levine and coauthors, this research found no differences in age, race, ethnicity, or socioeconomic status but found that men and people who identified themselves as LGB (especially bisexual) were significantly more likely to have practiced some form of CNM.[34]

CORNERSTONES OF CNM

Working with clients in CNM relationships involves many of the same strengths as working with people in dyadic relationships. Much of the work focuses on how people value themselves and handle attachment and intimacy. Due to stressors imposed by societal expectations, people in CNM relationships may need more support in dealing with societal constraints and expectations that stigmatize and oppress nonnormative identities and practices. Within this context, CNM individuals may also need more support for communicating clearly, navigating boundaries, and handling jealousy.

Many of the points about communication and intimacy made in chapter 7 also apply here. Using skills familiar to social workers, you can help clients develop their active listening skills and foster their capacity to ask open-ended questions. You can also support clients in the process of understanding their own needs and wants. Guiding clients to use "I" statements to clearly communicate what they need and want to all partners can also be critical to successful CNM. Working with clients as they refine their active listening skills adds an important layer to the work. Navigating multiple intimate relationships that each require different physical, emotional, and sexual energy within the bounded and limited notion of time requires the capacity to state needs while still hearing and responding to the needs of partners. Effectively communicating and establishing boundaries are important subsets of communication that require your clients to be attuned to their own desires and limits.

Franklin Veaux and Eve Rickert note that boundaries "derive from the idea that the only person you really control is yourself."[35] While leading proponents of CNM disagree on some aspects of CNM practice, there is a consensus that ethical CNM requires boundaries, not rules.[36] You should help your clients understand the distinction between the two. Rules are imposed externally upon a person, their behavior, or their relationship: e.g., if you have sex with someone else, you must use a barrier. Boundaries, in contrast, come from a place of "I": "If you have unbarriered sex with other people, then *I* will use barriers with you," or "*I* am okay with you having sex with someone when you are out of town for work, but not when you are home." If your client imposes strict rules on a partner or partners, you might explore their need for control. Work to help the client reframe their needs away from controlling another person and toward stating their personal boundaries. And while it is not unusual for boundaries to evolve over time, the constant softening of boundaries may be cause for concern. Your client may agree to concessions because they feel they have to and not because they want to.

Here are some boundaries to think through with clients as they establish their polyamorous practices: What constraints are there around how much time will be spent with different partners? When can sex with another occur? Where can it occur? Will encounters be discussed afterward or not? Will there be fluid bonding or not (for example, will condoms and dams be used to protect against infection)? How will holidays, anniversaries, and birthdays be navigated?

ABUNDANCE, COMPERSION, AND JEALOUSY

CNM is practiced from the principle of abundance. This is the idea that there is more than enough of everything to go around: enough love, intimacy, sex, and even time.

In the introduction to their groundbreaking book, *The Ethical Slut*, Janet Hardy and Dossie Easton note that while some people don't think it is possible to have all of the love, sex, and friendship that they dream of, others "persist and discover that being openly loving, intimate, [and] sexual with many people is not only possible but can be more rewarding than they ever imagined."[37]

CNM practitioners argue that people do not say, "If you have more children you will not love them enough," or "There is not enough love for more than one parent." So why would they say this about having only one emotional or sexual partner?[38] Practicing from a place of abundance addresses some of the fear of abandonment or jealousy that can arise when additional partners are introduced, especially during the exciting phase of new relationship energy.

There is a common misunderstanding that people who practice CNM do not experience jealousy. This is not true. While some people who practice CNM never experience jealousy, this is very rare and usually the result of a lot of personal work aimed at self-growth and understanding internal emotional responses. CNM practitioners often experience jealousy, particularly when they perceive that the safety and security of the relationship is threatened. However, CNM practitioners may have learned how to both manage their jealousy and use it as an opportunity for learning. As Klesse noted, "Jealousy can be taken as the starting point for self-exploration and changes in one's own emotional responses."[39] Like monogamous clients, poly clients may experience jealousy related to low self-esteem, so you may build their resilience by working with them on their feelings of self-esteem and -worth.

As we mentioned in chapter 7, Anita Wagner of the website Practical Polyamory has created a useful resource that explores different origins of jealousy and provides tools for use with polyamorous clients.[40] She identifies six types of fear that may underlie jealous feelings: fears of the unknown, change, losing power and control, scarcity, loss, and abandonment. Exploring which of these fears underlie your client's jealousy can facilitate the development of strategies and resiliency to overcome them.

Another strategy is to foster compersion—the feelings of joy and happiness at someone else's joy and happiness, or a sort of contagiousness of good feelings. In the case of CNM, seeing your partner happy and excited about another relationship may cause this positive feeling. Taormino suggests that compersion is the remedy for jealousy.[41] Certainly, not every CNM practitioner experiences compersion, but many do.[42]

AVOIDING ASSUMPTIONS AND DEALING WITH BIAS

As a sex-positive social worker, you are likely aware of the assumptions that we make in the regular course of practice. Interrupting these assumptions has been a critical focus of our work in this book. CNM is no different. The strong mononormative narrative socializes us to be skeptical of non-couple relationships, assuming that someone in such relationships is unhappy and looking for an exit, or that noncouple relationships are inferior, less stable, and less committed than traditional couple relationships. The sex-positive social worker doesn't assume that these relationships or poly practice in general are somehow less mature, less developed, or doomed to fail. In fact, the data suggest that a large percentage of monogamous relationships fail. The current divorce rate is 40–50 percent,[43] and the norm of lifelong monogamy is giving way to the norm of serial monogamy—a series of monogamous relationships over time.

Western norms are suspicious of those who identify as poly (as well as bisexual and pansexual people), who are seen as overly sexually permissive. In fact, CNM relationships are often "regarded as less moral, less sexually satisfying, lower in quality, and more sexually risky than monogamous relationships."[44] The assumption is that a person engages in CNM only to have even more (potentially unbarriered) sex. Stephanie Buehler points out that part of putting aside bias is "listen[ing] with compassion to what the client or clients might be saying about their feelings regarding social constriction or difficulties they may encounter in staying monogamous."[45]

She also notes that a person who "wants to practice solo polyamory may be seeking support for their decision in a monogamous world." Williams and Prior note that polyamorous clients may need help to decide what type of polyamory and what sort of relationships will suit them best: There can be a positive effect of opening up possibilities for your clients, since it is "empowering for clients to realize that relationships may be designed in different ways to better meet participants' needs."[46] In line with the notion of self-determination from the National Association of Social Workers' *Code of Ethics*,[47] Geri Weitzman and coauthors suggest that it may be easier to set aside bias or judgment if you focus on helping clients with "preserving and enriching their chosen relationships."[48] Adrienne Bairstow provided a series of helpful questions to uncover your feelings about and experiences with monogamy and CNM (see box 8.4).[49]

Box 8.4
QUESTIONS TO EXPLORE YOUR FEELINGS ABOUT POLYAMORY

- Where do my values and opinions on monogamy come from?
- What feelings come up when I think about people who have different values related to monogamy?
- What positive and negative examples of monogamy and CNM have I seen?
- What judgments do I make about people who engage in CNM?
- How might my attitudes impact my work with couples who want to explore opening their relationship?

This set of questions can be applied to many of the topics covered in this book. It's important for social workers to understand their personal values and explore the extent to which they can honor their ethical responsibility to be nonjudgmental and support self-determination. Keeping a countertransference journal can be especially helpful here, so that you can reflect upon your process within the therapeutic relationship.

As we discussed in chapter 4, the client should not have to educate you about consensual nonmonogamy. Instead, you should seek out background information. However, you should discuss with clients their understanding of their version of CNM so you are on the same page. Reflect your understanding to the client to test that what you hear from them is what they are actually trying to say. If you find that you cannot provide open, nonjudgmental care, then refer the client to someone who can. Some communities have directories of poly-friendly therapists that you can consult.

BECOMING A POLY-AWARE THERAPIST

To become a poly-aware social worker, you must recognize the way in which monogamy is the default organizing principle for relationships and interrogate any temptation to fall into that default.[50] As we have stressed throughout this book, never assume. Leave room for CNM as an option during intake questions and throughout your dialogues with your client.

Besides providing questions to uncover your biases about CNM, Bairstow also provided guidelines for therapists working with couples who are exploring CNM. Many of the guidelines can also be applied to people who already have an open relationship:

- Educate yourself about CNM
- Identify your own values and beliefs related to CNM
- Work with the couple's definition of CNM
- Be aware that partners may have varying concerns about CNM
- Address infidelity if present
- Avoid assumptions about the ways CNM will impact the relationship
- Recognize that opening a relationship is an ongoing process[51]

INTERSECTING IDENTITIES

The practices explored in this chapter and chapter 4 are not mutually exclusive. Many people have intersecting sexual and gender identities and practices, as well as racial or ethnic identities that influence how they experience the world. Lesbian, gay, bisexual, pansexual, and queer people have been strongly associated with the BDSM and poly movements.[52] Some posit that this is because their sexual identity already transgresses the dominant oppressive heterosexist paradigm, which gives them a greater sense of freedom to explore sexual behaviors and paradigms outside monogamous, vanilla sexuality.[53]

People who identify themselves as transgender, gender nonbinary, or gender queer (TGNBQ) are also often drawn to different aspects of BDSM. Here again the notion of freedom from cisnormative and heteronormative (sometimes called cisheteronormative) paradigms may play a role in feelings of freedom of expression. TGNBQ individuals may have had practice using clear communication within sexual encounters to establish boundaries about activities that are acceptable or not. For example, some TGNBQ people may say everything is permissible. Others may say it is okay to explore fully above the waist but not below the waist or allow nudity only in the dark. What people are comfortable with may be quite different at different times and within the context of different relationships. Having become comfortable in navigating sexual communication, establishing a contract for BDSM play may then seem like second nature.

People with disabilities are also drawn to BDSM as a sexual practice since it allows them to define sexuality and arousal outside conventional norms.[54] Focusing on sensations, intensity, and fantasy allows the sexual experience to go beyond the confines of the penetrative imperative and their physical limitations. BDSM practice allows people to define their own sexual experiences, rewriting static heteronormative scripts into dynamic, creative expressions of desire and arousal. Supporting this process is a critical role of the sex-positive social worker, as you work with clients to reimagine their notions of sexuality and sexual behavior to explore new realms beyond intercourse.

CHAPTER SUMMARY

This chapter explored alternative sexualities, those that to lesser or greater degrees transgress the dominant norms of monogamous, vanilla sex. It covered definitions related to BDSM and kink and the important distinction between coercive and noncoercive paraphilias. It explored some of the different types of paraphilias that people may be aroused by and the importance of consent and boundaries before and during play. It also explored the consent framework of safe, sane, and consensual kink, as well as RACK and the importance of agreeing on a safe word. It reminded us that a sex-positive social work practice never automatically pathologizes BDSM or kink behavior. And it highlighted the importance of assessing whether or not kink involvement is part of the presenting problem or causing significant distress. Rather than starting from an assumption that BDSM play is inherently problematic, the sex-positive social worker starts instead from the assumption that it is an important, healthy dimension of a client's sexuality.

Besides BDSM and kink, the chapter explored consensual nonmonogamy (CNM). It showed how the societal pressure imposed by mononormativity—the expectation and privileging of monogamy—is a potential area of distress for clients and an important area of social worker support. It discussed critical anchors to successful CNM, including strong communication skills, setting boundaries, and navigating monogamy. Finally, like many other chapters, it stressed the importance of not making assumptions and interrogating our biases, where they exist.

DISCUSSION QUESTIONS

1. Discuss the differences between a coercive and a noncoercive paraphilia.
2. Revisit Bairstow's questions to uncover any biases you may have against nonmonogamy. Reflect on each of them, then share your list of biases (if applicable) with someone to see where they are similar and where they differ.
3. Explore some of the boundaries that you anticipate you could help clients establish and negotiate as part of their CNM practices.

RESOURCES

American Association of Sexuality Educators, Counselors, and Therapists: www.aasect.org

Kink Aware Professionals Directory: https://ncsfreedom.org/key-programs/kink-aware -professionals-59776 (created by NCSF)

National Coalition for Sexual Freedom (NCSF): www.ncsfreedom.org

Practical Polyamory, Jealousy: http://www.practicalpolyamory.com/images/Jealousy_Up-dated_10-6-10.pdf

9

SEXUAL DYSFUNCTIONS AND DISORDERS

RELEVANT CSWE COMPETENCIES

Competency 2: Engage Diversity and Difference in Practice

Competency 6: Engage with Individuals, Families, Groups, Organizations, and Communities

Competency 8: Intervene with Individuals, Families, Groups, Organizations, and Communities

This chapter outlines some of the most common sexual disorders and dysfunctions you may encounter during your practice. While at first glance this may not seem to be a very sex-positive perspective, addressing sexual difficulties as they arise is a critical aspect of sexual health and well-being. Sexual difficulties, even those that go unacknowledged, can cause significant personal distress and lead to a range of sexual and relationship issues.

Our goal, then, is to look at some of the more typical sexual difficulties encountered through a sex-positive lens. It is beyond the scope of this book to give detailed attention to each different issue under consideration or to comprehensive treatment options. Instead, we will survey the main issues and make some general suggestions for maintaining a sex-positive perspective in treatment.

The chapter will begin by considering common issues related to desire, arousal, and orgasm, as well as those related to painful sex. Out-of-control sexual behavior (sometimes called sex addiction) will also be addressed. Finally, we will look again at paraphilias, introduced in chapter 8, this time focusing on those that involve coercion or cause clinically significant distress. We'll also consider the way in which these difficulties are pathologized in the *Diagnostic and Statistical Manual of Mental Disorders*, 5th ed. (*DSM*), of the American Psychiatric Association (APA).[1]

SCREENING AND ASSESSMENT

Sexual difficulties are typically characterized by disruption in a person's ability to respond to sexual stimulation or to experience sexual pleasure. It is not uncommon for someone to have several sexual dysfunctions simultaneously. *DSM* distinguishes between sexual issues that are lifelong or acquired and between those that are generalized (meaning it always occurs, regardless of partner or setting) or situational (meaning it occurs sometimes but not always, in some situations or with some partners but not in every situation or with every partner). Thus, you will want to assess when the difficulty arose. Is it something that the person has been dealing with since they began to be sexual, did it occur in response to a particular event, or did it develop over time? Here you are trying to assess whether something physical (e.g., a medical illness, injury, or change in medication), emotional, or traumatic may have had an impact on the person's functioning. Conversely, the difficulty may be lifelong, and the person has never experienced a different response. If it is not lifelong, you will want to get a sense of how long the issue has persisted. Most sexual issues in *DSM* require a minimum duration of six months and must occur 75–100 percent of the time for a diagnosis.

Your assessment should also include whether the difficulty is generalized or situational. Using the DOUPE (description, onset, understanding, past treatment efforts, and expectations) model we discussed in chapter 3 is a way for you to access this information with your client (see box 9.1 for a reminder of the model).[2]

Box 9.1
THE DOUPE MODEL OF SEXUAL PROBLEM ASSESSMENT

Description: What does the patient understand the problem to be?

Onset: When did the issue begin, how long has the problem occurred, and how has it changed over time?

Understanding: What does the client think caused the issue (e.g., was there any particular triggering event or illness)?

Past treatments: What has the client tried to do so far to address the issue? Has the client seen a physician, taken medication, or sought prior therapy?

Expectations: What are the client's expectations about what can be done and how the issue can be addressed?[3]

Besides assessing whether the issue is lifelong or acquired and generalized versus situational, there are other factors you should include as part of a comprehensive assessment. You will want to ask whether the person has been to a primary care provider. If so, what kind of screenings or testing have they undergone (e.g., blood tests) to determine whether there is a medical reason behind the sexual issue? You should also ask what medications the client takes, as side effects can often impair normal sexual functioning and decrease sexual desire. You should screen for other co-occurring mental health issues such as substance use, anxiety, depression, and trauma, which may impact sexual functioning.

Finally, if the person is partnered, you'll want to assess the extent to which they have been talking to their partner or partners about their sexual issues. Facilitating open and honest conversations between partners can be an important intervention. Quite often people make assumptions about what their partner is thinking and feeling, and often these assumptions are wrong. Allowing space to discuss the situation in a nonjudgmental, caring way, or providing partners with appropriate language to discuss it, can be an important first step toward addressing the problem.

DESIRE, AROUSAL, AND ORGASM ISSUES

In chapter 2, we addressed the anatomy and physiology of the sex organs and the sexual response cycle. Many of the problems that clients present are related to issues of anatomical anxiety, discomfort, or limitation, or to physiological or psychological aspects of the response cycle. The next sections of this chapter address difficulties that arise at various points in that cycle, including desire, arousal, and orgasm. As we explored in chapter 2, the linear view of the sexual response cycle put forward by William Masters and Virginia Johnson has come under criticism recently, especially related to female desire and arousal.[4] Responding to these criticisms and acknowledging newer models of arousal response in which desire may come after arousal (e.g., Rosemary Basson's model), the APA combined desire and arousal disorders for women in *DSM*, replacing hypoactive desire disorder and female arousal disorder with one category of female sexual interest or arousal disorder (FSAID).[5] Interestingly, the APA maintained male hypoactive sexual desire disorder as a distinct diagnosis. Since these categories are gendered in a way that is not inclusive, be careful when discussing potential diagnoses with clients. You can discuss the issue without assigning gender to it, or if necessary, you can focus on anatomy (e.g., people with a penis or people with a vagina) to distinguish categories.

While for simplicity's sake the sections that follow will be divided into distinct categories—desire, arousal, orgasm, and pain—in practice, the issues are often intertwined. For example, while premature ejaculation is an orgasm-related difficulty, repeated premature ejaculation can lead to a decrease in desire and subsequent sexual avoidance. Similarly, someone who is experiencing arousal difficulties and not becoming lubricated sufficiently may experience painful sex that decreases their desire or even manifests itself as sexual aversion. While it is helpful to think about the issues in the different phases of the sexual response cycle, remember that the interlocking sexual context can affect the overall picture.

DIFFICULTIES WITH DESIRE AND AROUSAL

We can define "desire" as interest in sex, sexual fantasies, and sexual activity. While there is no definitive research, there is evidence that sexual desire is strongly associated with testosterone levels in both women and men.[6] In fact, women's sexual desire can be especially sensitive to low levels of testosterone, and those levels may decrease with age.[7] One natural way to enhance testosterone is through eating certain foods. Fava beans and soybeans are thought to promote the manufacture of testosterone. Other foods are also thought to act as aphrodisiacs: oysters, okra, and pumpkin seeds, which are high in magnesium and potentially enhance testosterone production; pomegranates, which increase heart health; and chocolate, which improves overall mood.[8] However, research on the impact of natural aphrodisiacs is still limited.[9] Although diagnostic categories changed in *DSM* from the previous edition, there remain three key ways in which desire may present as an issue in practice: very low desire, very high desire, and mismatched levels of desire between partners.

Hypoactive sexual desire disorder—which remains its own category for males but is merged into FSAID for women—occurs when a person is uninterested in sex or has very low sexual desire. This absence of sexual desire, thoughts, and fantasies occurs prior to sex and may continue during sex as well. Alyson Spurgas argued that the conceptualization of desire is socioculturally constructed with a heteronormative, gendered narrative.[10] Basson highlighted the fact that some people with low desire first become aroused and then feel desire once the sexual experience has begun, arguing that a typical sexual response—especially for women—is to have desire increase after arousal.[11] This argument motivated the APA to collapse the categories in *DSM*. Nevertheless, issues related to desire are commonly presented by women in treatment.[12] Estimates of the share of women reporting low desire at some point are as high as 55 percent.[13] Perhaps related to the cultural construction of desire, only approximately 23 percent of women report experiencing distress as a result of their low desire. Consequently, Rebecca Frost and Caroline Donovan argued that treatment should focus on addressing societal messaging about what arousal and desire "should" look like and the experienced distress rather than the low desire itself.[14]. Although desire and arousal issues may appear to present separately in a clinical setting, Sabina Sarin, Rhonda Amsel, and Yitzchak Binik, studied the distinction between desire and arousal and noted a "high degree of overlap,"[15] which supported the inclusion of a combined criteria for FSAID in *DSM*.

In addition to low desire, there is sexual aversion, the active avoidance and fear of sex. Sexually averse people experience panic or anxiety at the prospect of sex. The diagnostic category for sexual aversion was removed from *DSM* as a specific disorder, as it closely resembles anxiety disorders and phobias and has limited empirical support.[16] However, you should still explore active avoidance during your assessment, as it may be present in people with FSAID or those who have a traumatic sexual history.

Conversely, hyperactive desire is when a person has a very high level of sexual desire and is constantly preoccupied with sex. Definitions vary regarding what extents of preoccupation or engagement in masturbation, pornography, or sexual activity merit diagnosis. For example, one definition used a rate of seven orgasms a week as the threshold, and another used a daily orgasm.[17] Nevertheless, preoccupation with sexual stimulation is consistent throughout the definitions. Hyperactive desire is not included as a diagnostic category in *DSM*, but it does present in practice as a source of distress for clients. Clinically, it is often discussed in the context of out-of-control sexual behavior or sexual compulsivity (sometimes referred to as sex addiction), which we will cover later in this chapter.

Another common presenting issue is discrepant desire, a mismatch of sexual desire between two or more partners. Often in such cases the person with the higher level of desire presents in distress or reports unmet needs.

For example, Nancy and Donald are in their early thirties and have been dating for four years. They have been talking about getting married but are scared that this commitment will make them feel tied down. They think of themselves as adventurous and outgoing. They have come to see you because of both their fears of marriage and their discrepant feelings about having children. Nancy is eager to start a family and does not think that they need to wait until they are married. Donald also wants to have children but wants to wait a little longer, "perhaps until they are married," he says almost flippantly. While addressing the relationship dynamics, you inquire about their sexual relationship. "It's fine," they both say in unison, but not very convincingly. After further prompting they reveal that Nancy is distressed because they don't have sex as frequently as they used to and it feels like Donald is almost uninterested in it. You take some time to explore their sexual history both prior to and during their relationship. You help them identify when the shift in interest emerged and how the discrepancy has played out within the relationship. Through supportive, nonjudgmental exploration, Nancy and Donald realize that Donald began to have less interest in sex as the conversations about starting a family gained in intensity. He also realized that he really did not want to have a child before he was married, whether with Nancy or with anyone else. Donald did not want Nancy to feel as though he was holding their sex life hostage for a wedding, although subconsciously he may have been. She did not want to feel held hostage either, but she could acknowledge that she did not understand how much being married meant to him. You encourage them both to continue to be direct in their communication, even through difficult conversations, as a way to maintain sexual intimacy.

As you can see from Nancy and Donald, when you address desire discrepancy, your assessment should include investigating why one partner does not want to have sex. It may be that that person is using sex to assert some degree of control over the relationship. It may also be that the person finds intimacy so overwhelming that sex comes to represent a threat. Avoiding sex, then, is a way to manage the feelings of merger and maintain distance.[18] Or perhaps there is a triangulation of power in the relationship, with one partner using work, their phone, substances such as drugs or alcohol, or another person to create distance. This can play out as a power struggle for attention through the sexual relationship. In fact, one approach to addressing issues of desire called syndyastic sexual therapy (SST) takes the focus away from sexual dysfunction or sexual desire and instead concentrates on improving overall relationship quality. This therapy focuses on the extent to which biopsychosocial needs are fulfilled (or frustrated) by the relationship and understands "sexuality as a way of communicating through body language."[19]

Besides mediating distance and intimacy, some underlying issues to consider in mismatched desire are whether the sex between partners is satisfying. Sometimes people find it easier to avoid having sex than to admit that they do not find it enjoyable or that their sexual needs are unmet. One way to assess whether satisfaction is a factor is by having your client complete a sexual satisfaction survey, like Walter Hudson's Index of Sexual Satisfaction.[20] Such a tool can provide both useful information and a jumping-off point for conversation.

Difficulties with excitement and arousal occur when someone cannot attain or maintain sexual arousal (lubrication, engorgement, or erection) in a situation that would typically produce an arousal response. Someone affected by arousal issues may be interested in sexual activity but unable to become sexually stimulated. As noted above, female arousal disorder was subsumed under FSAID in *DSM*, since women tend to have a much more intertwined experience of desire and arousal. A social, cultural, and religious context that repeatedly teaches women that they should either not be sexual or should be sexually passive can create internal conflict. This conflict produces shame and guilt, which can inhibit desire and the capacity for arousal. Addressing the sexual messaging a client may have received during adolescence and early adulthood can be an important starting point for addressing overall desire and arousal issues.

Increasingly unrealistic ideals related to body image and the intense pressure for perfection created by social and other media have also magnified body image issues that affect a person's sexual self-confidence.[21] The natural process of aging in women includes decreasing levels of estrogen, thinning of the vaginal walls, and decrease in lubrication, all of which can inhibit the arousal response. Perhaps because of the availability of over-the-counter lubricants, which can be relatively easily integrated into sexual practice, one study found that issues of reduced lubrication in women were not a cause of significant distress.[22] Therefore, providing information about the types of lubricants available and normalizing their use can be helpful if problems of vaginal dryness are presented.

Male erectile disorder (ED) remains listed as an arousal disorder in *DSM* for people with a penis.[23] Because notions of masculinity are centered on virility and the heterocentric coitus imperative,[24] ED can cause significant distress both for individuals and within relationships. Research suggests that people suffering from ED experience greater distress than their partners.[25]

Like many sexual issues, ED has many potential causes, from physiological issues or psychological issues to a combination of the two. While originally ED was thought to be predominantly psychological, new research suggests that approximately 80 percent of cases have underlying physiological causes.[26] Therefore, a social worker should recommend consulting a physician to determine whether there are underlying medical issues—such as with vascular, neurological, or endocrine systems—and to discuss potential side effects from any medications.[27] Potential psychological underpinnings may include performance anxiety, depression, or relationship dissatisfaction.

ED is much more common than most people think, with estimates suggesting that it affects about thirty million men in the United States.[28] The ever-increasing older adult population will likely consistently increase this number over time. ED becomes more common with age, though it can be an issue at any age. As with other sexual concerns, the social worker should conduct an assessment that includes questions from the DOUPE model. This is also a good time to explore past sexual responsiveness and assess any specific changes, such as those related to illnesses, injuries, surgeries, pregnancies, traumas, or changes in life situations like relationship stress or changes in employment. The social worker may guide clients as they explore their sexual selves by talking through their sexual fantasies and past positive experiences, if applicable. Encourage them to explore their body as it ages and changes, staying in touch with how their genitals and breasts look and feel and what stimulation may or may not be enjoyable. Encouraging the development of sexual agency and shifting the focus away from product-driven, orgasm-focused sex can help clients maintain sexual expression and satisfaction. Exercises with a sensory focus or mindfulness component can be effective interventions, especially if performance anxiety is an issue.[29] While a number of medications to treat ED are readily available, you should always explore potential underlying psychological concerns. And while testosterone treatment is not approved by the Food and Drug Administration for this purpose, it may be helpful to address some issues related to desire and arousal in peri- or postmenopausal people. However, the treatment has not yet had as successful results in this case as in that of ED.

DISORDERS RELATED TO ORGASM

Orgasm—an intense, pleasurable feeling accompanied by warmth, tingling, endorphin release, and involuntary pelvic floor contractions—is the dominant focus of Western sexuality. The term "sex" has become synonymous with the giving and receiving of orgasms. Despite the fact that a wide range of intensely pleasurable, sensual, and intimate experiences occur without an orgasmic release or climax, orgasm remains the focal point of the majority of sexual experiences. Therefore, it is often the presenting problem in treatment.

There are three orgasmic disorders (anorgasmia) in *DSM*: female orgasmic disorder, premature ejaculation, and delayed ejaculation (formerly called male orgasmic disorder).[30] As with other sexual disorders in *DSM*, diagnosis requires the inability to achieve orgasm despite adequate stimulation, and it must also be accompanied by distress and must occur 75–100 percent of the time.

Orgasmic disorders can be primary or lifelong—that is, the person has never experienced an orgasm. Or they can be secondary or acquired, when the person has experienced orgasm but can no longer. Secondary or acquired disorders are often related to a precipitating event. These disorders can also be distinguished by whether they are generalized (the person cannot achieve orgasm in any situation) or situational (they can achieve orgasm only in certain situations).

Estimates suggest that female orgasmic disorder impacts 10–25 percent of women.[31] Approximately 5–10 percent of women have never experienced orgasm.[32]

Delayed ejaculation is much less common, affecting less than 1 percent of people with a penis. The extended time required to achieve orgasm can result in soreness, rubbing, or exasperation and giving up.

There are lots of reasons why people may be unable to have an orgasm—some physiological and some learned. For example, take Barbara, a forty-seven-year-old who grew up in a close-knit and loving Caribbean family. She is close to her mom and two of her aunts, who were very influential in her earlier years. Barbara learned early that sex was taboo. She had little accurate information and accepted the notion that sex was for marriage and creating a family. Barbara came to you because she had so thoroughly internalized negative messages about sex that she has never had an orgasm. You work with Barbara to unpack the many different sociocultural messages she received about what types of people enjoyed sex; the sexual double standard that lauded male but not female sexuality; and her strong connections to her family, particularly her mom and aunts, whom she wants to make proud.

You create a sex-positive environment and model the expectation that sexual well-being is a key aspect of overall well-being. You help Barbara explore her sexual agency, starting slowly. First, you ask about aspects of affection that she enjoys, such as cuddling and kissing. You help her take ownership of how she likes to express affection intimately but not necessarily sexually, and then you work with her so she can permit herself to embrace her own sexuality. Over time, Barbara comes to believe that her sexual expression is not something of which to be afraid or ashamed. Eventually, you suggest that she explore masturbation, perhaps using a vibrator. After a few exploratory attempts, Barbara finally experiences orgasm. She does not experience orgasm every time she tries, either alone or with her husband, but she does sometimes. And she is continuing to unpack her underlying beliefs about sexuality, slowly embracing a sex-positive lens.

Barbara's is just one narrative that can be applied to anorgasmia. For some people the causes may be hormonal, but in most cases psychological factors play a key role. Potential areas for exploration include a lack of or diminished interest in current relationship(s); fear of intimacy; history of sexual abuse; historical, social, religious, and cultural notions of who enjoys sex; and the capacity to communicate sexual needs to partner(s), including the need for manual stimulation or additional stimulation after the climax of the partner(s). For all people, orgasm requires the loss of conscious control, so examining control issues can be a key focal point for therapy. Exploring anxiety, fear, anger, and guilt can be a helpful jumping-off point to uncover underlying issues that may be impacting a client's capacity to orgasm. It may also be important to give clients permission to have an orgasm. Take a sex-positive stance and encourage your clients to develop sexual agency to experience sexual pleasure (despite prior sociocultural messaging). One possible intervention is to gently encourage them to stop thinking quite so much. Often, performance pressure to have an orgasm interferes with one's capacity to focus on sensations, which then inhibits or interferes with the capacity to orgasm (which is probably why 58–62 percent of women have faked an orgasm).[33] As was emphasized previously, orgasm does not equate to sexual satisfaction, so it may be important to administer a sexual satisfaction scale (like Hudson's scale mentioned in the previous section) and establish the degree both of satisfaction and distress experienced by your client.[34]

Premature ejaculation (PE) is a different type of orgasmic disorder that involves rapid early ejaculation or the inability to delay ejaculation. Unchanged in *DSM* from previous editions, a diagnosis for premature ejaculation occurs when ejaculation occurs before or within one minute of penetration, and before it is wanted. PE is quite common, with most people with penises reporting experiencing it at some point. However, for diagnosis PE must have lasted for six months and occur during 75–100 percent of sexual encounters.[35] As a result of differing definitions and significant subjective distress, approximately 20–30 percent of men worldwide report concern with rapid ejaculation, but very few meet the diagnostic criteria.[36] PE can be an issue early in a person's sexual career, with overexcitement or lack of experience impacting timing, or it can occur if it has been a long time since the person has had sex. While PE is often thought of as psychologically based, it can be caused by issues with the prostate, side effects from medication, or substance use—all of which should be explored during assessment. Suggested treatments include James Semans's stop-start technique as an attempt to gain control over excitement levels, whereby the person begins stimulation but stops before climax.[37] The cycle is repeated multiple times during the sexual encounter. Masters and Johnson developed a variation on this technique, which involves not only stopping stimulation but also squeezing the frenulum of the penis to inhibit arousal.[38] It can be helpful to practice both techniques during masturbation first and then during partnered sex. It may also be helpful to focus on the arousal as it climbs, to help the client stay in the moment. Finally, desensitization creams or a small dose of antidepressant medication may be prescribed. A common myth is that distracted thinking—such as thinking about other, mundane topics during stimulation—is a way to reduce stimulation and delay orgasm, but that is not recommended.

In sessions, empathize with your clients who are venting, but do not treat the issue as tragic. Depathologize the occurrence if possible, educating the client about the typical nature of the concern. Try moving the focus away from the symptoms and toward the client's own understanding of what underlying causes might be, such as stress, relationship issues, medication, illness, and substance use.

PAINFUL SEX

DSM combined two categories previously related to painful sex—dyspareunia (genital pain or discomfort before, during, or after penetration) and vaginismus (involuntary contractions and pain upon penetration)—into genito-pelvic pain or penetration disorder and removed male dyspareunia completely. The diagnoses were combined because they are "highly comorbid and very difficult to distinguish."[39] Even studies designed to understand nuances in pelvic pain, including vaginismus and dyspareunia, have acknowledged that there was a "large overlap" between the two.[40] In *DSM*, for diagnosis to occur there should be persistent or recurring difficulty during penetration or attempted penetration, or fear and anxiety associated with the anticipated pain of penetration and a "tightening or tensing of the pelvic floor muscles during attempted penetration."[41] Since the new category is broad, the distinction between vaginismus and dyspareunia can still be helpful for clinical purposes.[42]

The types of vaginal pain can vary. It can be sharp, burning, or aching pain. Some people experience pain only during deep thrusting, while others always experience pain—even when inserting tampons. Others may experience a throbbing pain that is prolonged even after penetration. The symptoms formerly associated with vaginismus include pelvic muscle spasms upon the insertion of an object. As with other disorders, the condition can be lifelong or have begun after a period of experiences with no spasms. The condition may also be global, occurring during every situation and with any object, or situational, occurring only in certain circumstances. For example, some people experience spasms during gynecological exams.

Some physiological causes of pain or spasms include insufficient lubrication, bladder or urinary tract infection, inflammation, or injury. Underlying psychological causes can include prior trauma, such as sexual abuse or rape, anxiety, and stress. Start by exploring underlying medical conditions like urinary tract or yeast infections. Pelvic floor exercises like Kegel exercises can sometimes alleviate involuntary spasms, as can the use of dilators. In fact, one small study found that therapist-aided exposure therapy, involving the insertion of fingers (first the person's own and then a partner's, if applicable) or a dilator with the therapist and partner (if applicable) present, was successful in treating vaginismus in 89 percent of patients.[43] Facilitating communication between partners can promote dialogue that establishes pain-free sensuality and that can, over time, lead to clearer communication, increased intimacy, improved relationship satisfaction, and reduced anxiety.[44]

OUT-OF-CONTROL SEXUAL BEHAVIOR

Years ago, commercial phone sex and strip clubs were traditional outlets for people experiencing out-of-control sexual behavior, and both of them certainly still see their share of traffic. But the advent of the internet saw an exponential increase in access to sexually explicit material, especially pornography. Subsequently, a significant proportion of out-of-control sexual behavior (OCSB) shifted to the computer and cell phone via the internet and apps. In fact, pornography searches are ranked number one and "visits to pornography sites are said to account for half of all Internet traffic."[45] Access to chat rooms, sex and pornography sites, sex cam sites, and sex apps have led to a potentially seductive and never-ending stream of visual sexual stimulation and potential partners. This was enough to motivate some psychologists to propose that internet addiction disorder be added as a diagnosis in *DSM*.[46] While the diagnosis was ultimately not approved, psychologists are trying to understand cybersexuality.

During the drafting of *DSM*, Martin Kafka proposed the inclusion of hyperactive sexual disorder to encapsulate OCSB or compulsions with diagnostic criteria that included "increased frequency and intensity of sexual fantasies, urges, and overt behaviors."[47] Key characteristics also included the inability to stop despite wanting to, significant impairment in functioning, and negative consequences such as interfering with relationships or employment. There was not sufficient support for inclusion in *DSM*, partly because psychologists worried that the diagnosis would pathologize typical sexual behaviors.[48] However, sexual compulsivity does present in practice, and social workers must be prepared for it.

Because it is difficult to determine what defines problematic sexual preoccupation, and professionals disagree about how much is too much, prevalence estimates vary. Some put rates of people with sexual compulsions at 5–10 percent. Alfred Kinsey's famous sexuality study put male sexual compulsion at 7.6 percent, while a more contemporary review of several studies found rates of 3–6 percent.[49] Regardless of prevalence, when assessing symptoms, you should ascertain whether the preoccupation is leading to decreased functioning at work, relationship conflicts, decreased social relationships, increased isolation, or other negative consequences. As J. Christopher Barrilleaux points out, social workers are often unfamiliar with the notion of OCSB and therefore reluctant to engage in its treatment.[50]

Hyperactive sexual desire can manifest itself as compulsivity, impulsivity, or addiction.[51] Understanding hypersexuality as compulsivity frames it in relation to obsessive-compulsive disorder (OCD) and focuses on the sexual thoughts, fantasies, and behaviors as obsessions. A circular stress and tension pattern is created in which focus on the obsessive object leads to an increase in anxiety, to the point where engaging in the activity is vital to reducing the tension back to bearable levels.[52] However, the release does not relieve the obsessive focus, and the attention returns to the object until the stress builds up again to an unbearable level. The compulsive argument is supported by the degree of success that OCD medications (e.g., selective serotonin reuptake inhibitors [SSRIs]) have had in treating OCSB. However, skeptics note that decreased sexual desire is a side effect of such medications.[53]

Seeing hypersexuality as impulsivity centers on the notion that it represents an inability to regulate sexual behavior even though it is a significant source of distress, with negative personal, social, occupational, and even criminal consequences.[54] Again, supporting evidence for this theory centers on responsiveness to SSRIs, which also successfully treat impulse control disorder.[55]

The addiction model proposed by Patrick Carnes[56] posits that sexual addiction has a cycle of behavior similar to that in substance addiction: cravings, sex-seeking behavior, sexual behavior, and guilt or remorse. In this conceptualization, the person feels unable to stop even though they want to and despite negative consequences. Carnes's original model was abstinence-based.[57] More recently, Carnes and colleagues noted that there is a close association between OCSB and other addictive behaviors, triggering what they have coined "addiction interaction disorder"—in which the addictions exacerbate each other, such as when someone's alcohol and cocaine use lead to excessive sex.[58] Some argue that the addiction model is not a good fit, since there does not seem to be an increase in the tolerance level or a withdrawal response.[59]

Besides compulsivity, impulsivity, and addiction, some have argued for the association between OCSB and attachment issues and stressful life events. Specifically, hypersexual behavior has been associated with insecure attachment, causing difficulty with trust in relationships and fear of abandonment.[60] There are conflicting reports as to whether the association is specifically between OCSB and the anxious-attachment avoidant type, which was significant in one study but not another.[61] Regardless, attachment-informed treatment of hypersexuality is recommended.[62]

As with other sexual issues, social workers should conduct a comprehensive biopsychosocial assessment during the treatment of out-of-control sexual behavior. The biological aspect should assess whether there are underlying medical conditions, medications, substance use, or injuries that may be contributing factors. In fact, both brain injury and dementia can trigger out-of-control sexual behavior, and can be notable in the dramatic shift from prior functioning.[63] Your psychological assessment of your clients should include understanding their attachment, trauma, and relationship history. Finally, your social assessment should look at the impact on clients of sociocultural expectations, social functioning, and potential isolation.

Although there is little research regarding their efficacy, twelve-step groups such as Sex Addicts Anonymous, Sex and Love Addicts Anonymous, and Sexaholics Anonymous have been anecdotally reported as successfully treating some people. Perhaps two of the key roles of this type of group is to decrease feelings of isolation and neutralize feelings of shame and secrecy. Other treatments you may wish to consider for clients with OCSB include cognitive behavior therapy, covert sensitization, motivational interviewing, dialectical behavior therapy, and SSRIs.[64]

COERCIVE PARAPHILIAS

In chapter 8, we defined paraphilia as sexual arousal that occurs in relation to "objects, events, or people outside what is considered the norm."[65] There we focused on noncoercive activities, engaged in freely by consenting adults without explicit or implicit coercion. Coercive paraphilias involve an unwilling participant, some degree of coercion, or a minor. Examples of coercive paraphilias include voyeurism, telephone scatalogia, and exhibitionism. Coercive paraphilias cross the line from healthy sexual expression to problematic, potentially criminal behavior. *DSM* defines paraphilias as "any intense and persistent sexual interest other than sexual interest in genital stimulation or preparatory fondling with phenotypically normal physically mature, consenting human partners."[66] This definition includes the notion of recurrence: the paraphilia must be ongoing and not just a fleeting experience. As the definition outlines, to reach the status of a disorder, the paraphilia must have a duration of at least six months. Use of the word "intense" indicates that the fantasies and urges are strong, compelling, and difficult to ignore.

Box 9.2
EXAMPLES OF COERCIVE PARAPHILIAS

Exhibitionism: Exposing genitals to someone without their consent

Frotterism: Rubbing (usually genitals) against someone without their consent (e.g., a stranger in a crowded place such as a subway)

Necrophilia: Having sex with a corpse

Pedophilia: Having sex with a prepubescent child

Telephone scatalogia: Making obscene phone calls

Voyeurism: Watching others undressing or having sex without their knowledge or consent

Zoophilia or bestiality: Having sex with animals

While paraphilia appeared as a diagnosis in prior editions of the *Diagnostic and Statistical Manual of Mental Disorders*, the revised *DSM* includes the diagnosis "paraphilic disorder."[67] In a potentially progressive step toward sex positivity, the term "disorder" was included in this edition to differentiate paraphilias that cause distress or harm and those that do not. Specifically, the term "paraphilic disorder" is applied when a paraphilia causes "distress or impairment to the individual or . . . whereby [sexual] satisfaction entailed personal harm, or risk of harm, to others. This distinction was made in an effort to identify those sexual behaviors and interests that are of clinical significance."[68]

While not always feasible, in some cases it is possible to work with people who have been diagnosed with paraphilic disorder who practice it within a noncoercive environment, such as role-playing some of their potentially harmful fantasies with consenting adults through BDSM (bondage and discipline, dominance and submission, and sadism and masochism). The use of cognitive behavioral therapy has also been shown to be helpful in changing some of the negative behaviors associated with paraphilic disorders.[69]

CHAPTER SUMMARY

This chapter surveyed some of the common sex-related disorders and dysfunctions that may present in treatment. It considered the way in which sexual disorders have been categorized in *DSM* and how they changed from prior classifications. For most diagnoses, the problem has to have lasted for at least six months and occur 75–100 percent of the time. The chapter also considered out-of-control sexual behavior, even though it did not meet the threshold for inclusion in *DSM*. Clients regularly present in treatment with distress that they cannot adhere to limits they set around their sexual behaviors, such as time spent on hook-up apps or seeking out visual sexual stimulation.

The chapter also emphasized the need to screen for underlying causes of sexual difficulties, including medical conditions, medications, injuries, relationship issues, stress, depression, anxiety, and trauma. As we have emphasized throughout, experiencing sexual issues can depress self-esteem and may harm overall well-being. Thus, permitting clients to address their sexual issues, creating a space for open dialogue, and not minimizing their importance are all requisite for promoting your client's sexual health and well-being.

DISCUSSION QUESTIONS

1. Why is it important to understand when a sexual issue started and whether it occurs sometimes or always?
2. How can the DOUPE model help you in your assessment of sexual issues?

3. What are the similarities of or differences between sexual issues that occur during the desire and arousal phases? How has that been reflected by *DSM*?

4. What are the three dominant explanations for out-of-control sexual behavior? Which one resonates with you the most, and why?

RESOURCES

American Association of Sexuality Educators, Counselors and Therapists (AASECT): www.aasect.org

American Psychiatric Association: https://www.psychiatry.org/psychiatrists/practice/dsm/educational-resources (*DSM-5* Educational Resources)

Planned Parenthood: www.plannedparenthood.org

Sex Addicts Anonymous (SAA): https://saa-recovery.org

Sex and Love Addicts Anonymous (SLAA): https://slaafws.org

10

ETHICS AND THE SEX-POSITIVE SOCIAL WORKER

RELEVANT CSWE COMPETENCIES

Competency 1: Demonstrate Ethical and Professional Behavior

Competency 2: Engage Diversity and Difference in Practice

Competency 3: Advance Human Rights and Social, Economic, and Environmental Justice

Competency 6: Engage with Individuals, Families, Groups, Organizations, and Communities

Regardless of practice context or method, social workers are bound by the *Code of Ethics* of the National Association of Social Workers (NASW).[1] This chapter gives an overview of the six values that underpin the code and discusses how each principle may apply in relation to sex. This chapter addresses erotic transference (when a client has sexual, romantic, or erotic feelings about the therapist) and countertransference (when the therapist has such feelings about the client), dual relationships (which occur when a social worker and client see each other in a context outside of their work together), and general boundaries.

During practice, there are inevitably times when either a client is attracted to you or you are attracted to a client. This chapter discusses how to handle those situations. Most social workers recognize that they should not have sex with their clients,[2] (although reading the publicly posted ethics violations suggests that some do anyway). However, there are other less obvious ways in which sexuality and boundaries manifest in practice related to sex. Here we will raise some of the ethical concerns in practice and some suggestions for navigating them.

SOCIAL WORK VALUES AND ETHICS

While the terms "values" and "ethics" are used almost interchangeably, they are distinct concepts, so I often start my class by asking my students to define them. First, I ask the students to define "values." Some definitions they usually suggest are "core beliefs," "what's most important to you," and "ideas that guide your behavior." Even the definition I give them has the word "valuable" in it: values are something held to be "intrinsically valuable or good" to a society.[3] They can be personal, professional, religious, and/or cultural. As individuals, we have our own set of values that guide us and integrate these areas. Sometimes our personal and professional values may clash. For example, we may follow a religion that says abortion is a sin, but our professional code supports self-determination in matters of reproductive health. Values do not describe specific behaviors but refer instead to overarching principles. Values are malleable; they may change over time. Historically, the value of chastity before marriage was nearly universal. That value has shifted considerably, and while chastity is still an important value for some, maintaining chastity until marriage is not as important for everyone.

When I ask my students to define "ethics," they use words like "rules," "guides," "moral behavior," "conduct," and "relational standards." These are very good suggestions, as the word "ethics" stems from the Greek word *ethos*, meaning customs, character, and conduct. To distinguish between these two concepts, values offer overarching principles, and ethics are specifically related to behavior. Ralph Dolgoff and Louise Skolnick describe ethics as "values in operation, the guidelines for transforming values into action."[4]

The NASW *Code of Ethics* outlines the six values that underlie social work: service, social justice, dignity and worth of the person, importance of human relationships, integrity, and competence.[5] The code also lays out how we should act on those values by providing ethical principles and a description of how those principles might be interpreted in practice.

In the following sections, we will take a closer look at each of these values and how they relate to sexuality and social work.

SERVICE

Ethical Principle: "Social workers' primary goal is to help people in need and to address social problems."[6]

When they apply to graduate school, most would-be social workers write about service in their personal essay. They want to help people. In many ways, service is the primary function of social work on all levels: micro, mezzo, and macro. The ethical principles that apply to service include beneficence and nonmaleficence—that is, doing good when possible, or at least not doing harm.

Within sex-related ethics, you may run into a conflict between your personal values and your professional values, such as in cases addressing contraception, abortion, sexual identity, and gender identity. For example, imagine you are working in a community mental health program and fifteen-year-old Javier is assigned to you. Javier has been experiencing severe depressive symptoms that have begun to affect his grades at school. During the intake, you discover that Javier's depression stems from his struggle to reconcile his sexual identity, which seems to be pansexual or gay, with his families' cultural values. He fears that his close-knit family would be rocked by the news and is scared that someone will find out. Javier has become socially isolated and depressed. Preoccupied with his sexual orientation, he cannot focus on schoolwork, and his grades have dropped.

As a practicing Christian, you were taught that anything besides heterosexual relationships are wrong. You were taught very strongly to love the sinner and hate the sin, which is a position that makes you feel responsible to help Javier shut down that aspect of himself. Recognizing that this position would not validate Javier and who he is as a person, you realize that you have an obligation to do no harm (as well as to honor his self-determination). Because of this, you work with your colleagues and supervisor to provide Javier with referrals to practitioners who can provide him with a nonjudgmental, affirming environment, giving him the best opportunity to thrive. You realize that you must be careful when providing the referrals to emphasize why the other clinicians would offer better service, rather than telling him that you can't work with him—which could feel like rejection and cause him harm.

The situation with Javier is just one example of the many ways that personal and professional ethics may clash and potentially impair your capacity to provide service. The code notes that "social workers elevate service to others above self-interest."[7] While it is impossible to anticipate every situation in which your personal and professional ethics may collide, you should take time to reflect now. What potential conflicts will you experience between your personal and professional ethics? Do you have strong beliefs about contraception or abortion? What about infidelity, arranged marriages, and polyamorous relationships? Anticipating potential conflicts in advance and discussing them in supervision can prepare you to make better choices and act in your clients' best interest when they arise.

SOCIAL JUSTICE

Ethical Principle: "Social workers challenge social injustice."[8]

People are often drawn to the profession of social work rather than psychology or other human services because of the imperative to promote social justice. Central within this social work value is the notion of nondiscrimination. Social workers strive to serve clients in a way that does not judge them, and this applies especially to sexuality. As we have seen throughout this book, there are wide ranges of sexual behaviors and relationships that may challenge your norms and go beyond your comfort zone. The key for the sex-positive social worker is to acknowledge your process and remain open and nonjudgmental in your practice. If you feel unable to provide competent and nonjudgmental service, you may offer appropriate referrals that will best serve the client.

Consider how this ethical principle is articulated. It is not just a call for social workers to promote social justice issues like supporting same-sex marriage, access to reproductive health care, or trans-inclusive legislation. It is also an active statement, urging social workers to fight social injustice. In this light, social workers must challenge policies that disadvantage women who have been trafficked; discriminate against lesbian, gay, bisexual, queer, and questioning (LGBTQ) people in health care, housing, and employment; exclude people living with HIV/AIDS; create roadblocks to comprehensive, inclusive sex education; or criminalize sex trades. Social workers also have a responsibility to take an active role in discussing sexual citizenship worldwide and sexual health as a human right, promoting sexual agency for all people.

I often have community organizing students in my class who embrace this aspect of the work fully. But I tell my clinical students that this call to action is just as much for them. It is our ethical responsibility to widen the focus from the client in front of us to understand what structural barriers and systemic policies have created the discriminatory situation. Then we can work to remove those barriers and change those policies.

DIGNITY AND WORTH OF THE PERSON

Ethical Principle: "Social workers respect the inherent dignity and worth of the person."[9]

Social work sees every person as valuable and important. Relevant here is the ethical idea of autonomy, the notion of governing yourself or "self-rule."[10] Autonomy means that people should make decisions for themselves.

Historically, professions like medicine have operated from a patriarchal perspective, making decisions on behalf of people who were thought unable to make suitable choices for themselves. Social workers have moved away from their more prescriptive past to honor the dignity and worth of the person through the application of autonomy and self-determination.

Unless someone is not competent or is in imminent danger of harming themselves or someone else, the code of ethics calls on us to trust people to make choices for themselves. The concepts of autonomy and self-determination can be difficult to put into practice when you are just starting out in social work. It is easy to think that we know better than the client and that we can see a fuller picture. This can be especially true when working with adolescents or people using substances. But our ethical obligation is clear: we must provide a nonjudgmental therapeutic environment to explore the immediate and underlying issues and provide information and access to concrete resources. It is not for us to make decisions about which relationships a person should be in or the sexual behaviors in which they should engage.

You may find this especially difficult when working with people involved in sex trades. There is a temptation to want to "rescue" them from their circumstances. While people who have been trafficked certainly need assistance escaping their circumstances, many in the sex trades feel a great deal of autonomy in their actions and do not want to be "rescued." However, they want to be respected and supported as they gain access to appropriate services, including health care and employment protections. As one report about sex workers' experiences in health care noted, "No Lectures or Stink-Eye."[11] While it can be difficult watching someone struggle in a painful relationship or try to manage out-of-control sexual behavior, we must honor the dignity of each person and trust their process when it doesn't pose an immediate threat to them or others.

Another key ethical idea is the right to privacy, which we apply through confidentiality. Confidentiality is a cornerstone of social work practice, and this is especially true for issues related to sex. Assurances of confidentiality—except when there is imminent harm to self or others or a legal request—engenders trust between the client and social worker. Given the sociocultural taboos about sexuality, establishing trust is part of creating a sex-positive practice. The client's confidentiality is theirs to break. That is why you must have their permission to discuss their case with other providers.

That is also why when you see a client in public, perhaps at a store or on the street, you should not acknowledge the client unless they acknowledge you first. You do not know who they might be with. Take the client's lead: if they say a simple hello, respond in kind. If they ignore you, do the same. If they introduce you as their therapist, match that acknowledgment in your interactions. Whatever happens, it is usually good to discuss the interaction in the next treatment session. Ask the client how it felt to see you in a public context. This conversation can be especially important if you did not acknowledge the client. Sometimes clients are confused and even hurt that you did not speak to them. Explaining the concept of confidentiality and how it applies can ease that confusion and reassure them.

IMPORTANCE OF HUMAN RELATIONSHIPS

Ethical Principle: "Social workers recognize the central importance of human relationships."[12]

Human relationships are the key intervention of social work. No matter what our practice method is, we do our work through relationships with our clients, community members, or coworkers. This is more obvious in the clinical setting, but it is just as true in agency administration and community organizing. As the *Code of Ethics* states, "Social workers understand that relationships between and among people are an important vehicle for change."[13] An instrumental part of using human relationships to create change is maintaining clear, unambiguous boundaries and navigating dual relationships. Establishing boundaries that maintain the professional nature of the relationship are the key to creating a safe therapeutic space. As Anne Dailey writes, "People have good boundaries when they are able to restrain their impulses, to limit desire, to hold back, to tolerate frustration."[14] If boundaries become permeable or unclear, ambiguity can creep into the relationship and compromise the client's trust and safety.

Some types of mental health practitioners argue that once the therapeutic relationship has ended, it is appropriate to shift to a different type of (nonsexual) relationship. Some professional associations go even further and require that a certain amount of time must have passed since treatment ended before you begin a sexual relationship with a former client.

Social work does not hold this position. The danger remains: there was a power differential when the relationship was formed that cannot be undone. You will always hold a position of power within the relationship. And should life circumstances change and the client decide to reenter treatment, you are no longer an available therapeutic option.

The nature of the therapeutic relationship means that clients will often test boundaries. They may ask personal questions, give you gifts, flirt with you, or invite you to events. Part of the work with certain clients may even revolve around this testing and how you maintain the relationship to model appropriate boundaries. The use of texting, a typically informal medium, to communicate with clients can lead to trouble in some cases. Make sure that you retain your professional self in any communication you have with your clients, whether in person or via technology. The professional boundary is yours to enforce, and the protection of yourself and your client depends on it.

The clearest boundary for you to maintain is never to have sex with a client. We will explore the concepts of erotic transference and countertransference more fully in a later section of the same name. Here the point is simply that honoring the professional boundary is an ethical responsibility. The *Code of Ethics* states, "Social workers should under no circumstances engage in sexual activities, inappropriate sexual communications through the use of technology or in person, or sexual contact with current clients, whether such contact is consensual or forced."[15] The code also states that social workers should not engage in sexual relationships with a client's family member or anyone else with whom the client is close, and where such a relationship may cause harm.

For social workers, the rule is once a client, always a client. I caution my students that if they open their office door and they are desperately attracted to the person standing there, it's bad luck. Even if they shut the door immediately, they're shutting it on someone who came to them for professional help.

Here, sometimes my community organizing students push back. They argue that in the process of organizing they meet lots of people casually. I too push back, once again raising the idea of their authentic professional self. I challenge them to admit that they know when they are working and when they meet someone in a professional capacity, even if the setting is casual. And as frustrating as the limit might be, you cannot pursue a personal relationship with the person. Maintaining clear boundaries is an ethical imperative for social workers.

Despite the code's clear statement regarding sexual involvement with clients or close relatives of clients, and despite the fact that 95 percent of BSW and MSW students think sex with clients is inappropriate,[16] sexual impropriety was involved in nearly 20 percent of malpractice insurance claims through NASW in the period 1961–1990[17] and in 12 percent of violations of the code in 1986–1997.[18] Srinika Jayaratne, Tom Croxton, and Debra Mattison found that 1.1 percent of the social workers in their study reported having sex with a former client.[19] The true percentage is likely even higher.

Among mental health professionals in general there are varying estimates of the prevalence of sexual impropriety. Frederic Reamer summarized findings from several studies that reported rates of sexual contact being lower with female therapists than with males. The studies' estimates ranged from 1.7 percent to 3.0 percent for female therapists and from 8.0 percent to 16.0 percent for males.[20] And these estimates are likely underestimates, between a quarter and a half of practicing therapists reported treating clients who reported sexual contact with a former therapist.[21]

Perhaps some of the issues with sexual misconduct arose from too little education and training about sexual ethics—an area where there seem to have been improvements. In a study of social work students, Cathy Berkman and coauthors found that, there was concern students did not feel adequately trained in sexual ethics and "many felt unprepared to handle sexual feelings from or toward a client."[22] Over 30 percent reported that sexual contact with a client was acceptable if the professional relationship had terminated more than five years before. However, in a follow-up study, Gloria Aguilar and Carol Williams found that 95.0 percent of both bachelor and master of social work students felt that sexual contact between social workers and clients was inappropriate, and 78.1 percent felt that they had received moderate to significant instruction on sexual ethics.[23] This may be a sign that sexual ethics education is improving and the numbers of ethical violations will decrease.

There is also the danger of a sexual relationship between social workers. In the section of the *Code of Ethics*, which discusses ethical responsibility to colleagues in supervision and education, it is clear that social workers must not engage in sexual relationships with someone over whom they have power. Terry Koenig and Richard Spano draw attention to the serious issue: "Sexual boundary violations in supervisory relationships . . . are harmful and often emotionally devastating to the parties involved."[24] The authors point out that we tend to shy away from addressing sexual feelings and argue for specific supervisory training related to discussing sexuality in supervision, which would ultimately better prepare supervisees. The information in the *Code of Ethics* related to sexual relations between colleagues is less clear, although it does specify that such relationships should be avoided if there is the "potential for a conflict of interest."[25]

Dual relationships are another example of the need for boundaries. For example, in a small community you might see some of your clients at your child's school, church, or an Alcoholics Anonymous (AA) meeting. In some cases, such as exercise classes, it may be possible to shift schedules to avoid the conflict. In other situations, it may not. For instance, there may be only one AA meeting in town. Whenever you have to maintain a dual relationship, remember that the boundary is yours to hold. You are responsible for presenting your authentic professional self in the situation and maintaining the integrity of the therapeutic relationship for your client.

INTEGRITY

Ethical Principle: "Social workers behave in a trustworthy manner."[26]

The social worker with integrity speaks truthfully and acts honestly. The main avenue for change within social work is via relationships, and relationships are built on trust. Only practicing in a way that is trusting and trustworthy will nurture such relationships. Creating an environment that feels authentic and honest encourages expressions of authenticity and honesty from our clients. Creating an honest and affirming environment can facilitate change. The issue related to integrity that is raised most often in class is navigating working with adolescents about sexuality, contraception, and sexual identity issues and how much to disclose to their parents. There is no one answer because different states have different (and changing) laws related to disclosure requirements. For example, in New York, adolescents seeking information about reproductive health and wellness do not need parental permission, whereas other states may require parental disclosure. The Guttmacher Institute's "An Overview of Consent to Reproductive Health Services by Young People" is an excellent reference if you are unsure of the requirements in your area.[27]

Other issues that are raised when discussing integrity have to do with diagnosis and billing. Occasionally, agencies have a practice of adjusting a client's diagnosis so they may qualify for more sessions or better reimbursement rates. As I have noted in a study of ethical issues encountered by social work students during field placement, the most egregious example of this reported by study participants was the case of a student who was asked to write a biopsychosocial assessment on a client they had never seen.[28] While it is tempting to adjust a diagnosis to secure more sessions, honesty is our ethical imperative. You have no way of knowing how an inaccurate diagnosis may affect the client in the future. Veracity is an important ethical principle to honor in the service of sex-positive social work.

COMPETENCE

Ethical Principle: "Social workers practice within their areas of competence and develop and enhance their professional expertise."[29]

Social work education covers a wide range of topics and prepares people for practice in a wide range of settings. During that education there may be opportunities to specialize in different practice settings, such as child welfare agencies, schools, health care settings, community-based agencies, and within the criminal justice system. You can also specialize in practices, such as aging, trauma, substance use, and sexuality and gender. The central tenet of this ethical principle is to be honest about your training and to practice within the scope of competence you have developed.

If you have a specialty in substance use, then it is appropriate for you to work with people who are addressing issues of addiction. If you have a specialty in working with people who are transgender or nonbinary, it is appropriate for you to work with people who are exploring their gender identity. But if you have not received any training in substance use or gender-identity issues, then you should not present yourself as having such training. If the client needs specialized treatment, you should provide referrals to people with the appropriate expertise.

Another dimension to practicing within your scope of competence is not to practice a modality in which you are not trained—like yoga or Reiki—or in which the client did not request services. For example, suppose that in addition to being a social worker you are a certified yoga instructor. If a client comes to you to address underlying attachment issues they have related to their parent's divorce when they were eight years old, and you think they could benefit from a yoga practice to help them feel more grounded, you cannot just launch into yoga during your session. They came to you expecting talk therapy, not yoga. You can certainly tell them that you are a certified yoga instructor and explain how they might benefit from practicing during sessions, but you should not introduce yoga without their full and informed permission.

Another dimension of competence is the ethical imperative to develop your professional knowledge and skill by staying abreast of new information, theories, policies, and practices. Many states require licensed social workers to obtain continuing education credits as part of license renewal, but even if that is not required, you should push yourself to stay on top of innovations in the field. Joining peer supervision groups, attending conferences, and pursuing advanced education are all good ways to keep on top of new knowledge. In the area of sexuality, you might consider earning sexuality-related continuing education unit credits or attending the annual conference of the American Association of Sexuality Educators, Counselors and Therapists.

EROTIC TRANSFERENCE AND COUNTERTRANSFERENCE

In this section we explore in more depth a particular ethical issue that can arise in sexuality and practice: erotic transference and countertransference. Glen Gabbard distinguished between different types of erotic transference, highlighting the distinction between erotic transference as a recognition of romantic or erotic feelings and sexualized (or eroticized) transference, which involves a desperate need to be sexual with the therapist.[30] Sarah Mourra explores this distinction, noting that with erotic transference the client recognizes the fantasies are unrealistic, whereas with sexualized transference the client experiences an "irrational preoccupation" with being sexual with the therapist.[31] Despite these distinctions, Alberto Stefana points out that all types of erotic transference involve idealization and fit within a "pleasure . . . continuum."[32]

There is some evidence to suggest that people who have experienced child abuse may be more likely to exhibit erotic transference.[33] Mourra further explains that the "experience of being cared for and being sexual may be conflated."[34] Some also suggest that clients with borderline personality disorder may be especially susceptible to erotic transference, given their tendency to develop strong feelings about their therapist.[35]

What do you do with a sexually provocative client? First, acquire good supervision. A good supervisor can help you explore the case and determine whether you should provide a referral or whether you can work through the situation. Supervision can also help you determine how to construct a firm boundary and how to explore the dynamics of the relationship to address the provocative behavior.[36]

Another good tool is a countertransference journal, in which you write down your process and identify what issues are coming up for you. Although used mostly for countertransference, it can be used to process transference as well. Such a journal can also provide a place for you to process your interventions and gain some perspective on your therapeutic approach. For instance, how is countertransference affecting your behavior toward the client?

Consulting with colleagues can also be helpful, and many social workers rely on peer supervision groups as a way to work through sexual content that arises during treatment.[37] Maintaining consistent policies and actions will create a strong precedent for your behavior, and you'll thus be more alert to any deviations from your own norm.

Finally, ensure that you thoroughly document both your client's actions and your own.

COUNTERTRANSFERENCE

Not only may clients be attracted to you, but you may also be attracted to clients. In Jayaratne, Croxton and Mattison's study, 52.4 percent of the social workers reported having been sexually attracted to a client.[38] The chances are that you are probably going to be in such a situation. What should you do?

First, don't panic! This is a common occurrence. You do not have to feel alone or ashamed. Again, seek out good supervision. Be open and honest with yourself and your supervisor. Don't minimize what is happening, but don't blow it out of proportion either. You may be tempted to pretend it is not happening: resist that temptation.

A countertransference journal is helpful here, too. It is a space for you to explore your feelings and understand your own process. If your ability to work with the client is compromised, then you may need to provide a referral or transfer the case to a colleague. A key concept here is to be honest with yourself about your feelings. Have you started to adjust your schedule so that you do not have a time restriction at the end of a session with this client? Are you paying extra attention to what you are wearing on the days when the client is coming to see you? Are you skipping details about the case in supervision? All of these are warning signs that you should analyze your actions and be forthcoming in supervision. If appropriate and necessary, you may even want to discuss the case with your own therapist.

CHAPTER SUMMARY

This chapter explored the six values outlined in the NASW *Code of Ethics*[39] and the ethical principles attached to them. It explored the ways in which social work training on sexual ethics appears to have improved,[40] although sexual misconduct violations remain prevalent in practice.[41] It also explored the fact that, unlike other mental health professions, social work holds that a sexual relationship with a former client is never appropriate.

In addition, the chapter explored some of the ways in which sexual content may be related to six key social work principles: confidentiality (e.g., around sexual identity or reproductive justice), dual relationships and boundary violations, and practicing within your scope of competence. The ethical social worker engages in lifelong learning about issues related to sexuality, as the field is dynamic and language and best practices change rapidly. Finally, the chapter encouraged you to anticipate when your personal and professional ethics may conflict, so you are prepared when they do.

DISCUSSION QUESTIONS

1. What are some of the key steps you can take when trying to resolve an ethical issue?
2. Explore some of the situations related to sexuality in which your personal and professional ethics may conflict.

3. What is a dual relationship?
4. Identify some potential dual relationships that you may encounter in your practice. What are some of the steps you would take to navigate the situation?

RESOURCES

Guttmacher Institute: https://www.guttmacher.org

National Association of Social Workers:https://www.socialworkers.org/about/ethics/code-of -ethics/code-of-ethics-english (read the *Code of Ethics*)

CONCLUSION

At the beginning of this book, we discussed its purposes: to raise the visibility of the sexual dimension within social work, address the taboo that renders sex invisible within social work education and practice, look at clients through a sex-positive lens rather than one based on risks, and challenge you to step out of your comfort zone and engage with sexuality in your practice.

Early in the book we addressed why this process is necessary, and we assessed where you had knowledge and comfort and where you had room for growth. I tell my students that if they feel they want to avoid a topic, that usually means it's one they need to address. For you, perhaps it was your discomfort with conversations about anatomy or physiology, feeling insecure about your understanding of sexual or gender identity or your comprehension of disorders and dysfunction, or your tendency to pathologize BDSM (bondage and discipline, dominance and submission, and sadism and masochism) play and noncoercive paraphilias. Social work practice is a journey. We keep discovering and growing. Your areas of interest and growth will shift over time. Topics you resisted earlier will become more familiar, and new topics will emerge that put you on edge. I encourage you to revisit some of the chapters in this book regularly to see how your interaction with them changes over time. I also encourage you to engage colleagues in conversation about positive sexuality and encourage others to take responsibility for this dimension of their own practice. If we do, social work will be stronger, and our clients will be better served.

Issues of sexuality arise not just with clients but also in supervision. Whether you are the supervisor or the supervisee, I encourage you to discuss the sexual dimension of your clients' lives and address the issues of erotic transference and countertransference. Do not pretend they aren't there, as that is a sure way to invite problems. Acknowledge any situation involving transference or countertransference, bring it into the open, explore it with colleagues, and raise it in supervision and even in your own treatment if applicable. Don't let it become powerful and problematic in its secrecy.

On the last day of class, I remind my students to create a sex-positive practice environment; focus on positive aspects of sexuality along with the common risks and dangers; not to make assumptions; engage with sexuality in working with all clients, regardless of age or ability; find your authentic professional self; and keep learning.

When creating a sex-positive environment, analyze your intake forms. Are they inclusive? Do they use nonjudgmental language? Can they accommodate continually evolving identities so your clients see themselves represented in your forms? Review your office and agency decor to ensure that it represents diversity in race, ethnicity, age, gender identity, sexual identity, and physical ability. Have magazines or materials that are diverse, inclusive, and affirming, so your clients see themselves mirrored in your office. And my favorite recommendation: have a book on display that says "sex" on the spine in large letters. This sends clients important implicit messages about the relevance and appropriateness of sex as a subject in their work with you. It may also be the nudge that gives someone the courage they need to share their sex-related concerns.

Too often social work, mirroring the broader cultural context, focuses on aspects of sexuality that are negative, dangerous, traumatic, and "bad." The purpose of this book was not to ignore those aspects but to maintain a sex-positive lens, acknowledging that despite those risk-based or even traumatic experiences of sexuality, people still have an inherent right to sexual agency, well-being, and fulfillment. I hope that you ask your clients about desire and pleasure, peak sexual experiences, and ways to communicate needs and wants. I encourage you to engage in conversations about sex and sexuality with all clients regardless of their age, health, or ability and across a range of practice settings. Do not assume that sex is not a pertinent topic for them. You will likely be surprised.

In keeping with the imperative of competence in the National Association of Social Workers' *Code of Ethics*,[1] I hope you will continue your lifelong learning and stay abreast of the dynamic nature of sexuality and gender. Terminology is always changing, and so is our understanding of concepts critical to our clients' lives. Always test your ideas and ask the client if you don't understand an expression they use—but don't leave it to the client to educate you on a topic. It is your responsibility to become an expert and become educated in the key areas that are important to your clients' lives.

Advocate for comprehensive, inclusive sex education. As it stands now, the majority of adults who take my class report having had only limited or negative experiences with sex education. Very few feel that they received clear, comprehensive education about developing into healthy sexual beings. My students describe spending their early adulthood unlearning messages of fear and shame about sex. Some still struggle with those messages well into later life. We have an opportunity to change this pattern. Comprehensive sex education can provide people with information to make choices that are right for them. It does not mandate sexual activity. It provides tools for making decisions, navigating consent, communicating, and coming to understand desire and pleasure. The current practice of excluding sexual and gender minorities from sex education conversations leaves people feeling isolated and alone—with potentially dire consequences. Providing sex education that questions hetero-, cis-, and mononormative assumptions will prepare our adolescents to make choices for themselves that are based on information rather than fear and stigma.

Do not ignore sexuality with your older adult clients. Older adults are often seen as asexual, but they are not. Older adults engage in a wide range of sensual and sexual activities with established partners, new partners, and on their own. Thus, they may need some guidance on how to navigate dating apps or new relationships, prevent or treat sexually transmitted infections, make physical adjustments for pain-free sex, or navigate privacy in assisted or congregate living situations in a way that optimizes sexual satisfaction and safety. I hope that this book inspired you to address rather than ignore sexuality issues in your older adult clients.

Sex-positive social work also means helping your clients build their capacity for communication about sex and intimacy; supporting them as they understand how their early experiences with attachment have influenced their current relationship style; and fostering communication skills such as active listening, which can change relationship dynamics and foster agency. I challenge you to be open to and affirming of a range of alternative sexual behaviors that may be satisfying and positive for your clients, including BDSM/kink, noncoercive paraphilias, fetishes, and polyamory. The goal is to create an affirming therapeutic environment in which clients feel seen and supported for exactly who they are. We should never pathologize their behavior or assume that it is relevant to the presenting problem, unless the client identifies it as such or if it is causing obvious distress or harm.

Since culturally we have been conditioned to talk about sex only with our closest friends or intimate partners, it can be hard to find the right professional voice. Throughout this book, I encouraged you to find your authentic professional self—one that is not so stiff that people don't want to open up to you, but one using a genuine voice that both allows you to admit when you don't know something or make a mistake and firmly maintains professional boundaries and is not overly familiar or slangy in tone. At first the notion of an authentic professional self may seem elusive, but with practice you can find the right tone. In fact, your tone and approach may shift as you become experienced working with clients in matters to do with the sexual dimension. What's most important is that you continue to practice through role-playing and with clients, so you can develop the professional voice for discussing sexuality that works for you.

In the two decades that I've been teaching human sexuality, understanding of sexual identity has become noticeably more expansive and inclusive. There have also been legal changes, including the legal recognition of same-sex relationships—first through domestic partnerships, then civil unions, and eventually marriage. And while not all people's relationships currently enjoy legal protection, these changes are a significant shift from the dominant heterosexual norm of the twentieth century. Legal changes also provide LGBTQ people with some protections in housing, health care, and employment. However, these protections are not universal, and there have also been legal setbacks—especially in the more recent, divisive political climate. For example, there have been attempts to block adoptions by people who identify themselves as LGBTQ. Actions have also been taken to reverse measures aimed at transgender people's inclusion in the military. In fact, transgender and gender nonbinary discrimination is an area where there's still considerable room for growth and improvement. There are ever-increasing attempts at the federal and state level to limit reproductive health options and abortion access. There are also policies related to sex trades that need to change to improve both service provision and legal protection. Currently, in most places in America, people engaged in sex trades are criminalized and liable to be turned over to the carceral state. This leads to a negative spiral in which people get caught up in systems that then limit their access to other resources and opportunities, such as federal loans for education and employment options. Sex-positive social work involves accepting people as they are, meeting them where they are, and working toward social justice for all.

The purposes of this book are to raise the pivotal nature of the sexual dimension of the biopsychosocial and encourage you to engage with that dimension in your practice. I hope the book has provided you with some tools to finally bring social work out of the "conspiracy of silence" around sex and place it squarely into your practice.[2] I also hope that you remain interested and inquisitive and keep learning. I wish you good luck on your sex-positive journey.

NOTES

INTRODUCTION

1. SJ Dodd and D. Tolman, "Reviving a Positive Discourse on Sexuality Within Social Work," *Social Work* 62, no. 3 (2017): 227–234; P. Dunk, "Everyday Sexuality and Social Work: Locating Sexuality in Professional Practice and Education," *Social Work and Society* 5, no. 2 (2007): 135–142; E. McCave, B. Shepard, and V. Winter, "Human Sexuality as a Critical Subfield in Social Work," *Advances in Social Work* 15, no. 2 (2014): 409–427.
2. J. Gochros, "Talking about Sex," in *Human Sexuality and Social Work*, ed. H. Gochros and L. Schultz (New York: Association Press, 1972), 97.
3. International Society for Sexual Medicine, (2017). "What Does 'Sex Positive' mean?" https://www.issm.info/sexual-health-qa/what-does-sex-positive-mean/.
4. J. Kim and K. Bolton, "Strengths Perspective," in *Encyclopedia of Social Work*, ed. L. Davis and T. Mizrahi, online ed. (Washington, DC: NASW Press, 2019).

1. CREATING A SEX-POSITIVE ENVIRONMENT FOR YOUR CLIENTS

All CSWE competencies can be found in Council on Social Work Education, "2015 Educational Policy and Accreditation Standards," June 11, 2015, https://cswe.org /Accreditation/Standards-and-Policies/2015-EPAS.

1. R. Crooks and K. Baur, *Our Sexuality*, 13th ed. (Belmont, CA: Thomas Wadsworth, 2017).

2. J. Bywater and R. Jones, *Sexuality and Social Work* (Exeter, UK: Learning Matters, 2007); E. McCave, B. Shepard, and V. Winter, "Human Sexuality as a Critical Subfield in Social Work," *Advances in Social Work* 15, no. 2 (2014): 409–427.

3. H. R. Wineburg, "Social Work and Human Sexuality: An Examination of the Country's Top 25-CWSE Ranked MSW Curricula" (master's thesis, Smith College, 2015).

4. SJ Dodd and D. Tolman, "Reviving a Positive Discourse on Sexuality Within Social Work," *Social Work* 62, no. 3 (2017): 227–234; J. Gochros, "Talking About Sex," in *Human Sexuality and Social Work*, ed. H. Gochros and L. Schultz (New York: Association Press, 1972), 92–101.

5. R. Roberts, "Importance of the Sexual Dimension in Psychosocial Assessment," *Australian Social Work* 45, no. 3 (1992): 37–42.

6. Gochros, "Talking About Sex," 97.

7. C. Graham and M. Smith, "Operationalizing the Concept of Sexuality Comfort: Applications for Sexuality Educators," *Journal for Sexual Health* 54, no. 11 (1984): 439–442.

8. S. Harris and K. Hays, "Family Therapist Comfort with and Willingness to Discuss Client Sexuality," *Journal of Marital and Family Therapy* 34, no. 2 (2008): 239–250.

9. Harris and Hays, "Family Therapist Comfort," 246.

10. L. Bay-Cheng, "Human Sexuality," in *Encyclopedia of Social Work*, ed. C. Franklin (online ed., Washington, DC: NASW Press, 2013), https://oxfordre.com/socialwork; M. Fine, "Sexuality, Schooling, and Adolescent Females: The Missing Discourse of Desire," *Harvard Educational Review* 58, no. 1 (1988): 29–54; V. Oliver et al., "If You Teach Them, They Will Come: Providers' Reactions to Incorporating Pleasure Into Youth Sexual Education," *Revue Canadienne de Sante Publique* 104, no. 2 (2013): 142–146.

11. J. Kirkpatrick, "Human Sexuality: A Survey of What Counselors Need to Know," *Counselor Education and Supervision* 19, no. 4 (1980): 276–282.

12. Harris and Hays, "Family Therapist Comfort," 239–250.

13. J. Sitron and D. Dyson, "Validation of a Sexological Worldview: A Construct for Use in the Training of Sexologists in Sexual Diversity," *SAGE Open,* 2, no. 1 (2012): 1–16.

14. Sitron and. Dyson, "Validation of a Sexological Worldview; R. Francoeur, *Becoming a Sexual Person*, 2nd ed. (New York: Macmillan, 1991).

15. Sitron and Dyson, "Validation of a Sexological Worldview," 7.

16. Sitron and Dyson, "Validation of a Sexological Worldview."

17. B. Newman, P. Dannenfelser, and L. Benishek, "Assessing Beginning Social Work and Counseling Students' Acceptance of Lesbians and Gay Men," *Journal of Social Work Education* 38, no. 2 (2002): 273–288.

18. R. Roberts, "Importance of the Sexual Dimension in Psychosocial Assessment," 37–42.

19. Williams Institute, *Adult LGBT Population in the United States* (Los Angeles: University of California, Los Angeles, 2019); The Joint Commission: *Advancing Effective Communication, Cultural Competence, and Patient- and Family- Centered Care for the Lesbian, Gay, Bisexual, and Transgender (LGBT) Community: A Field Guide* (Oak Brook, IL, Oct. 2011), LGBTFieldGuide.pdf.

20. SJ Dodd and C. C. Katz, "Sex Positive Social Work: Integrating Content Into HBSE and Beyond," *Journal of Teaching in Social Work* 40, no. 1 (2020): 48–57; SJ Dodd and

D. Tolman, "Reviving a Positive Discourse on Sexuality Within Social Work," 227–234; Roberts, "Importance of the Sexual Dimension in Psychosocial Assessment," *Australian Social Work*, 45, no. 3 (1992): 37–42.

21. S. Myers and J. Milner, *Sexual Issues in Social Work* (Bristol, UK: Policy Press, 2007); National Association of Social Workers, *Code of Ethics* (Washington, DC: National Association of Social Workers, 2017).

22. M. Ballon, "Disability and Sexuality Within Social Work Education in the USA and Canada: The Social Model of Disability as a Lens for Practice," *Social Work Education* 27, no. 2 (2008): 194–202; L. Bay-Cheng, "Justifying Sex: The Place of Women's Sexuality on a Social Justice Agenda," *Families in Society* 91, no. 1 (2010): 97–103; N. Claiborne and V. M. Rizzo, "Addressing Sexual Issues in Individuals with Chronic Health Conditions [Practice Forum]," *Health and Social Work* 31 (2006): 221–224; N. Giunta and N. Rowan, *Lesbian, Gay, Bisexual, and Transgender Aging: The Role of Gerontological Social Work* (London: Routledge, 2015).

23. Centers for Disease Control and Prevention, *A Guide to Taking a Sexual History*, accessed November 23, 2019, https://www.cdc.gov/std/treatment/sexualhistory.pdf; B. Johnson, "Sexually Transmitted Infections and Older Adults," *Journal of Gerontological Nursing* 39, no. 11 (2013): 53–60; M. Poynten, A. Grulich, and D. Templeton, "Sexually Transmitted Infections in Older Populations: Current Opinions," *Infectious Diseases* 26, no. 1 (2013): 80–85. See also ageisnotacondom.org, home page, accessed November 23, 2019, http://ageisnotacondom.org/en/home/.

24. J. Gochros, "Talking About Sex," 92–101; Roberts, "Importance of the Sexual Dimension in Psychosocial Assessment," 37–42.

2. ANATOMY, PHYSIOLOGY, AND AROUSAL

1. V. Oliver et al., "If You Teach Them, They Will Come: Providers' Reactions to Incorporating Pleasure Into Youth Sexual Education," *Revue Canadienne de Sante Publique* 104, no. 2 (2013): 142–146.

2. I dislike the word "normal," since it is loaded with all sorts of judgment and othering.

3. L. Moore, "Polishing the Pearl: Discoveries of the Clitoris," in *Introducing the New Sexuality Studies*, 3rd ed., ed. N. Fischer and S. Seidman (London: Routledge, 2016), 69.

4. L. Blonna and R. Carter, *Healthy Sexuality*, 3rd ed. (Dubuque, IA: Kendall Hunt, 2013); S. M. Lindberg, J. S. Hyde, and N. M. McKinley, "A Measure of Objectified Body Consciousness for Preadolescent and Adolescent Youth," *Psychology of Women Quarterly* 30, no. 1 (2006): 65–76; E. J. Strahan et al., "Victoria's Dirty Secret: How Sociocultural Norms Influence Adolescent Girls and Women," *Personality and Social Psychology Bulletin* 34, no. 2 (2008): 288–301.

5. Lindberg, Hyde, and McKinley, "A Measure of Objectified Body Consciousness"; J. Mustapic, D. Marcinko, and P. Vargek, "Body Shame and Disordered Eating in Adolescents," *Current Psychology* 36, no. 3 (2017): 447–452.

6. A. Slater and M. Tiggemann, "Body Image and Disordered Eating in Adolescent Girls and Boys: A Test of Objectification Theory," *Sex Roles* 63, nos. 1–2 (2010): 42–49; M. M. Bucchianeri et al., "Body Dissatisfaction: Do Associations with Disordered Eating and Psychological Well-Being Differ Across Race/Ethnicity in Adolescent Girls and Boys?," *Cultural Diversity and Ethnic Minority Psychology* 22, no. 1 (2016): 137–146.

7. P. Schwartz and M. Kempner, *50 Great Myths of Human Sexuality* (New York: Wiley, 2015).

8. V. Braun and L. Tiefer, "The 'Designer Vagina' and the Pathologisation of Female Genital Diversity: Interventions for Change," Radical Psychology 8, no. 1 (2010), http://www.radicalpsychology.org/vol8-1/brauntiefer.html.

9. D. Veale et al., "Psychological Characteristics and Motivation of Women Seeking Labiaplasty," *Psychological Medicine* 44, no. 3 (2014): 555–566.

10. S. LeVay, J. I. Baldwin, and J. D. Baldwin, *Discovering Human Sexuality*, 3rd ed. (Sunderland, MA: Sinauer Associates, 2015), 81.

11. LeVay, Baldwin, and Baldwin, *Discovering Human Sexuality*, 81.

12. R. Crooks and K. Baur, *Our Sexuality*, 13th ed. (Belmont, CA: Thomson Wadsworth, 2017).

13. Moore, "Polishing the Pearl," 72.

14. A. Kinsey et al., *Sexual Behavior in the Human Female* (Philadelphia: Saunders, 1953). See also Moore, "Polishing the Pearl."

15. Moore, "Polishing the Pearl," 73.

16. J. Greenberg, C. Bruess, and S. Oswalt, *Exploring the Dimensions of Human Sexuality*, 5th ed. (Burlington, MA: Jones and Bartlett Learning, 2017), 102.

17. D. Herbenick et al., "Pubic Hair Removal Among Women in the United States: Prevalence, Methods, and Characteristics," *Journal of Sexual Medicine* 7, no. 10 (2010): 3322–3330.

18. LeVay, Baldwin, and Baldwin, *Discovering Human Sexuality*, 26.

19. LeVay, Baldwin, and Baldwin, *Discovering Human Sexuality*, 26.

20. Schwartz and Kempner, *50 Great Myths of Human Sexuality*, 6.

21. Schwartz and Kempner, *50 Great Myths of Human Sexuality*, 8.

22. C. E. Ekpenyong and E. A. Etukumana, "Ethnicity, Family Socioeconomic Inequalities, and Prevalence of Vaginal Douching Among College Students: The Implication for Health," *Journal of American College Health* 61, no. 4 (2013): 222–230, 222. On regular use of douching, see N. De La Cruz et al., "Attitudes and Sociocultural Factors Influencing Vaginal Douching Behavior Among English-Speaking Latinas," *American Journal of Health Behavior* 33, no. 5 (2009): 558–568; E. Funkhouser, T. D. Hayes, and S. H. Vermund, "Vaginal Douching Practices Among Women Attending a University in the Southern United States," *Journal of American College Health* 50, no. 4 (2002): 177–182.

23. B. H. Cottrell and F. T. Close, "Vaginal Douching Among University Women in the Southeastern United States," *Journal of American College Health* 56, no. 4 (2008): 415–421; N. De La Cruz et al., "Attitudes and Sociocultural Factors Influencing Vaginal Douching Behavior Among English-Speaking Latinas," 558–568; D. M. Grimley et al.,

"Vaginal Douches and Other Feminine Hygiene Products: Women's Practices and Perceptions of Product Safety," *Maternal and Child Health Journal* 10, no. 3 (2006): 303–310.

24. Funkhouser, Hayes, and Vermund, "Vaginal Douching Practices Among Women Attending a University in the Southern United States," 177–182.

25. Ekpenyong and Etukumana, "Ethnicity, Family Socioeconomic Inequalities, and Prevalence of Vaginal Douching Among College Students," 222–230.

26. For instructions on how to conduct a breast examination, see Breastcancer.org, "Breast Self-Exam," October 24, 2019, https://www.breastcancer.org/symptoms/testing/types /self_exam.

27. Crooks and Baur, *Our Sexuality.*

28. *Physicians' Desk Reference*, 71st ed. (Montvale, NJ: PDR Network, 2017).

29. LeVay, Baldwin, and Baldwin, *Discovering Human Sexuality.*

30. Greenberg, Bruess, and Oswalt, *Exploring the Dimensions of Human Sexuality.*

31. See https://cancerstatisticscenter.cancer.org/?_ga=2.230434074.764725653.1578066681 -1090919082.1578066681#!/cancer-site/Prostate.

32. See https://testicularcancersociety.org/pages/self-exam-how-to; https://www.testicular cancerawarenessfoundation.org.

33. World Health Organization and UNAIDS, *Male Circumcision: Global Trends and Determinants of Prevalence, Safety and Acceptability* (Geneva: WHO Press, 2007).

34. T. B. Nippoldt, "Is There Any Safe Way to Naturally Boost a Man's Testoterone Level?," Mayo Clinic, July 19, 2017, https://www.mayoclinic.org/healthy-lifestyle/sexual-health /expert-answers/testosterone-level/faq-20089016.

35. P. A. Costa et al., "Andropause Symptoms Severity Inventory (ASSI): Preliminary Study with a Portuguese Sample," *Maturitas, 100* (2017): 182–183.

36. N. Bassil, S. Alkaade, and J. E. Morley, "The Benefits and Risks of Testosterone Replacement Therapy: A Review," *Therapeutics and Clinical Risk Management* 5, no. 3 (June 2009): 427–448; E. Osterberg, A. Bernie, and R. Ramasamy, "Risks of Testosterone Replacement Therapy in Men," *Indian Journal of Urology* 30, no. 1 (January–March 2014): 2–7.

37. Bassil, Alkaade, and Morley, "The Benefits and Risks of Testosterone Replacement Therapy."

38. *Physicians' Desk Reference.*

39. LeVay, Baldwin, and Baldwin, *Discovering Human Sexuality.* 32.

40. M. Blackless et al., "How Sexually Dimorphic Are We? Review and Synthesis," *American Journal of Human Biology* 12, no. 2 (2000): 151–166.

41. Historically the term was "ambiguous genitalia," wording that many intersex people find offensive.

42. J. Shelton and SJ Dodd, "Beyond the Binary: Addressing Cisnormativity in the Social Work Classroom," *Journal of Social Work Education* 56, no. 1 (2020): 179–185.

43. N. Fischer and S. Seidman, eds., *Introducing the New Sexuality Studies*, 3rd ed. (London: Routledge, 2016). See editor's note in Part 2, 57.

44. Fischer and Seidman, *Introducing the New Sexuality Studies*, 57.

45. W. Masters and V. Johnson, *Human Sexual Response* (Bronx, NY: Ishi Press, 2010).

46. R. Basson, "Human Sex-Response Cycles," *Journal of Sex and Marital Therapy* 27, no. 1 (January–February 2001): 33–43, and "Women's Sexual Dysfunction: Revised and Expanded Definitions," *Canadian Medical Association Journal* 172, no. 10 (2005): 1327–1333; S. Leiblum, "Critical Overview of the New Consensus-Based Definitions and Classifications of Sexual Dysfunction," *Journal of Marital and Sex Therapy* 27, no. 2 (2001): 159–168; B. Whipple and K. Brash-McGreer, "Management of Female Sexual Dysfunction," in *Sexual Function in People with Disability and Chronic Illness: A Health Professional's Guide*, ed. M. L. Sipski and C. J. Alexander (Gaithersburg, MD: Aspen, 1997), 509–534.

47. R. Basson, "Human Sex-Response Cycles," *Journal of Sex and Marital Therapy* 27, no. 1 (January–February 2001): 33–43, and "Women's Sexual Dysfunction: Revised and Expanded Definitions," *Canadian Medical Association Journal* 172, no. 10 (2005): 1327–1333.

48. B. Whipple and K. Brash-McGreer, "Management of Female Sexual Dysfunction."

49. Basson, "Human Sex-Response Cycles."

50. Leiblum, "Critical Overview of the New Consensus-Based Definitions and Classifications of Sexual Dysfunction." See also Basson, "Human Sex-Response Cycles."

51. Leiblum, "Critical Overview of the New Consensus-Based Definitions and Classifications of Sexual Dysfunction."

52. Basson, "Women's Sexual Dysfunction."

53. E. B. Vance and N. N. Wagner, "Written Descriptions of Orgasm: A Study of Sex Differences," *Archives of Sexual Behavior* 5, no. 1 (1976): 87–98.

54. H. Fisher, *Why We Love* (New York: Henry Holt, 2004), 89.

55. Masters and Johnson, *Human Sexual Response*; A. Kaplan, *Women's Self Development in Late Adolescence* (Wellesley, MA: Stone Center for Developmental Services and Studies, Wellesley College, 1985); Basson, "Human Sex-Response Cycles" and "Women's Sexual Dysfunction."

3. TAKING A SEXUAL HISTORY

1. D. Tolman, *Dilemmas of Desire: Teenage Girls Talk About Sexuality* (Cambridge, MA: Harvard University Press, 2002).

2. L. Bay-Cheng, "Recovering Empowerment: De-Personalizing and Re-Politicizing Adolescent Female Sexuality (Commentary)," *Sex Roles* 66 (2012): 713–717; M. Fine and S. McClelland, "Sexuality Education and Desire: Still Missing After All These Years," *Harvard Education Review* 76, no. 3 (2006): 297–338; Tolman, *Dilemmas of Desire*.

3. G. Engle, "Anal Sex: Safety, How Tos, Tips, and More," *Teen Vogue*, November 12, 2019, https://www.teenvogue.com/story/anal-sex-what-you-need-to-know; A. Henley, "Why Sex Education for Disabled People Is So Important," *Teen Vogue*, October 5, 2017, https://www.teenvogue.com/story/disabled-sex-ed.

3. TAKING A SEXUAL HISTORY

4. E. Harris-Hastick and C. Modeste-Curwen, *Journal of HIV/AIDS Prevention and Education for Adolescents and Children* 4, no. 4 (2001): 5–22; K. Kempadoo, "Caribbean Sexuality: Mapping the Field," *Caribbean Review of Gender Studies* no. 3 (2009): 1–24.

5. V. Guilamo-Ramos et al., "The Content and Process of Mother-Adolescent Communication About Sex in Latino Families," *Social Work Research* 30, no. 3 (2006): 169–181.

6. Guilamo-Ramos et al., "The Content and Process of Mother-Adolescent Communication About Sex in Latino Families."

7. E. Laumann et al., *The Social Organization of Sexuality: Sexual Practice in the United States* (Chicago: University of Chicago Press, 1994).

8. L. Diamond, *Sexual Fluidity: Understanding Women's Love and Desire* (Cambridge, MA: Harvard University Press, 2008).

9. Centers for Disease Control and Prevention, *A Guide to Taking a Sexual History*, accessed November 23, 2019, https://www.cdc.gov/std/treatment/sexualhistory.pdf.

10. P. Pahwa and S. Foley, "Biopsychosocial Evaluation of Sexual Dysfunctions," in *The Textbook of Clinical Sexual Medicine*, ed. W. W. IsHak (Cham, Switzerland: Springer International, 2017), 79–94.

11. National Association of Social Workers, *Code of Ethics* (Washington, DC: National Association of Social Workers, 2017).

12. Council on Social Work Education, "2015 Educational Policy and Accreditation Standards," 5.

13. Council on Social Work Education, "2015 Educational Policy and Accreditation Standards," 9.

14. R. Crooks and K. Baur, *Our Sexuality: Instructor's Manual*, 11th ed. (Belmont, CA: Wadsworth/Cengage Learning, 2011), 205–206.

15. J. Gagnon and W. Simon, *Sexual Conduct: The Social Sources of Human Sexuality* (Chicago: Aldine, 1973).

16. S. Buehler, *What Every Mental Health Professional Needs to Know About Sex* (New York: Springer, 2017); U. Bronfenbrenner, *The Ecology of Human Development: Experiments by Nature and Design.* (Cambridge, MA: Harvard University Press, 1979).

17. Buehler, *What Every Mental Health Professional Needs to Know About Sex*, 64–66.

18. Buehler, *What Every Mental Health Professional Needs to Know About Sex*, 64.

19. Buehler, *What Every Mental Health Professional Needs to Know About Sex*, 64–66.

20. Buehler, *What Every Mental Health Professional Needs to Know About Sex*, 64–69.

21. Buehler, *What Every Mental Health Professional Needs to Know About Sex*, 66.

22. Buehler, *What Every Mental Health Professional Needs to Know About Sex.*

23. S. Iasenza, "What Is Queer About Sex? Expanding Sexual Frames in Theory and Practice," *Family Process* 49, no. 3 (2010): 291–308.

24. Iasenza, "What Is Queer About Sex?," 300.

25. Iasenza, "What Is Queer About Sex?," 300.

26. Iasenza, "What Is Queer About Sex?," 300.

27. Iasenza, "What Is Queer About Sex?," 300.

28. J. Morin, *The Erotic Mind* (New York: Harper Perennial, 1995).

29. S. Foley, "Biopsychosocial Assessment and Treatment of Sexual Problems in Older Age," *Current Sexual Health Reports* 7, no. 2 (2015): 80–88.

30. Foley, "Biopsychosocial Assessment and Treatment of Sexual Problems in Older Age"; Pahwa and Foley, "Biopsychosocial Evaluation of Sexual Dysfunctions."

31. Buehler, *What Every Mental Health Professional Needs to Know About Sex.*

32. Centers for Disease Control and Prevention, *A Guide to Taking a Sexual History.*

33. Foley, "Biopsychosocial Assessment and Treatment of Sexual Problems in Older Age."

4. SEXUAL IDENTITY

1. S. Stryker and P. Burke, "The Past, Present, and Future of an Identity Theory," *Social Psychology Quarterly* 63, no. 4 (2000): 284.

2. A. Schmidt, "Prevalence, Predictors, and Negative Outcomes Associated with Discordant Sexual Identity, Sexual Attraction and Sexual Behavior" (PhD diss., City University of New York, 2010), 14.

3. S. Freud, *Three Essays on the Theory of Sexuality*, trans. James Strachey (New York: Basic Books, 1962).

4. E. H. Erikson, *Identity and the Life Cycle* (New York: International Universities Press, 1959).

5. L. Diamond, *Sexual Fluidity: Understanding Women's Love and Desire* (Cambridge, MA: Harvard University Press, 2008); Schmidt, "Prevalence, Predictors, and Negative Outcomes."

6. A. Kinsey, W. Pomeroy, and C. Martin, *Sexual Behavior in the Human Male* (Philadelphia: Saunders, 1948); A. Kinsey et al., Sexual Behavior in the Human Female (Philadelphia: Saunders, 1953).

7. American Psychiatric Association, *Diagnostic and Statistical Manual of Mental Disorders* (Washington, DC: Author, 1952); American Psychiatric Association, *Diagnostic and Statistical Manual of Mental Disorders*, 2nd ed. (Washington, DC: American Psychiatric Association, 1968); American Psychiatric Association, *Diagnostic and Statistical Manual of Mental Disorders*, 5th ed. (Arlington, VA: American Psychiatric Association, 2013).

8. E. Hooker, "The Adjustment of the Male Overt Homosexual," *Journal of Projective Techniques* 21, no. 1 (1957): 18–31.

9. American Psychiatric Association, *Diagnostic and Statistical Manual of Mental Disorders*, 6th printing (Arlington, VA: American Psychiatric Association, 1974).

10. American Psychiatric Association, Diagnostic and Statistical Manual of Mental Disorders, 3rd ed. (Arlington, VA: American Psychiatric Association, 1980).

11. American Psychiatric Association, *Diagnostic and Statistical Manual of Mental Disorders*, 3rd ed. Revised (III-R) (Arlington, VA: American Psychiatric Association, 1987).

12. R. Shilts, *And the Band Played On: Politics, People, and the AIDS Epidemic* (New York: St. Martin's Press, 1987).

13. Shilts, *And the Band Played On.*

14. National Coalition of Anti-Violence Programs, *A Crisis of Hate: A Report on Homicides Against Lesbian, Gay, Bisexual and Transgender People: Emily Waters, Larissa Pham, Chelsea Convery* (New York: National Coalition of Anti-Violence Programs, 2018).

15. J. G. Kosciw et al., *The 2017 National School Climate Survey: The Experiences of Lesbian, Gay, Bisexual, Transgender, and Queer Youth in Our Nation's Schools* (New York: GLSEN, 2018).

16. Kosciw et al., *The 2017 National School Climate Survey*, xix.

17. SJ Dodd, "LGBTQ Poverty in NYC: Busting the Gay Affluence Myth," in *Worse Than You Think: The Dimensions of Poverty in NYC*, ed. M. Sullivan. (New York: National Association of Social Workers, New York City Chapter, 2014), 55–58.

18. S. D. Cochran, V. M. Mays, and J. G. Sullivan, "Prevalence of Mental Disorders, Psychological Distress, and Mental Health Services Use Among Lesbian, Gay, and Bisexual Adults in the United States," *Journal of Consulting and Clinical Psychology* 71, no. 1 (2003): 53–61; S. T. Russell and J. N. Fish, "Mental Health in Lesbian, Gay, Bisexual, and Transgender (LGBT) Youth," *Annual Review of Clinical Psychology* 12 (2016): 465–487.

19. B. S. Mustanski, R. Garofalo, and E. M. Emerson, "Mental Health Disorders, Psychological Distress, and Suicidality in a Diverse Sample of Lesbian, Gay, Bisexual, and Transgender Youths," *American Journal of Public Health* 100, no. 12 (2010): 2426–2432.

20. Williams Institute, *Adult LGBT Population in the United States* (Los Angeles: University of California, Los Angeles, 2019).

21. U.S. Census Bureau, American Community Survey (U.S. Census Bureau, 2017), https://www.census.gov/library/stories/2019/09/where-same-sex-couples-live.html.

22. K. I. Fredriksen-Goldsen and H. J. Kim, "The Science of Conducting Research with LGBT Older Adults: An Introduction to Aging with Pride: National Health, Aging, and Sexuality/Gender Study," *Gerontologist* 57, issue supplement 1 (2017): S1–S14.

23. Fredriksen-Goldsen and Kim, "The Science of Conducting Research with LGBT Older Adults," S2.

24. National Association of Social Workers, *Code of Ethics* (Washington, DC: National Association of Social Workers, 2017).

25. V. Cass, "Homosexual Identity Formation: A Theoretical Model," *Journal of Homosexuality* 4, no. 3 (1979): 219–235.

26. Donna Ann Kenneady, Sara B. Oswalt, "Is Cass's Model of Homosexual Identity Formation Relevant to Today's Society?," *American Journal of Sexuality Education* 9, no. 2 (2014): 229–246.

27. K. I. Fredriksen-Goldsen, "The Future of LGBTQ+ Aging: A Blueprint for Action in Services, Policies and Research," *Generations* 40, no. 2 (2016): 6–15.

28. L. Brotto and M. Yule, "Asexuality: Sexual Orientation, Paraphilia, Sexual Dysfunction, or None of the Above?," *Archives of Sexual Behavior* 46 (2017): 619–627.

29. Brotto and Yule, "Asexuality," 619.

30. S. Cranney, "Does Asexuality Meet the Stability Criterion for a Sexual Orientation?," *Archives of Sexual Behavior* 46 (2017): 637–638.

31. M. Peixoto, "Sex and Sexual Orientation," in *The Textbook of Clinical Sexual Medicine*, ed. W. W. IsHak (Cham, Switzerland: Springer International, 2017), 433–445.

32. S. Buehler, *What Every Mental Health Professional Needs to Know About Sex* (New York: Springer, 2017); A. Bogaert, "Asexuality: Prevalence and Associated Factors in a National Probability Sample," *Journal of Sex Research* 41, no. 3 (2004): 279–287.

33. A. Bogaert, "Asexuality," 282.

34. Peixoto, "Sex and Sexual Orientation," 433–445.

35. M. Yule, L. Brotto, and B. Gorzalka, "Sexual Fantasy and Masturbation Among Asexual Individuals," *Canadian Journal of Human Sexuality* 23, no. 2 (2014): 89–95.

36. Yule, Brotto, and Gorzalka, "Sexual Fantasy and Masturbation Among Asexual Individuals."

37. N. Robbins, K. Graff Low, and A. Query, "An Exploration of the 'Coming Out' Process for Asexual Individuals," *Archives of Sexual Behavior* 45, no. 3 (2016): 751–760.

38. Robbins, Graff Low, and Query, "An Exploration of the 'Coming Out' Process for Asexual Individuals," 751.

39. Robbins, Graff Low, and Query, "An Exploration of the 'Coming Out' Process for Asexual Individuals," 758.

40. Robbins, Graff Low, and Query, "An Exploration of the 'Coming Out' Process for Asexual Individuals," 759.

41. S. Monro, S. Hines, and A. Osborne, "Is Bisexuality Invisible? A Review of Sexualities Scholarship, 1970–2015," *Sociological Review* 65, no. 4 (2017): 663–681.

42. P. Schwartz and M. Kempner, *50 Great Myths of Human Sexuality* (New York: Wiley, 2015), 44.

43. A. Callis, "Beyond Bi: Sexual Fluidity, Identity, and the Post-Bisexual Revolution," in *Introducing the New Sexuality Studies*, 3rd ed., ed. N. Fischer and S. Seidman (London: Routledge, 2016), 215–224.

44. R. Ochs, "Biphobia: It Goes Both Ways," in *Bisexuality: The Identity Politics of an Invisible Minority*, ed. B. A. Firestein (Thousand Oaks, CA: Sage, 1996), and "What's in a Name? Why Women Embrace or Resist Bisexual Identity," in *Becoming Visible: Counseling Bisexuals Across the Lifespan*, ed. B. A. Firestein (New York: Columbia University Press, 2007).

45. Callis "Beyond Bi"; Ochs, "Biphobia."

46. Ochs, "What's in a Name?"

47. C. Flanders et al., "Positive Identity Experiences of Young Bisexual and Other Nonmonosexual People: A Qualitative Inquiry," *Journal of Homosexuality* 64, no. 8 (2017): 1014–1032.

48. M. Bradford, "The Bisexual Experience: Living in a Dichotomous Culture," *Journal of Bisexuality* 4, nos. 1–2 (2004): 7–23.

49. G. Weber, "Practice with Bisexual People," in *Social Work Practice with Lesbian, Gay, Bisexual and Transgender People*, 3rd ed., ed. G. P. Mallon (New York: Routledge, 2018), 30–41.

50. B. Dodge and T. Sandfort, "A Review of Mental Health Research on Bisexual Individuals When Compared to Homosexual and Heterosexual Individuals," in *Becoming Visible: Counseling Bisexuals Across the Lifespan*, ed. B. A. Firestein (New York: Columbia University Press, 2007), 28–51; Flanders et al., "Positive Identity Experiences."

51. G. Bauer and D. Brennan, "The Problem with 'Behavioral Bisexuality': Assessing Sexual Orientation in Survey Research," *Journal of Bisexuality* 13, no. 2 (2013): 148–165.

52. Weber, "Practice with Bisexual People," 31.

53. Weber, "Practice with Bisexual People," 39.

54. Weber, "Practice with Bisexual People," 40.

55. J. Parsons et al., "Alternatives to Monogamy Among Gay Male Couples in a Community Survey: Implications for Mental Health and Sexual Risk," *Archives of Sexual Behavior* 42, no. 2 (2013): 308–312.

56. E. Sheff, *The Polyamorists Next Door: Inside Multiple-Partner Relationships and Families* (Lanham, MD: Rowman and Littlefield, 2014), 1; C. Klesse, "Contesting the Culture of Monogamy: Consensual Nonmonogamies and Polyamory," in *Introducing the New Sexuality Series*, 3rd ed., ed. N. Fischer and S. Seidman (London: Routledge, 2016), 332.

57. Klesse, "Contesting the Culture of Monogamy," 325–336; D. Williams and E. Prior, "Contemporary Polyamory: A Call for Awareness and Sensitivity in Social Work," *Social Work* 60, no. 3 (2015): 268–270.

58. Sheff, *The Polyamorists Next Door*, 3.

59. Williams and Prior, "Contemporary Polyamory."

60. Diamond, *Sexual Fluidity*; M. Chivers, G. Rieger, E. Latty, and Bailey. "A Sex Difference in the Specificity of Arousal," *Psychological Science* 15, no. 11 (2004): 736–744.

61. Chivers et al. "A Sex Difference in the Specificity of Arousal."

62. Diamond, *Sexual Fluidity*.

63. Robbins, Graff Low, and Query, "An Exploration of the 'Coming Out' Process for Asexual Individuals."

64. W. B. Bostwick et al., "Discrimination and Mental Health Among Lesbian, Gay, and Bisexual Adults in the United States," *American Journal of Orthopsychiatry* 84, no. 1 (2014): 35–45; S. K. Choi et al., *Serving Our Youth 2015: The Needs and Experiences of Lesbian, Gay, Bisexual, Transgender, and Questioning Youth Experiencing Homelessness* (Los Angeles: Williams Institute, 2015); G. L. Ream, "What's Unique About Lesbian, Gay, Bisexual, and Transgender (LGBT) Youth and Young Adult Suicides? Findings from the National Violent Death Reporting System," *Journal of Adolescent Health* 64, no. 5 (2019): 602–607; M. Shelton, *Fundamentals of LGBT Substance Use Disorders: Multiple Identities, Multiple Challenges* (New York: Harrington Park Press, 2017).

65. Williams Institute, Adult LGBT Population in the United https://williamsinstitute.law .ucla.edu/research/lgbt-adults-in-the-us/; Choi et al., *Serving Our Youth 2015*, 4.

66. Choi et al., *Serving Our Youth 2015*, 4.

67. Choi et al., *Serving Our Youth 2015*, 5.

68. R. DiAngelo, "Heterosexism: Addressing Internalized Dominance," *Journal of Progressive Human Service* 8, no. 1 (1997): 6.

69. G. M. Herek, "The Psychology of Sexual Prejudice," *Current Directions in Psychological Science* 9, no. 1 (2000): 19–22.

70. J. Fjelstrom, "Sexual Orientation Change Efforts and Search for Authenticity," *Journal of Homosexuality* 60, no. 6 (2013): 801.

5. GENDER IDENTITY

1. American Psychiatric Association, *Diagnostic and Statistical Manual of Mental Disorders*, 5th ed. (Arlington, VA: American Psychiatric Association, 2013).

2. Gender Identity Project, "Transgender Basics," August 10, 2009, https://www.youtube.com/watch?v=UXI9woPbBXY.

3. R. Crooks and K. Baur, *Our Sexuality*, 13th ed. (Belmont, CA: Thomson Wadsworth, 2017).

4. Crooks and Baur, *Our Sexuality*, 12th ed. (Belmont, CA: Thomson Wadsworth, 2014), 111.

5. B. Burdge, "Bending Gender, Ending Gender: Theoretical Foundations for Social Work Practice with the Transgender Community," *Social Work* 52, no. 3 (2007): 243–250.

6. K. Farrell, N. Gupta, and M. Queen, *Interrupting Heteronormativity: Lesbian, Gay, Bisexual, and Transgender Pedagogy and Responsible Teaching at Syracuse University* (Syracuse, NY: Syracuse University Press, 2004).

7. C. Berkman and G. Zinberg, "Homphobia and Heterosexism in Social Workers," *Social Work* 42, no. 4 (1997): 320.

8. J. G. Kosciw et al., *The 2017 National School Climate Survey: The Experiences of Lesbian, Gay, Bisexual, Transgender, and Queer Youth in Our Nation's Schools* (New York: GLSEN, 2018): xviii.

9. Human Rights Campaign, "Violence Against the Transgender Community in 2018," accessed November 28, 2019, https://www.hrc.org/resources/violence-against-the-transgender-community-in-2018.

10. S. James et al., *The Report of the 2015 U.S. Transgender Survey* (Washington, D.C.: National Center for Transgender Equality, 2016); B. Mustanski, R. Andrews, and J. A. Puckett, "The Effects of Cumulative Victimization on Mental Health Among Lesbian, Gay, Bisexual, and Transgender Adolescents and Young Adults," *American Journal of Public Health* 106, no. 3 (2016): 527–533; B. Mustanski and R. T. Liu, "A Longitudinal Study of Predictors of Suicide Attempts Among Lesbian, Gay, Bisexual, and Transgender Youth," *Archives of Sexual Behavior* 42, no. 3 (2013): 437–448; S. Pardor and A. Devor, "Transgender and Gender Nonconforming Identity Development," in *The Sage Encyclopedia of Psychology and Gender*, ed. K. Nadal (Thousand Oaks, CA: Sage Publications, 2017), 1689–1692.

11. James et al., *The Report of the 2015 U.S. Transgender Survey*, 5.

12. SJ Dodd, "LGBTQ Poverty in NYC: Busting the Gay Affluence Myth," in *Worse Than You Think: The Dimensions of Poverty in NYC*, ed. M. Sullivan (New York: National Association of Social Workers, New York City Chapter, 2014), 55–58.

13. S. Ferro, "Homophobia Is Bad for the Economy," *Business Insider*, July 2015, http://www.businessinsider.com/ubs-homophobia-is-bad-for-the-economy-2015-7.

14. A. Enke, *Transfeminist Perspectives in and Beyond Transgender Studies* (Philadelphia: Temple University Press, 2012), 63. See also J. Butler, *Gender Trouble: Feminism and the Subversion of Identity* (New York: Routledge, 2006).

15. Y. G. Ansara and I. Berger, "Cisgenderism," in *The Wiley Blackwell Encyclopedia of Gender and Sexuality Studies*, ed. N. Naples et al. (Oxford: Blackwell, 2016), 137–160.

16. J. Pyne, "Unsuitable Bodies: Trans People and Cisnormativity in Shelter Services," *Canadian Social Work Journal* 28, no. 1 (2011): 131.

17. Farrell, Gupta, and Queen, *Interrupting Heteronormativity*. 3.

18. A. Austin, S. L. Craig, and L. B. McInroy, "Toward Transgender Affirmative Social Work Education," *Journal of Social Work Education* 52, no. 3 (2016): 308; J. Serano, *Outspoken: A Decade of Transgender Activism and Trans Feminism* (Oakland, CA: Switch Hitter Press, 2016), 6.

19. Austin, Craig, and McInroy, "Toward Transgender Affirmative Social Work Education," 308; Serano, *Outspoken*, 6.

20. Austin, Craig, and McInroy, "Toward Transgender Affirmative Social Work Education," 308.

21. Crooks and Baur, *Our Sexuality*, 111.

22. https://apastyle.apa.org/style-grammar-guidelines/grammar/singular-they; https://www.merriam-webster.com/words-at-play/word-of-the-year/they.

23. American Psychiatric Association, *Diagnostic and Statistical Manual of Mental Disorders*. 3rd ed. (Arlington, VA: American Psychiatric Association, 1980), 261.

24. American Psychiatric Association, *Diagnostic and Statistical Manual of Mental Disorders*, 4th ed. (Arlington, VA: American Psychiatric Association, 1994), 493.

25. American Psychiatric Association, *Diagnostic and Statistical Manual of Mental Disorders*, 5th ed., 451–459.

26. K. J. Zucker, "The DSM-5 Diagnostic Criteria for Gender Dysphoria," in *Management of Gender Dysphoria: A Multidisciplinary Approach*, ed. C. Trombetta, G. Liguori, and M. Bertolotto (Trieste, Italy: Springer-Verlag Italia, 2015), 34.

27. I. Sherer et al., "Affirming Gender: Caring for Gender-Atypical Children and Adolescents," *Contemporary Pediatrics* 32, no. 1 (2015): 16–19; T. Steensma et al., "Factors Associated with Desistance and Persistence of Childhood Dysphoria: A Quantitative Follow-Up Study," *Journal of the American Academy of Child and Adolescent Psychiatry* 52, no. 6 (2013): 582–590.

28. Pardor and Devor, "Transgender and Gender Nonconforming Identity Development," 1689–1692.

29. American Psychiatric Association, *What Is Gender Dysphoria?* n.d., https://www.psychiatry.org/patients-families/gender-dysphoria/what-is-gender-dysphoria.

30. C. Davis, "Practice with Transgender People," in *Social Work Practice with Lesbian, Gay, Bisexual, and Transgender People*, 3rd ed., ed. G. P. Mallon (New York: Routledge, 2018), 42–65.

31. American Psychiatric Association, *Diagnostic and Statistical Manual of Mental Disorders*, 5th ed., 452–453.

32. K. Whalen, "(In)validating Transgender Identities: Progress and Trouble in the DSM-5," National LGBTQ Task Force, accessed November 28, 2019, https://www.thetaskforce.org/invalidating-transgender-identities-progress-and-trouble-in-the-dsm-5/.

33. Davis, "Practice with Transgender People," 45.

34. J. DeLameter and W. Friedrich, "Human Sexual Development," *Journal of Sex Research* 39, no. 1 (2002): 10–14.

35. J. Butler, *Gender Trouble*; James et al., *The Report of the 2015 U.S. Transgender Survey*; J. K. Schulman and L. Erickson-Schroth, "Mental Health in Sexual Minority and Transgender Women," *Medical Clinics of North America* 103, no. 4 (2019): 723–733.

36. James et al., *The Report of the 2015 U.S. Transgender Survey*, 5.

37. A. I. Lev, *Transgender Emergence: Therapeutic Guidelines for Working with Gender-Variant People and Their Families* (Binghamton, NY: Haworth Press, 2004).

38. Lev, *Transgender Emergence*, 234.

39. Lev, *Transgender Emergence*, 234.

40. Lev, *Transgender Emergence*, 234.

41. American Psychiatric Association, *Diagnostic and Statistical Manual of Mental Disorders*, 5th ed., 451–459.

42. Lev, *Transgender Emergence*, 234.

6. SEX ACROSS THE LIFE SPAN

1. K. Robinson, "Children's Sexual Citizenship," in *Introducing the New Sexuality Studies*, 3rd ed., ed. N. Fischer and S. Seidman (London: Routledge, 2016), 485–493.

2. Robinson, "Children's Sexual Citizenship."

3. Robinson, "Children's Sexual Citizenship," 487.

4. S. LeVay, J. I. Baldwin, and J. D. Baldwin, *Discovering Human Sexuality*, 3rd ed. (Sunderland, MA: Sinauer Associates, 2015); J. Money, *The Lovemap Guidebook: A Definitive Statement* (New York: Continuum. 1999); J. Richardson and M. A. Schuster, *Everything You Never Wanted Your Kids to Know About Sex (but Were Afraid They'd Ask): The Secrets to Surviving Your Child's Sexual Development from Birth to the Teens* (New York: Three Rivers Press, 2003).

5. H. Harlow, "The Nature of Love," *American Psychologist* 13, no. 12 (1958): 673–685.

6. LeVay, Baldwin, and Baldwin, *Discovering Human Sexuality*; Richardson and Schuster, *Everything You Never Wanted Your Kids to Know About Sex*.

7. See, for example, American Academy of Pediatrics, Promoting Healthy Sexual Development and Sexuality in Bright Futures: Guidelines for Health Supervision of Infants, Children, and Adolescents, 217–227. https://brightfutures.aap.org/Bright%20Futures%20Documents/BF4_HealthySexuality.pdf; National Sexual Violence Resource Center, Preventing Child Sexual Abuse Resources. https://www.nsvrc.org/preventing-child-sexual-abuse-resources.

8. Hutchinson, *Dimensions of Human Behavior*, 154.

9. Hutchinson, *Dimensions of Human Behavior*, 154.

10. Hutchinson, *Dimensions of Human Behavior*, 154.

11. Hutchinson, *Dimensions of Human Behavior*, 154.

12. American Academy of Pediatrics, Promoting Healthy Sexual Development and Sexuality in Bright Futures, 217–227.

13. S. Buehler, *What Every Mental Health Professional Needs to Know About Sex* (New York: Springer, 2017).

14. LeVay, Baldwin, and Baldwin, *Discovering Human Sexuality*, 319.

15. Hutchinson, *Dimensions of Human Behavior*, 251.

16. L. Kann et al., "Youth Risk Behavior Surveillance—United States, 2017," *Morbidity and Mortality Weekly Report*, June 15, 2018, https://www.cdc.gov/healthyyouth/data/yrbs /pdf/2017/ss6708.pdf.

17. E. H. Erikson, *Identity and the Life Cycle* (New York: International Universities Press, 1959).

18. Kann et al., "Youth Risk Behavior Surveillance."

19. C. F. Roy, D. L. Tolman, and F. Snowden, "Heterosexual Anal Intercourse Among Black and Latino Adolescents and Young Adults: A Poorly Understood High-Risk Behavior," *Journal of Sex Research* 50, no. 7 (2013): 715–722.

20. Hutchinson, *Dimensions of Human Behavior*, 251–252.

21. M. Fine and S. McClelland, "Sexuality Education and Desire: Still Missing After All These Years," *Harvard Education Review* 76, no. 3 (2006): 297–338; D. Tolman, *Dilemmas of Desire: Teenage Girls Talk About Sexuality* (Boston, MA: Harvard University Press, 2005).

22. D. Hernandez, "The Effects of Consuming Pornography: Men's Attitudes Toward Violence Against Women, Dominance Over and Objectification of Women, and Sexual Expectations of Women," *Perspectives* 3, no. 1 (2011): 116–123.

23. Unitarian Universalist Association, "Our Whole Lives: Lifespan Sexuality Education," https://www.uua.org/re/owl.

24. D. Carter, "Comprehensive Sex Education for Teens Is More Effective Than Abstinence." *American Journal of Nursing* 112, no. 3 (2012): 15.

25. J. Crolley-Simic, M. E. Vonk, and W. Ellsworth, "A School Social Worker's Impact on a Human Sexuality Program," *School Social Work Journal* 31, no. 2 (2007): 17–32.

26. Erikson, *Identity and the Life Cycle*; see also Hutchinson, *Dimensions of Human Behavior*, 112.

27. R. Blonna and L. Carter, *Healthy Sexuality*, 3rd ed. (Dubuque, IA: Kendall Hunt, 2013).

28. T. J. Mathews and B. E. Hamilton, "Mean Age of Mothers Is on the Rise: United States, 2000–2014," NCHS Data Brief no. 232, January 2016, https://www.cdc.gov /nchs/data/databriefs/db232.pdf.

29. R. Crooks and K. Baur, *Our Sexuality*, 13th ed. (Belmont, CA: Thomson Wadsworth, 2017), 425.

30. S. T. Lindau and N. Gavrilova, "Sex, Health, and Years of Sexually Active Life Gained Due to Good Health: Evidence from Two US Population Based Cross Sectional Surveys of Ageing," *BMJ* 340 (2010): c810.

31. A. Karraker, J. Delamater, and C. R. Schwartz, "Sexual Frequency Decline from Midlife to Later Life," *Journals of Gerontology: Series B: Psychological Sciences and Social Sciences* 66, no. 4 (2011): 502–512; Lindau and Gavrilova, "Sex, Health, and Years of Sexually Active Life Gained Due to Good Health."

32. M. E. Dunn and N. Cutler, "Sexual Issues in Older Adults," *AIDS Patient Care and STDs* 14, no. 2 (2000): 67–69.

33. Dunn and Cutler, "Sexual Issues in Older Adults," 67.

34. Dunn and Cutler, "Sexual Issues in Older Adults," 67.

35. A. R. Helgason et al., "Sexual Desire, Erection, Orgasm, and Ejaculatory Functions and Their Importance to Elderly Swedish Men: A Population Based Study," *Age and Ageing* 25, no. 4 (1996): 285.

36. M. L. Meijer, dir., *69: Love Sex Senior* (Netherlands, 2013).

37. N. Gavey, "Viagra and the Coital Imperative." In *Introducing the New Sexuality Studies*, 3rd ed., ed. N. Fischer and S. Seidman (London: Routledge, 2016), 74–80.

38. A. Taylor and M. A. Gosney, "Sexuality in Older Age: Essential Considerations for Healthcare Professionals," *Age and Ageing* 40, no. 5 (2011): 538–543.

39. Crooks and Baur, *Our Sexuality*, 423.

40. J. Bywater and R. Jones, *Sexuality and Social Work* (Exeter, UK: Learning Matters, 2007).

41. A. Taylor and Gosney, "Sexuality in Older Age," 541.

42. Centers for Disease Control and Prevention, *HIV Surveillance Report, 2017*, vol. 29, November 2018, https://www.cdc.gov/hiv/pdf/library/reports/surveillance/cdc-hiv -surveillance-report-2017-vol-29.pdf.

43. New York City Health Department. *Health of Older Adults in New York City*, https:// www1.nyc.gov/assets/doh/downloads/pdf/episrv/2019-older-adult-health.pdf.

44. Centers for Disease Control and Prevention. *Sexually Transmitted Disease Surveillance 2018,* https://www.cdc.gov/std/stats18/syphilis.htm.

45. J. S. Annon, *Behavioral Treatment of Sexual Problems: Brief Therapy* (Oxford, UK: Harper and Row, 1976).

46. American Sexual Health Association, "Sexual Rights for Seniors," accessed November 29, 2019, http://www.ashasexualhealth.org/sexual-rights-for-seniors.

7. COMMUNICATING ABOUT LOVE AND INTIMACY

1. J. G. Rosier and J. M. Tyler, "Finding the Love Guru in You: Examining the Effectiveness of a Sexual Communication Training Program for Married Couples," *Marriage and Family Review* 53, no. 1 (2017): 66.

2. R. Sternberg, "A Triangular Theory of Love," *Psychological Review* 93, no. 2 (1986): 119–135, and "Triangulating Love," in *The Psychology of Love*, ed. R. Sternberg and M. Barnes (New Haven, CT: Yale University Press, 1988), 119–138.

3. Sternberg, "A Triangular Theory of Love," 124.

4. Sternberg, 124.

5. A. De Boer, E. Van Buel, and G. Ter Horst, "Love Is More Than Just a Kiss: A Neurobiological Perspective on Love and Affection." *Neuroscience*, 201 (2012): 114–124.

6. M. Reese-Weber, "Intimacy, Communication, and Aggressive Behaviors: Variations by Phases of Romantic Relationship Development," *Personal Relationships* 22 (2015): 206.

7. De Boer, van Buel, and Ter Horst, "Love Is More Than Just a Kiss."

8. Sternberg, "A Triangular Theory of Love," 124.

9. De Boer, van Buel, and Ter Horst, "Love Is More Than Just a Kiss."

10. R. Crooks and K. Baur, *Our Sexuality*, 13th ed. (Belmont, CA: Thomson Wadsworth, 2017), 191.

11. Crooks and Baur, *Our Sexuality*, 424.

12. Sternberg, "A Triangular Theory of Love," 124.

13. S. Buehler, *What Every Mental Health Professional Needs to Know About Sex* (New York: Springer, 2017), 117; S. Iasenza, "What Is Queer About Sex? Expanding Sexual Frames in Theory and Practice," *Family Process* 49, no. 3 (2010): 291–308.

14. S. Tatkin, *Wired for Love* (Oakland, CA: New Harbinger, 2011), xi.

15. J. Bowlby, *Attachment and Loss* (New York: Basic Books, 1969); M. Ainsworth et al., *Patterns of Attachment: A Psychological Study of the Strange Situation* (Hillsdale, NJ: Erlbaum, 1978).

16. E. D. Hutchinson, *Dimensions of Human Behavior: The Changing Life Course* (Thousand Oaks, CA: SAGE Publications, 2015), 116.

17. Bowlby, *Attachment and Loss*.

18. Ainsworth et al., *Patterns of Attachment*.

19. Ainsworth et al., *Patterns of Attachment*.

20. Tatkin, *Wired for Love*, and *Wired for Dating* (Oakland, CA: New Harbinger, 2016).

21. Ainsworth et al., *Patterns of Attachment*.

22. Tatkin, *Wired for Love*.

23. Tatkin, *Wired for Love*, *Wired for Dating*, and *Your Brain on Love* (Audible, 2013, https://www.audible.com/pd/Your-Brain-on-Love-Audiobook/B00DMCBEOE).

24. Tatkin, *Your Brain on Love*.

25. De Boer, van Buel, and Ter Horst, "Love Is More Than Just a Kiss."

26. H. Fisher, *Why We Love* (New York: St. Martin's Griffin, 2004), 86; Tatkin, *Your Brain on Love*.

27. Fisher, *Why We Love*, 86; Tatkin, *Your Brain on Love*.

28. De Boer, Van Buel, and Ter Horst, "Love Is More Than Just a Kiss," 118.

29. Tatkin, *Your Brain on Love*.

30. Tatkin, *Your Brain on Love*.

31. Crooks and Baur, *Our Sexuality*, 196.

32. Rosier and Tyler, "Finding the Love Guru in You."

33. A. Godow, "Playful Sexuality," *Contemporary Sexuality* 33, nos. 1–2 (1999).

34. J. Gottman, "The 6 Things That Predict Divorce," *Gottman Relationship Blog*, accessed November 29, 2019, https://www.gottman.com/blog/the-6-things-that-predict-divorce/.

35. E. Liu and M. E. Roloff, "Regret for Complaint Withholding," *Communication Quarterly* 64 (2016): 72–92.

36. J. Morin, *The Erotic Mind* (New York: Harper Perennial, 2012).

37. Rosier and Tyler, "Finding the Love Guru in You," 65.

38. J. Gottman, *Why Marriages Succeed or Fail* (New York: Simon and Schuster, 1994).

39. Gottman, *Why Marriages Succeed or Fail*.

40. Tatkin, *Wired for Love*, and *Wired for Dating*.

41. T. Koike et al., "Neural Substrates of Shared Attention as Social Memory: A Hyperscanning Functional Magnetic Resonance Imaging Study," *Neuroimage* 125 (2016): 401–412.

42. C. E. Murray and E. C. Campbell, "The Pleasures and Perils of Technology in Intimate Relationships," *Journal of Couple and Relationship Therapy* 14, no. 2 (2015): 116–140.

43. A. Wagner, "Making Peace with Jealousy in Polyamorous Relationships," accessed November 29, 2019, http://www.practicalpolyamory.com/images/Jealousy_Updated_10-6-10.pdf.

44. E. C. Campbell and C. E. Murray, "Measuring the Impact of Technology on Couple Relationships: The Development of the Technology and Intimate Relationship," *Journal of Couple and Relationship Therapy* 14 (2015): 255.

45. A. Ben-Ze'ev and L. Brunning, "How Complex Is Your Love? The Case of Romantic Compromises and Polyamory," *Journal for the Theory of Social Behaviour* 48, no. 1 (2018): 98–116; Campbell and Murray, "Measuring the Impact of Technology on Couple Relationships."

46. B. Mileham, "Online Infidelity in Internet Chat Rooms: An Ethnographic Exploration," *Computers in Human Behavior* 23, no. 1 (2007): 11–31.

47. L. Leon, "Texting Amor: Emerging Intimacies in Textually Mediated Romance Among Tzotzil Mayan Youth," *Ethos* 45, no. 4 (2017): 462–488.

48. Y. Amichai-Hamburger and S. Etgar, "Intimacy and Smartphone Multitasking—A New Oxymoron?," *Psychological Reports* 119, no. 3 (2016): 826.

49. Sternberg, "A Triangular Theory of Love" and "Triangulating Love."

8. ALT SEX

1. P. J. Kleinplatz, "Learning from Extraordinary Lovers," *Journal of Homosexuality* 50, no. 2 (2006): 325–348.

2. M. Yost and L. Hunter, "BDSM Practitioners' Understandings of Their Initial Attraction to BDSM Sexuality: Essentialist and Constructionist Narratives," *Journal of Psychology and Human Sexuality* 3, no. 3 (2012): 244.

3. S. Buehler, *What Every Mental Health Professional Needs to Know About Sex* (New York: Springer, 2017), 279.

4. American Psychiatric Association, *Diagnostic and Statistical Manual of Mental Disorders*, 5th ed. (Arlington, VA: American Psychiatric Association, 2013).

5. S. LeVay, J. I. Baldwin, and J. D. Baldwin, *Discovering Human Sexuality*, 3rd ed. (Sunderland, MA: Sinauer Associates, 2015).

6. M. Yost and L. Hunter, "BDSM Practitioners' Understandings of Their Initial Attraction to BDSM Sexuality: Essentialist and Constructionist Narratives," *Journal of Psychology and Human Sexuality* 3, no. 3 (2012): 244–259.

7. Yost and Hunter, "BDSM Practitioners' Understandings of Their Initial Attraction to BDSM Sexuality," 245. See also G. W. Taylor and J. M. Ussher, "Making Sense of S&M: A Discourse Analytic Account," *Sexualities* 4, no. 3 (2001): 293–314; M. S. Weinberg, C. J. Williams, and C. Moser, "The Social Constituents of Sadomasochism," *Social Problems* 31, no. 4 (1984): 379–389.

8. K. Kolmes, W. Stock, and C. Moser, "Investigating Bias in Psychotherapy with BDSM Clients," *Journal of Homosexuality* 50, nos. 2–3 (2006): 301–324.

9. C. C. Joyal, A. Cossette, and V. Lapierre, "Sexual Fantasies in the General Population," *Journal of Sexual Medicine* 12, no. 2 (2015): 328–340.

10. World Health Organization, Defining Sexual Health: Report of a Technical Consultation on Sexual Health 28–31 January 2002 (Geneva, 2006), https://www.who.int/reproductivehealth/publications/sexual_health/defining_sexual_health.pdf.

11. L. Moore, T. Pincus, and D. Rodemaker, "What Professionals Need to Know About BDSM," National Coalition for Sexual Freedom, accessed November 30, 2019, https://www.ncsfreedom.org/images/stories/pdfs/Activist/What_Professionals_Need_to_Know_About_BDSM_1.pdf.

12. Yost and Hunter, "BDSM Practitioners' Understandings of Their Initial Attraction to BDSM Sexuality," 244.

13. Yost and Hunter, "BDSM Practitioners' Understandings of Their Initial Attraction to BDSM Sexuality," 244.

14. E. Jozifkova, "Consensual Sadomasochistic Sex (BDSM): The Roots, the Risks, and the Distinctions Between BDSM and Violence," Current Psychiatric Reports 15, no. 9 (2013): 392.

15. J. Morin, The Erotic Mind (New York: Harper Perennial, 1995).

16. J. Powls and J. Davies, "A Descriptive Review of Research Relating to Sadomasochism: Considerations for Clinical Practice," Deviant Behavior 33, no. 3 (2012): 231.

17. L. Iannotti, "I Didn't Consent to That: Secondary Analysis of Discrimination Against BDSM Identified Individuals" (PhD diss., City University of New York, June 2014, https://academicworks.cuny.edu/gc_etds/229).

18. Buehler, What Every Mental Health Professional Needs to Know About Sex, 287.

19. R. Crooks and K. Baur, Our Sexuality, 13th ed. (Belmont, CA: Thomson Wadsworth, 2017).

20. C. Klesse, "Contesting the Culture of Monogamy: Consensual Nonmonogamies and Polyamory," in Introducing the New Sexuality Series, 3rd ed., ed. N Fischer and S. Seidman (London: Routledge, 2016), 325–336.

21. Klesse, "Contesting the Culture of Monogamy."

22. E. Levine, et al., "Open Relationships, Nonconsensual Nonmonogamy, and Monogamy Among U.S. Adults: Findings from the 2012 National Survey of Sexual Behavior and Health," Archives of Sexual Behavior 47 (2018): 1439–1450.

23. H. Fisher, Why We Love (New York: St Martin's Griffin, 2004), 121.

24. E. Sheff, The Polyamorists Next Door: Inside Multiple-Partner Relationships and Families (Lanham, MD: Rowman and Littlefield, 2014), 1.

25. Klesse, "Contesting the Culture of Monogamy," 332.

26. D. Williams and E. Prior, "Contemporary Polyamory: A Call for Awareness and Sensitivity in Social Work," Social Work 60, no. 3 (2015): 268.

27. Sheff, The Polyamorists Next Door, xi.

28. Sheff, The Polyamorists Next Door, 3.

29. Klesse, "Contesting the Culture of Monogamy"; Williams and Prior, "Contemporary Polyamory."

30. Crooks and Baur, Our Sexuality, 416.

31. Levine et al., "Open Relationships, Nonconsensual Nonmonogamy, and Monogamy Among U.S. Adults," 1439.

32. M. Haupert, et al., "Prevalence of Experiences with Consensual Nonmonogamous Relationships: Findings from Two National Samples of Single Americans." *Journal of Sex and Marital Therapy* 43, no. 5 (2017): 424.

33. Haupert et al., "Prevalence of Experiences with Consensual Nonmonogamous Relationships."

34. Haupert et al., "Prevalence of Experiences with Consensual Nonmonogamous Relationships," 424.

35. F. Veaux and E. Rickert, *More than Two: A Practical Guide to Ethical Polyamory* (Portland, OR: Thorntree Press, 2014), 150.

36. J. Hardy and D. Easton, *The Ethical Slut*, 3rd ed. (New York: Ten Speed Press, 2017); T. Taormino, *Opening Up: A Guide to Creating and Sustaining Open Relationships* (San Francisco: Cleis Press, 2008); Veaux and Rickert, *More than Two*.

37. Hardy and Easton, *The Ethical Slut*, 1.

38. Taormino, *Opening Up*.

39. Klesse, "Contesting the Culture of Monogamy," 333.

40. A. Wagner, "Making Peace with Jealousy in Polyamorous Relationships," accessed November 29, 2019, http://www.practicalpolyamory.com/images/Jealousy_Updated_10-6-10.pdf.

41. Taormino, *Opening Up*, 175.

42. Veaux and Rickert, *More than Two*, 399.

43. American Psychological Association, "Marriage and Divorce," accessed November 30, 2019, https://www.apa.org/topics/divorce/; Klesse, "Contesting the Culture of Monogamy," 328.

44. Levine et al., "Open Relationships, Nonconsensual Nonmonogamy, and Monogamy Among U.S. Adults," 1440.

45. Buehler, *What Every Mental Health Professional Needs to Know About Sex*, 120.

46. Williams and Prior, "Contemporary Polyamory," 269.

47. National Association of Social Workers, *Code of Ethics* (Washington, DC: National Association of Social Workers, 2017), 5.

48. G. Weitzman et al., "What Psychology Professionals Should Know About Polyamory," National Coalition for Sexual Freedom, accessed November 30, 2019, https://ncsfreedom.org/images/stories/pdfs/KAP/2010_poly_web.pdf, 17.

49. A. Bairstow, "Couples Exploring Nonmonogamy: Guidelines for Therapists," *Journal of Sex and Marital Therapy* 43, no. 4 (2017): 346.

50. K. Zimmerman, "Clients in Sexually Open Relationships: Considerations for Therapists." *Journal of Feminist Family Therapy* 24, no. 3 (2012): 272–289.

51. Bairstow, "Couples Exploring Nonmonogamy," 344.

52. Weitzman et al. "What Psychology Professionals Should Know About Polyamory."

53. Klesse, "Contesting the Culture of Monogamy."

54. D. Reynolds, "Disability and BDSM: Bob Flanagan and the Case for Sexual Rights," *Sexuality Research and Social Policy* 4 (2007): 40–52.

9. SEXUAL DYSFUNCTIONS AND DISORDERS

1. American Psychiatric Association, *Diagnostic and Statistical Manual of Mental Disorders*, 5th ed. (Arlington, VA: American Psychiatric Association, 2013).
2. S. Foley, "Biopsychosocial Assessment and Treatment of Sexual Problems in Older Age," *Current Sexual Health Reports* 7 (2015): 80–88.
3. Foley, "Biopsychosocial Assessment and Treatment of Sexual Problems in Older Age," 81.
4. R. Basson, "Human Sex-Response Cycles," *Journal of Sex and Marital Therapy* 27, no. 1 (January–February 2001): 33–43; A. Spurgas, "Interest, Arousal, and Shifting Diagnoses of Female Sexual Dysfunction, or: How Women Learn About Desire," *Studies in Gender and Sexuality* 14, no. 3 (2013): 187–205, and "Low Desire, Trauma, and Femininity in the DSM-5: A Case for Sequelae," *Psychology and Sexuality* 7, no. 1 (2016): 48–67.
5. American Psychiatric Association, *Diagnostic and Statistical Manual of Mental Disorders*, 5th ed., 433–437; Basson, "Human Sex-Response Cycles."
6. R. Crooks and K. Baur, *Our Sexuality*, 13th ed. (Belmont, CA: Thomson Wadsworth, 2017), 166–167.
7. Crooks and Baur, *Our Sexuality*, 166–167.
8. W. W. IsHak et al., "Sex and Natural Sexual Enhancement: Sexual Techniques, Aphrodisiac Foods, and Nutraceuticals," in *The Textbook of Clinical Sexual Medicine*, ed. W. W. IsHak (Cham, Switzerland: Springer International, 2017, 413–432.
9. IsHak et al., , "Sex and Natural Sexual Enhancement," 415.
10. Spurgas, "Interest, Arousal, and Shifting Diagnoses of Female Sexual Dysfunction," 187.
11. Basson, "Human Sex-Response Cycles."
12. C. Meston and A. Stanton, "Evaluation of Female Sexual Interest/Arousal Disorder," in *The Textbook of Clinical Sexual Medicine*, ed. W. W. IsHak (Cham, Switzerland: Springer International, 2017), 155–163.
13. R. Frost and C. Donovan, "Low Sexual Desire in Women: Amongst the Confusion, Could Distress Hold the Key?," *Sexual and Relationship Therapy* 30, no. 3 (2015): 338.
14. Frost and Donovan, "Low Sexual Desire in Women," 347.
15. S. Sarin, R. Amsel, and Y. Binik, "A Streetcar Named 'Derousal'? A Psychophysiological Examination of the Desire-Arousal Distinction in Sexually Functional and Dysfunctional Women," *Journal of Sex Research* 53, no. 6 (2016): 727.
16. W. W. IsHak and G. Tobia, "DSM-5 Changes in Diagnostic Criteria of Sexual Dysfunctions," *Reproductive System and Sexual Disorders* 2, no. 2 (2013): 1000122.
17. W. W. IsHak, "Evaluation and Treatment of Hypersexual and Other Sexual Dysfunctions," in *The Textbook of Clinical Sexual Medicine*, ed. W. IsHak (Cham, Switzerland: Springer International Publishing, 2017), 359.
18. SJ Dodd and L. Booker, "Practice with Lesbian Individuals and Couples," in *Social Work Practice with Lesbian, Gay, Bisexual, and Transgender People*, 3rd ed., ed. G. P. Mallon (New York: Haworth Press, 2018), 66–89.

19. K. Beier and K. Loewit, "Biopsychosocial Treatment of Sexual Dysfunctions," in *The Textbook of Clinical Sexual Medicine*, ed. W. W. IsHak (Cham, Switzerland: Springer International, 2017), 97.

20. W. W. Hudson, *Index of Sexual Satisfaction: The WALMYR Assessment Scales Scoring Manual* (Tallahassee, FL: WALMYR, 1993).

21. S. M. Lindberg, J. S. Hyde, and N. M. McKinley, "A Measure of Objectified Body Consciousness for Preadolescent and Adolescent Youth," *Psychology of Women Quarterly* 30, no. 1 (2006): 65–76; J. Mustapic, D. Marinko, and P. Vargek, "Body Shame and Disordered Eating in Adolescents," *Current Psychology* 36, no. 3 (2017): 447–452.

22. Meston and Stanton, "Evaluation of Female Sexual Interest/Arousal Disorder," 155.

23. American Psychiatric Association, *Diagnostic and Statistical Manual of Mental Disorders*, 5th ed., 426–429.

24. L. Sandberg, "Inventions of Hetero-Sex in Later Life: Beyond Dysfunction and the Coital Imperative," in *Introducing the New Sexuality Studies*, 3rd ed., ed. N. Fischer and S. Seidman (London: Routledge, 2016), 304–312.

25. P. Kempeneers et al., "Sexual Cognitions, Trait Anxiety, Sexual Anxiety, and Distress in Men with Different Subtypes of Premature Ejaculation and in Their Partners," *Journal of Sexual and Marital Therapy* 44, no. 4 (2018): 319–332.

26. A. El-Sakka, "Evaluation of Erectile Disorder," in *The Textbook of Clinical Sexual Medicine*, ed. W. W. IsHak (Cham, Switzerland: Springer International, 2017), 169–185.

27. El-Sakka, "Evaluation of Erectile Disorder," 169.

28. El-Sakka, "Evaluation of Erectile Disorder," 169.

29. C. Meston and A. Stanton, "Treatment of Female Sexual Interest/Arousal Disorder," in *The Textbook of Clinical Sexual Medicine*, ed. W. W. IsHak (Cham, Switzerland: Springer International, 2017), 165–168.

30. American Psychiatric Association, *Diagnostic and Statistical Manual of Mental Disorders*, 5th ed., 424–426, 429–432, 443–446.

31. S. Brody, "Evaluation of Female Orgasmic Disorder," in *The Textbook of Clinical Sexual Medicine*, ed. W. W. IsHak (Cham, Switzerland: Springer International, 2017), 203.

32. Crooks and Baur, *Our Sexuality*, 436.

33. Crooks and Baur, *Our Sexuality*, 438.

34. W. W. Hudson, *Index of Sexual Satisfaction*.

35. American Psychiatric Association, *Diagnostic and Statistical Manual of Mental Disorders*, 5th ed., 443.

36. M. Waldinger, "Evaluation of Rapid Ejaculation," in *The Textbook of Clinical Sexual Medicine*, ed. W. W. IsHak (Cham, Switzerland: Springer International, 2017), 273.

37. Crooks and Baur, *Our Sexuality*, 459.

38. M. Waldinger, "Evaluation of Rapid Ejaculation," 271.

39. American Psychiatric Association, DSM-5 Self-Exam: Sexual Dysfunctions. Psychiatric News (2013), https://doi.org/10.1176/appi.pn.2013.10b11.

40. M. A. Lahaie et al., "Can Fear, Pain, and Muscle Tension Discriminate Vaginismus from Dyspareunia/Provoked Vestibulodynia? Implications for the New DSM-5 Diag-

nosis of Genito-Pelvic Pain/Penetration Disorder," *Archives of Sexual Behavior* 44 (2015): 1538.

41. Quoted in IsHak and Tobia, "DSM-5 Changes in Diagnostic Criteria of Sexual Dysfunctions," 122.

42. Crooks and Baur, *Our Sexuality*, 458.

43. M. Ter Kuile et al., "Therapist-Aided Exposure for Women with Lifelong Vaginismus: A Randomized Waiting-List Control Trial of Efficacy," *Journal of Clinical Psychology* 81, no. 6 (2013): 1127–1136.

44. K. Merwin, L. O'Sullivan, and N. Rosen, "We Need to Talk: Disclosure of Sexual Problems Is Associated with Depression, Sexual Functioning, and Relationship Satisfaction in Women," *Journal of Sex and Marital Therapy* 43, no. 8 (2017): 786–800.

45. S. Buehler, *What Every Mental Health Professional Needs to Know About Sex* (New York: Springer, 2017), 291.

46. H. Cash et al., "Internet Addiction: A Brief Summary of Research and Practice," *Current Psychiatry Review* 8, no. 4 (2012): 292–298.

47. M. Kafka, "Hypersexual Disorder: A Proposed Diagnosis for DSM-V," *Archives of Sexual Behavior* 39, no. 2 (2010): 379.

48. M. Kafka, "What Happened to Hypersexual Disorder?," *Archives of Sexual Behavior* 43, no. 7 (2014): 1259–1261.

49. Kinsey, W. Pomeroy, and C. Martin, *Sexual Behavior in the Human Male* (Philadelphia: Saunders, 1948); L. Karila, A. Wery, A. Weinstein, O. Cottencin, A. Petit, M. Reynaud and J. Billieux, "Sexual Addiction or Hypersexual Disorder: Different Terms for the Same Problem?," *Current Pharmaceutical Design*, 20, 25, (2014): 4012; K. Rosenberg, P. Carnes, and S. O'Connor, "Evaluation and Treatment of Sex Addiction," *Journal of Sex and Marital Therapy* 40, no. 2 (2014): 77–91.

50. J. C. Barrilleaux, "Sexual Addiction: Definitions and Interventions," *Journal of Social Work Practice in the Addictions* 16, no. 4 (2016): 421–438.

51. Buehler, *What Every Mental Health Professional Needs to Know About Sex*, 292–293; W. W. IsHak, "Evaluation and Treatment of Hypersexual and Other Sexual Dysfunctions," 359–360; Rosenberg, Carnes, and O'Connor, "Evaluation and Treatment of Sex Addiction" 77; M. Walton et al., "Hypersexuality: A Critical Review and Introduction to the 'Sexhavior Cycle,'" *Archives of Sexual Behavior* 46, no. 8 (2017): 2231.

52. W. W. IsHak, "Evaluation and Treatment of Hypersexual and Other Sexual Dysfunctions."

53. W. W. IsHak, Evaluation and Treatment of Hypersexual and Other Sexual Dysfunctions."

54. W. W. IsHak, "Evaluation and Treatment of Hypersexual and Other Sexual Dysfunctions"; Walton et al., "Hypersexuality."

55. W. W. IsHak, "Evaluation and Treatment of Hypersexual and Other Sexual Dysfunctions."

56. P. Carnes, *Don't Call It Love: Recovering from Sexual Addiction* (New York: Bantam Books, 1991).

57. P. Carnes, *Don't Call It Love.*

58. P. Carnes, R. Murray, and L. Charpentier, "Bargains with Chaos: Sex Addicts and Addiction Interaction Disorder," *Sexual Addiction and Compulsivity* 12, nos. 2–3 (2005): 84. See also Rosenberg, Carnes, and O'Connor, "Evaluation and Treatment of Sex Addiction."

59. Buehler, *What Every Mental Health Professional Needs to Know About Sex*. 293; S. LeVay, J. I. Baldwin, and J. D. Baldwin, *Discovering Human Sexuality*, 3rd ed. (Sunderland, MA: Sinauer Associates, 2015), 451.

60. M. Crocker, "Out-of-Control Sexual Behavior as a Symptom of Insecure Attachment in Men," *Journal of Social Work Practice in the Addictions* 15, no. 4 (2015): 373–393; D. Timberlake et al., "Sexually Compulsive Behaviors: Implications for Attachment, Early Life Stressors, and Religiosity," *Sexual Addiction and Compulsivity* 23, no. 4 (2016): 361–373.

61. Crocker, "Out-of-Control Sexual Behavior as a Symptom of Insecure Attachment in Men," 373; Timberlake et al., "Sexually Compulsive Behaviors," 363.

62. Crocker, "Out-of-Control Sexual Behavior as a Symptom of Insecure Attachment in Men," 371.

63. LeVay, Baldwin, and Baldwin, *Discovering Human Sexuality*, 451.

64. Barrilleaux, "Sexual Addiction"; Buehler, *What Every Mental Health Professional Needs to Know About Sex*; W. W. IsHak, "Evaluation and Treatment of Hypersexual and Other Sexual Dysfunctions"; Kafka, "Hypersexual Disorder"; LeVay, Baldwin, and Baldwin, *Discovering Human Sexuality*; Rosenberg, Carnes, and O'Connor, "Evaluation and Treatment of Sex Addiction."

65. Buehler, *What Every Mental Health Professional Needs to Know About Sex*, 279.

66. American Psychiatric Association, *Diagnostic and Statistical Manual of Mental Disorders*, 5th ed., 685.

67. American Psychiatric Association, *Diagnostic and Statistical Manual of Mental Disorders*, 5th ed., 685–705.

68. R. Sorrentino, "DSM-5 and Paraphilias: What Psychiatrists Need to Know," *Psychiatric Times* 33, no. 11 (November 28, 2016), https://www.psychiatrictimes.com/dsm-5/dsm-5-and-paraphilias-what-psychiatrists-need-know.

69. M. Kaplan and R. Krueger, "Cognitive-Behavioral Treatment for Paraphilias," *Israel Journal of Psychiatry and Related Sciences* 49, no. 4 (2012): 291–296.

10. ETHICS AND THE SEX-POSITIVE SOCIAL WORKER

1. National Association of Social Workers, *Code of Ethics* (Washington, DC: National Association of Social Workers, 2017).

2. G. Aguilar and C. Williams, "Sexual Ethics: A Comparative Study of MSWs and BSWs," *Journal of Baccalaureate Social Work* 11, no. 1 (2005): 58–70.

3. R. Dolgoff and L. Skolnik, "Ethical Decision Making, the NASW Code of Ethics and Group Work Practice: Beginning Explorations," *Social Work with Groups* 15, no. 4 (1992): 100.

4. Dolgoff and Skolnik, "Ethical Decision Making," 100.

5. National Association of Social Workers, *Code of Ethics*, 1.

6. National Association of Social Workers, *Code of Ethics*, 5.

7. National Association of Social Workers, *Code of Ethics*, 5.

8. National Association of Social Workers, *Code of Ethics*, 5.

9. National Association of Social Workers, *Code of Ethics*, 5.

10. F. Reamer, *Social Work Values and Ethics*, 4th ed. (New York: Columbia University Press, 2013), 33.

11. C. P. McCullough and S. E. Patterson, "'No Lectures or Stink-Eye': The Healthcare Needs of People in the Sex Trade in New York City," Persist Health Project, April 2014, http://media.wix.com/ugd/6ddedf_5c3c4b0d5fe84af89a543f8eeacead4c.pdf.

12. National Association of Social Workers, *Code of Ethics*, 6.

13. National Association of Social Workers, *Code of Ethics*, 6.

14. A. Dailey, "Violating Boundaries," *Studies in Gender and Sexuality* 18, no. 1 (2017): 13.

15. National Association of Social Workers, *Code of Ethics*, 15.

16. Aguilar and Williams, "Sexual Ethics," 63.

17. F. Reamer, "Boundary Issues in Social Work: Managing Dual Relationships," *Social Work* 48, no. 1 (2003): 124.

18. K. J. Strom-Gotfried, "Professional Boundaries: An Analysis of Violations by Social Workers" *Families in Society* 80, no. 5 (1999): 442.

19. S. Jayaratne, T. Croxton, and D. Mattison, "Social Work Professional Standards: An Exploratory Study," *Social Work* 42, no. 2 (1997): 191.

20. Reamer, *Social Work Values and Ethics*. 167.

21. L. Housman and J. Stake, "The Current State of Ethics Training in Clinical Psychology: Issues of Quantity, Quality, and Effectiveness," *Professional Psychology* 30, no. 3 (1999): 302–311.

22. C. Berkman et al., "Sexual Contact with Clients: Assessment of Social Workers' Attitudes and Educational Preparation," *Social Work* 45, no. 3 (2000): 223.

23. Aguilar and Williams, "Sexual Ethics," 63–64.

24. T. Koenig and R. Spano, "Sex, Supervision, and Boundary Violations: Pressing Challenges and Possible Solutions," *Clinical Supervisor* 22, no. 1 (2003): 4.

25. National Association of Social Workers, *Code of Ethics*, 19.

26. National Association of Social Workers, *Code of Ethics*, 6.

27. Guttmacher Institute, "An Overview of Consent to Reproductive Health Services by Young People," November 1, 2019, https://www.guttmacher.org/state-policy/explore/overview-minors-consent-law.

28. SJ Dodd, "Identifying the Discomfort: An Examination of Ethical Issues Encountered by MSW Students During Field Placement," *Journal of Teaching in Social Work* 27, nos. 1–2 (2007): 1–19.

29. National Association of Social Workers, *Code of Ethics*, 6.

30. G. Gabbard, "On Love and Lust in Erotic Transference," *Journal of the American Psychoanalytic Association* 42, no. 2 (1994): 385–403.

31. S. Mourra, "Sexualized Transference in Older Adults," *Psychiatric Times*, September 26, 2014, 1.

32. A. Stefana, "Erotic Transference," *British Journal of Psychotherapy* 33, no. 4 (2017): 505–513.

33. A. Rachman, R. Kennedy, and M. Yard, "Erotic Transference and Its Relationship to Childhood Seduction," *Psychoanalytic Social Work* 16 (2009): 12–30.

34. Mourra, "Sexualized Transference in Older Adults," 1.

35. A. Frias et al., "Sexual Feelings Toward the Therapist Among Patients with Borderline Personality Disorder: A Case of Erotomanic Delusional Disorder," *Archives of Sexual Behavior* 44 (2015): 3–4.

36. S. Buehler, *What Every Mental Health Professional Needs to Know About Sex* (New York: Springer, 2017), 305–306.

37. E. Jackson, "Too Close for Comfort: The Challenges of Engaging with Sexuality in Work with Adolescents," *Journal of Child Psychotherapy* 43, no. 1 (2017): 6–22.

38. Jayaratne, Croxton, and Mattison, "Social Work Professional Standards," 192.

39. National Association of Social Workers, *Code of Ethics*.

40. Berkman et al., "Sexual Contact with Clients"; Aguilar and Williams, "Sexual Ethics."

41. Housman and Stake, "The Current State of Ethics Training in Clinical Psychology"; Reamer, *Social Work Values and Ethics*, 124.

CONCLUSION

1. National Association of Social Workers, *Code of Ethics* (Washington, DC: National Association of Social Workers, 2017).

2. J. Gochros, "Talking About Sex," in *Human Sexuality and Social Work*, ed. H. Gochros and L. Schultz (New York: Association Press, 1972), 97.

BIBLIOGRAPHY

Ageisnotacondom.org. Home page. Accessed November 23, 2019. http://ageisnotacondom.org
/en/home/.

Aguilar, G., and Williams, C. "Sexual Ethics: A Comparative Study of MSWs and BSWs."
Journal of Baccalaureate Social Work 11, no. 1 (2005): 58–70.

Ainsworth, M. "Attachments Beyond Infancy." *American Psychologist* 44 (1989): 709–716.

——. "Infant-Mother Attachment." *American Psychologist* 34 (1979): 932–937.

Ainsworth, M., M. Blehar, E. Walters, and S. Walls. *Patterns of Attachment: A Psychological
Study of the Strange Situation.* Hillsdale, NJ: Erlbaum, 1978.

American Academy of Pediatrics, Promoting Healthy Sexual Development and Sexuality. In
Bright Futures. Guidelines for Health Supervision of Infants, Children, and Adolescents.
217–227. https://brightfutures.aap.org/Bright%20Futures%20Documents/BF4_Healthy
Sexuality.pdf.

American Cancer Society. "Key Statistics for Testicular Cancer." January 8, 2019. https://www
.cancer.org/cancer/testicular-cancer/about/key-statistics.html.

American Psychiatric Association. *Diagnostic and Statistical Manual of Mental Disorders.* Washington, DC: Author, 1952.

——. *Diagnostic and Statistical Manual of Mental Disorders.* 2nd ed. Washington, DC: American Psychiatric Association, 1968.

——. *Diagnostic and Statistical Manual of Mental Disorders.* 3rd ed. Arlington, VA: American
Psychiatric Association, 1980.

——. *Diagnostic and Statistical Manual of Mental Disorders.* 3rd ed. Revised (III-R) Arlington,
VA: American Psychiatric Association, 1987.

——. *Diagnostic and Statistical Manual of Mental Disorders*. 5th ed. Arlington, VA: American Psychiatric Association, 2013.

——. *Diagnostic and Statistical Manual of Mental Disorders*. 6th ed. Arlington, VA: American Psychiatric Association, 1974.

——. *What Is Gender Dysphoria?* n.d. https://www.psychiatry.org/patients-families/gender -dysphoria/what-is-gender-dysphoria.

American Psychological Association. "Marriage and Divorce." Accessed November 30, 2019. https://www.apa.org/topics/divorce.

American Sexual Health Association. "Sexual Rights for Seniors." Accessed November 29, 2019. http://www.ashasexualhealth.org/sexual-rights-for-seniors/.

Amichai-Hamburger, Y., and S. Etgar. "Intimacy and Smartphone Multitasking—a New Oxymoron?" *Psychological Reports* 119, no. 3 (2016): 826–838.

Annon, J. S. *Behavioral Treatment of Sexual Problems: Brief Therapy*. Oxford, UK: Harper and Row, 1976.

Ansara, Y. G., and I. Berger. "Cisgenderism." In *The Wiley Blackwell Encyclopedia of Gender and Sexuality Studies*, ed. N. Naples, R. C. Hoogland, M. Wickramasinghe, and W. C. A. Wong. Oxford: Blackwell, 2016.

Association of Reproductive Health Professionals. "What You Need to Know About Female Sexual Response." Fact sheet. March 2008. http://www.arhp.org/uploadDocs/FSRfactsheet .pdf#search=%22intimacy%22.

Austin, A., S. L. Craig, and L. B. McInroy. "Toward Transgender Affirmative Social Work Education." *Journal of Social Work Education* 52, no. 3 (2016): 297–310.

Bairstow, A. "Couples Exploring Nonmonogamy: Guidelines for Therapists." *Journal of Sex and Marital Therapy* 43, no. 4 (2017): 343–353.

Ballon, M. "Disability and Sexuality Within Social Work Education in the USA and Canada: The Social Model of Disability as a Lens for Practice." *Social Work Education* 27, no. 2 (2008): 194–202.

Barrilleaux, J. C. "Sexual Addiction: Definitions and Interventions." *Journal of Social Work Practice in the Addictions* 16, no. 4 (2016): 421–438.

Bassil, N., S. Alkaade, and J. E. Morley. "The Benefits and Risks of Testosterone Replacement Therapy: A Review." *Therapeutics and Clinical Risk Management* 5, no. 3 (June 2009): 427–448.

Basson, R. "Human Sex-Response Cycles." *Journal of Sex and Marital Therapy* 27, no. 1 (January–February 2001): 33–43.

——. "Women's Sexual Dysfunction: Revised and Expanded Definitions." *Canadian Medical Association Journal* 172, no. 10 (2005): 1327–1333.

Bauer, G., and D. Brennan. "The Problem with 'Behavioral Bisexuality': Assessing Sexual Orientation in Survey Research." *Journal of Bisexuality* 13, no. 2 (2013): 148–165.

Bay-Cheng, L. Y. "Human Sexuality." In *Encyclopedia of Social Work*, ed. C. Franklin. Online ed. Washington, DC: NASW Press, 2013. https://oxfordre.com/socialwork.

——. "Justifying Sex: The Place of Women's Sexuality on a Social Justice Agenda." *Families in Society* 91, no. 1 (2010): 97–103.

———. "Recovering Empowerment: De-Personalizing and Re-Politicizing Adolescent Female Sexuality (Commentary)." *Sex Roles* 66, nos. 11–12 (2012): 713–717.

Beier, K., and K. Loewit. "Biopsychosocial Treatment of Sexual Dysfunctions." In *The Textbook of Clinical Sexual Medicine*, ed. W. W. IsHak, 95–120. Cham, Switzerland: Springer International, 2017.

Ben-Ze'ev, A., and L. Brunning. "How Complex Is Your Love? The Case of Romantic Compromises and Polyamory." *Journal for the Theory of Social Behaviour* 48, no. 1 (2018): 98–116.

Berkman, C., S. Turner, M. Cooper, D. Polnerow, and M. Swartz. "Sexual Contact with Clients: Assessment of Social Workers' Attitudes and Educational Preparation." *Social Work* 45, no. 3 (2000): 223–235.

Berkman, C., and G. Zinberg. "Homphobia and Heterosexism in Social Workers." *Social Work* 42, no. 4 (1997): 319–332.

Blackless, M., A. Charuvastra, A. Derryck, and A. Faustos. "How Sexually Dimorphic Are We? Review and Synthesis." *American Journal of Human Biology* 12, no. 2 (2000):151–166.

Blonna, L., and R. Carter. *Healthy Sexuality.* 3rd ed. Dubuque, IA: Kendall Hunt, 2013.

Bogaert, A. "Asexuality: Prevalence and Associated Factors in a National Probability Sample." *Journal of Sex Research* 41, no. 3 (2004): 279–287.

Bostwick, W. B., C. J. Boyd, T. L. Hughes, B. T. West, and S. E. McCabe. "Discrimination and Mental Health Among Lesbian, Gay, and Bisexual Adults in the United States." *American Journal of Orthopsychiatry* 84, no. 1 (2014): 35–45.

Bowlby, J. *Attachment and Loss.* New York: Basic Books, 1969.

Bradford, M. "The Bisexual Experience: Living in a Dichotomous Culture." *Journal of Bisexuality* 4, nos. 1–2 (2004): 7–23.

Braun, V., and L. Tiefer. "The 'Designer Vagina' and the Pathologisation of Female Genital Diversity: Interventions for Change." *Radical Psychology* 8, no. 1 (2010).

Breastcancer.org. "Breast Self-Exam." October 24, 2019. https://www.breastcancer.org/symptoms /testing/types/self_exam.

Brody, S. "Evaluation of Female Orgasmic Disorder." In *The Textbook of Clinical Sexual Medicine*, ed. W. W. IsHak, 203–218. Cham, Switzerland: Springer International, 2017.

Bronfenbrenner, U. *The Ecology of Human Development: Experiments by Nature and Design.* Cambridge, MA.: Harvard University Press, 1979.

Brotto, L., and M. Yule. "Asexuality: Sexual Orientation, Paraphilia, Sexual Dysfunction, or None of the Above?" *Archives of Sexual Behavior* 46 (2017): 619–627.

Bucchianeri, M. M., N. Fernandes, K. Loth, P. J. Hannan, M. E. Eisenberg, and D. Neumark-Sztainer. "Body Dissatisfaction: Do Associations with Disordered Eating and Psychological Well-Being Differ Across Race/Ethnicity in Adolescent Girls and Boys?" *Cultural Diversity and Ethnic Minority Psychology* 22, no. 1 (2016): 137–146.

Buehler, S. *What Every Mental Health Professional Needs to Know About Sex.* New York: Springer, 2017.

Burdge, B. "Bending Gender, Ending Gender: Theoretical Foundations for Social Work Practice with the Transgender Community." *Social Work* 52, no. 3 (2007): 243–250.

Butler, J. *Gender Trouble: Feminism and the Subversion of Identity.* New York: Routledge, 2006.

Butler, R. M., A. Horenstein, M. Gitlin, R. J. Testa, S. C. Kaplan, M. B. Swee, and R. G. Heimberg. "Social Anxiety Among Transgender and Gender Nonconforming Individuals: The Role of Gender-Affirming Medical Interventions." Journal of Abnormal Psychology 128, no. 1 (2019): 25–31.

Bywater, J., and R. Jones. *Sexuality and Social Work*. Exeter, UK: Learning Matters, 2007.

Callis, A. "Beyond Bi: Sexual Fluidity, Identity, and the Post-Bisexual Revolution." In *Introducing the New Sexuality Studies*, 3rd ed., ed. N. Fischer and S. Seidman, 215–224. London: Routledge, 2016.

Campbell, E. C., and C. E. Murray. "Measuring the Impact of Technology on Couple Relationships: The Development of the Technology and Intimate Relationship." *Journal of Couple and Relationship Therapy* 14 (2015): 254–276.

Carnes, P. *Don't Call It Love: Recovering from Sexual Addiction*. New York: Bantam Books, 1991.

Carnes, P., R. Murray, and L. Charpentier. "Bargains with Chaos: Sex Addicts and Addiction Interaction Disorder." *Sexual Addiction and Compulsivity* 12, nos. 2–3 (2005): 79–120.

Carter, D. "Comprehensive Sex Education for Teens Is More Effective Than Abstinence." *American Journal of Nursing* 112, no. 3 (2012): 15.

Cash, H., C. Rae, A. Steel, and A. Winkler. "Internet Addiction: A Brief Summary of Research and Practice." *Current Psychiatry Review* 8, no. 4 (2012): 292–298.

Cass, V. "Homosexual Identity Formation: A Theoretical Model." *Journal of Homosexuality* 4, no. 3 (1979): 219–235.

Centers for Disease Control and Prevention. *A Guide to Taking a Sexual History*. Accessed November 23, 2019. https://www.cdc.gov/std/treatment/sexualhistory.pdf.

——. *HIV Surveillance Report, 2017*, vol. 29. November 2018. https://www.cdc.gov/hiv/pdf/library/reports/surveillance/cdc-hiv-surveillance-report-2017-vol-29.pdf.

——. *Sexually Transmitted Disease Surveillance, 2018*. https://www.cdc.gov/std/stats18/syphilis.htm.

Chivers, M., G. Rieger, E. Latty, and J. Bailey. "A Sex Difference in the Specificity of Arousal." *Psychological Science* 15, no. 11 (2004): 736–744.

Choi, S. K., B. D. M. Wilson, J. Shelton, and G. Gates. *Serving Our Youth 2015: The Needs and Experiences of Lesbian, Gay, Bisexual, Transgender, and Questioning Youth Experiencing Homelessness*. Los Angeles: Williams Institute, 2015.

Claiborne, N., and V. M. Rizzo. "Addressing Sexual Issues in Individuals with Chronic Health Conditions [Practice Forum]." *Health and Social Work* 31, no. 3 (2006): 221–224.

Cochran, S. D., V. M. Mays, and J. G. Sullivan. "Prevalence of Mental Disorders, Psychological Distress, and Mental Health Services Use Among Lesbian, Gay, and Bisexual Adults in the United States." *Journal of Consulting and Clinical Psychology* 71, no. 1 (2003): 53–61.

Costa, P. A., R. Rosas, F. Pimenta, J. Maroco, and I. Leal. "Andropause Symptoms Severity Inventory (ASSI): Preliminary Study with a Portuguese Sample." *Maturitas* no. 100 (2017): 182–183.

Cottrell, B. H., and F. T. Close. "Vaginal Douching Among University Women in the Southeastern United States." *Journal of American College Health* 56, no. 4 (2008): 415–421.

Council on Social Work Education. "2015 Educational Policy and Accreditation Standards."
June 11, 2015. https://www.cswe.org/getattachment/Accreditation/Accreditation-Process
/2015-EPAS/2015EPAS_Web_FINAL.pdf.aspx.

——. *EPAS Handbook.* 2017. https://www.cswe.org/Accreditation/Standards-and-Policies
/EPAS-Handbook.

Cranney, S. "Does Asexuality Meet the Stability Criterion for a Sexual Orientation?" *Archives
of Sexual Behavior* 46, no. 3 (2017): 637–638.

Crocker, M. "Out-of-Control Sexual Behavior as a Symptom of Insecure Attachment in Men."
Journal of Social Work Practice in the Addictions 15, no. 4 (2015): 373–393.

Crolley-Simic, J., M. E. Vonk, and W. Ellsworth. "A School Social Worker's Impact on a
Human Sexuality Program." *School Social Work Journal* 31, no. 2 (2007): 17–32.

Crooks, R., and K. Baur. *Our Sexuality.* 13th ed. Belmont, CA: Thomson Wadsworth, 2017.

——. *Our Sexuality.* 12th ed. Belmont, CA: Thomson Wadsworth, 2014.

——. *Our Sexuality: Instructor's Manual.* 11th ed. Belmont, CA: Wadsworth/Cengage Learning, 2011.

Dailey, A. "Violating Boundaries." *Studies in Gender and Sexuality* 18, no. 1 (2017): 13–18.

Davis, C. "Practice with Transgender People." In *Social Work Practice with Lesbian, Gay,
Bisexual, and Transgender People*, 3rd ed., ed. G. P. Mallon, 42–65. New York: Routledge,
2018.

De Boer, A., E. Van Buel, and G. Ter Horst. "Love Is More Than Just a Kiss: A Neurobiological Perspective on Love and Affection." *Neuroscience*, 201 (2012): 114–124.

De La Cruz, N., D. L. Cornish, R. Mccree-Hale, L. Annang, and D. M. Grimley. "Attitudes
and Sociocultural Factors Influencing Vaginal Douching Behavior Among English-
Speaking Latinas." *American Journal of Health Behavior* 33, no. 5 (2009): 558–568.

DeLameter, J., and W. Friedrich. "Human Sexual Development." *Journal of Sex Research* 39,
no. 1 (2002): 10–14.

Diamond, L. *Sexual Fluidity: Understanding Women's Love and Desire.* Cambridge, MA: Harvard University Press, 2008.

DiAngelo, R. "Heterosexism: Addressing Internalized Dominance." *Journal of Progressive
Human Service* 8, no. 1 (1997): 5–21.

Dodd, SJ. "Identifying the Discomfort: An Examination of Ethical Issues Encountered by
MSW Students During Field Placement." *Journal of Teaching in Social Work* 27, nos. 1–2
(2007): 1–19.

——. "LGBTQ Poverty in NYC: Busting the Gay Affluence Myth." In *Worse Than You Think:
The Dimensions of Poverty in NYC.*, ed. M. Sullivan, 55–58. New York: National Association of Social Workers, New York City Chapter, 2014.

Dodd, SJ, and L. Booker. "Practice with Lesbian Individuals and Couples." In *Social Work Practice with Lesbian, Gay, Bisexual, and Transgender People*, 3rd ed., ed. G. P. Mallon, 66–89.
New York: Routledge, 2018.

Dodd, SJ, and C. Katz. "Sex Positive Social Work: Integrating Content Into HBSE and Beyond." *Journal of Teaching in Social Work* 40, no. 1 (2020): 48–57.

Dodd, SJ, and D. Tolman. "Reviving a Positive Discourse on Sexuality Within Social Work."
Social Work 62, no. 3 (2017): 227–234.

Dodge, B., and T. Sandfort. "A Review of Mental Health Research on Bisexual Individuals When Compared to Homosexual and Heterosexual Individuals." In *Becoming Visible: Counseling Bisexuals Across the Lifespan*, ed. B. A. Firestein, 28–51. New York: Columbia University Press, 2007.

Dolgoff, R., and L. Skolnik. "Ethical Decision Making, the NASW Code of Ethics and Group Work Practice: Beginning Explorations." *Social Work with Groups* 15, no. 4 (1992): 99–112.

Dunk, P. "Everyday Sexuality and Social Work: Locating Sexuality in Professional Practice and Education." *Social Work and Society* 5, no. 2 (2007): 135–142.

Dunn, M. E., and N. Cutler. "Sexual Issues in Older Adults." *AIDS Patient Care and STDs* 14, no. 2 (2000): 67–69.

Ekpenyong, C. E., and E. A. Etukumana. "Ethnicity, Family Socioeconomic Inequalities, and Prevalence of Vaginal Douching Among College Students: The Implication for Health." *Journal of American College Health* 61, no. 4 (2013): 222–230.

El-Sakka, A. "Evaluation of Erectile Disorder." In *The Textbook of Clinical Sexual Medicine*, ed. W. W. IsHak, 169–185. Cham, Switzerland: Springer International, 2017.

Engle, G. "Anal Sex: Safety, How Tos, Tips, and More." *Teen Vogue*, November 12, 2019. https://www.teenvogue.com/story/anal-sex-what-you-need-to-know.

Enke, A. *Transfeminist Perspectives in and Beyond Transgender Studies*. Philadelphia: Temple University Press, 2012.

Erikson, E. H. *Identity and the Life Cycle*. New York: International Universities Press, 1959.

Farrell, K., N. Gupta, and M. Queen. *Interrupting Heteronormativity: Lesbian, Gay, Bisexual, and Transgender Pedagogy and Responsible Teaching at Syracuse University*. Syracuse, NY: Syracuse University Press, 2004.

Ferro, S. "Homophobia Is Bad for the Economy." *Business Insider*, July 1, 2015. http://www.businessinsider.com/ubs-homophobia-is-bad-for-the-economy-2015-7.

Fine, M. "Sexuality, Schooling, and Adolescent Females: The Missing Discourse of Desire." *Harvard Educational Review* 58, no. 1 (1988): 29–54.

Fine, M., and S. McClelland. "Sexuality Education and Desire: Still Missing After All These Years." *Harvard Educational Review* 76, no. 3 (2006): 297–338.

Firestein, B., ed. *Bisexuality: The Psychology and Politics of an Invisible Minority*. Thousand Oaks, Calif.: Sage.

Fischer, N., and S. Seidman, eds. *Introducing the New Sexuality Studies*. 3rd ed. London: Routledge, 2016.

Fisher, H. *Why We Love*. New York: Henry Holt, 2004.

Fjelstrom, J. "Sexual Orientation Change Efforts and Search for Authenticity." *Journal of Homosexuality* 60, no. 6 (2013): 801–827.

Flanders, C., L. Tarasoff, M. Legge, M. Robinson, and G. Gos. "Positive Identity Experiences of Young Bisexual and Other Nonmonosexual People: A Qualitative Inquiry." *Journal of Homosexuality* 64, no. 8 (2017): 1014–1032.

Foley, S. "Biopsychosocial Assessment and Treatment of Sexual Problems in Older Age." *Current Sexual Health Reports* 7, no. 2 (2015): 80–88.

Francoeur, R. *Becoming a Sexual Person*. 2nd ed. New York: Macmillan, 1991.

Fredriksen-Goldsen, K. I. "The Future of LGBT+ Aging: A Blueprint for Action in Services, Policies, and Research." *Generations* 40, no. 2 (2016): 6–15.

Fredriksen-Goldsen, K. I., and H. J. Kim. "The Science of Conducting Research with LGBT Older Adults: An Introduction to Aging with Pride: National Health, Aging, and Sexuality/Gender Study." *Gerontologist* 57, no. 1 (2017): S1–S14.

Freud, S. *Three Essays on the Theory of Sexuality*. Trans. James Strachey. New York: Basic Books, 1962.

Frias, A., C. Palma, N. Farriols, and B. Martinez. "Sexual Feelings Toward the Therapist Among Patients with Borderline Personality Disorder: A Case of Erotomanic Delusional Disorder." *Archives of Sexual Behavior* 44 (2015): 3–4.

Frost, R., and C. Donovan. "Low Sexual Desire in Women: Amongst the Confusion, Could Distress Hold the Key?" *Sexual and Relationship Therapy* 30, no. 3 (2015): 338–350.

Funkhouser, E., T. D. Hayes, and S. H. Vermund. "Vaginal Douching Practices Among Women Attending a University in the Southern United States." *Journal of American College Health* 50, no. 4 (2002): 177–182.

Funkhouser, E., L. Pulley, G. Lueschen, C. Costello, E. I. Hook, and S. H. Vermund. "Douching Beliefs and Practices Among Black and White Women." *Journal of Women's Health and Gender-Based Medicine* 11, no. 1 (2002): 29–37.

Gabbard, G. "On Love and Lust in Erotic Transference." *Journal of the American Psychoanalytic Association* 42, no. 2 (1994): 385–403.

Gagnon, J., and W. Simon. *Sexual Conduct: The Social Sources of Human Sexuality*. Chicago: Aldine, 1973.

Gavey, N. "Viagra and the Coital Imperative." In *Introducing the New Sexuality Studies*, 3rd ed., ed. N. Fischer and S. Seidman, 74–80. London: Routledge, 2016.

Gender Identity Project. "Transgender Basics." August 10, 2009. https://www.youtube.com/watch?v=UXI9woPbBXY.

Giunta, N., and N. Rowan. *Lesbian, Gay, Bisexual, and Transgender Aging: The Role of Gerontological Social Work*. London: Routledge, 2015.

Gochros, J. "Talking About Sex." In *Human Sexuality and Social Work*, ed. H. Gochros and L. Schultz, 92–101. New York: Association Press, 1972.

Godow, A. "Playful Sexuality." *Contemporary Sexuality* 33, nos. 1–2 (1999).

Gottman, J. "The 6 Things That Predict Divorce." *Gottman Relationship Blog*. Accessed November 29, 2019. https://www.gottman.com/blog/the-6-things-that-predict-divorce/.

——. *Why Marriages Succeed or Fail*. New York: Simon and Schuster, 1994.

Graham, C., and M. Smith. "Operationalizing the Concept of Sexuality Comfort: Applications for Sexuality Educators." *Journal for Sexual Health* 54 (1984): 439–442.

Greenberg, J., C. Bruess, and S. Oswalt. *Exploring the Dimensions of Human Sexuality*. 5th ed. Burlington, MA: Jones and Bartlett Learning, 2017.

Grimley, D. M., L. Annang, H. R. Foushee, F. C. Bruce, and J. S. Kendrick. "Vaginal Douches and Other Feminine Hygiene Products: Women's Practices and Perceptions of Product Safety." *Maternal and Child Health Journal* 10, no. 3 (2006): 303–310.

Guilamo-Ramos, V., P. Dittus, J. Jaccard, V. Goldberg, E. Casillas, and A. Bouris. "The Content and Process of Mother-Adolescent Communication About Sex in Latino Families." *Social Work Research* 30, no. 3 (2006): 169–181.

Guttmacher Institute. "An Overview of Consent to Reproductive Health Services by Young People." November 1, 2019. https://www.guttmacher.org/state-policy/explore/overview-minors-consent-law.

Hardy, J., and D. Easton. *The Ethical Slut*. 3rd ed. New York: Ten Speed Press, 2017.

Harlow, H. "The Nature of Love." *American Psychologist* 13, no. 12 (1958): 673–685.

Harris, S., and K. Hays. "Family Therapist Comfort with and Willingness to Discuss Client Sexuality." *Journal of Marital and Family Therapy* 34, no. 2 (2008): 239–250.

Harris-Hastick, E., and C. Modeste-Curwen. "The Importance of Culture in HIV/AIDS Prevention in Grenada." *Journal of HIV/AIDS Prevention and Education for Adolescents and Children* 4, no. 4 (2001): 5–22.

Haupert, M., A. Gesselman, A. Moors, H. Fisher, and J. Garcia. "Prevalence of Experiences with Consensual Nonmonogamous Relationships: Findings from Two National Samples of Single Americans." *Journal of Sex and Marital Therapy* 43, no. 5 (2017): 424–440.

Helgason, A. R., J. Adolfsson, P. Dickman, S. Arver, M. Fredrikson, M. Gothberg, and G. Steinbeck. "Sexual Desire, Erection, Orgasm, and Ejaculatory Functions and Their Importance to Elderly Swedish Men: A Population Based Study." *Age and Ageing* 25, no. 4 (1996): 285–291.

Henley, A. "Why Sex Education for Disabled People Is So Important." *Teen Vogue*, October 5, 2017. https://www.teenvogue.com/story/disabled-sex-ed.

Herbenick, D., V. Schick, M. Reece, S. Sanders, and J. Fortenberry. "Pubic Hair Removal Among Women in the United States: Prevalence, Methods, and Characteristics." *Journal of Sexual Medicine* 7, no. 10 (2010): 3322–3330.

Herek, G. M. "The Psychology of Sexual Prejudice." *Current Directions in Psychological Science* 9, no. 1 (2000): 19–22.

Hernandez, D. "The Effects of Consuming Pornography: Men's Attitudes Toward Violence Against Women, Dominance Over and Objectification of Women, and Sexual Expectations of Women." *Perspectives* 3, no. 1 (2011): 116–123.

Hooker, E. "The Adjustment of the Male Overt Homosexual." *Journal of Projective Techniques* 21, no. 1 (1957): 18–31.

Housman, L., and J. Stake. "The Current State of Ethics Training in Clinical Psychology: Issues of Quantity, Quality, and Effectiveness." *Professional Psychology* 30, no. 3 (1999): 302–311.

Hudson, W. W. *Index of Sexual Satisfaction*. The WALMYR Assessment Scales Scoring Manual. Tallahassee, FL: WALMYR, 1993.

Human Rights Campaign. "Violence Against the Transgender Community in 2018." Accessed November 28, 2019. https://www.hrc.org/resources/violence-against-the-transgender-community-in-2018.

Hutchinson, E. D. *Dimensions of Human Behavior: The Changing Life Course*. Thousand Oaks, CA: SAGE Publications 2015.

Iannotti, L. "I Didn't Consent to That: Secondary Analysis of Discrimination Against BDSM Identified Individuals." PhD diss., City University of New York, June 2014. https://academicworks.cuny.edu/gc_etds/229.

BIBLIOGRAPHY

Iasenza, S. "What Is Queer About Sex? Expanding Sexual Frames in Theory and Practice." *Family Process* 49, no. 3 (2010): 291–308.

International Society for Sexual Medicine, (2017). "What Does 'Sex Positive' Mean?" https://www.issm.info/sexual-health-qa/what-does-sex-positive-mean/.

IsHak, W. W. "Evaluation and Treatment of Hypersexual and Other Sexual Dysfunctions." In *The Textbook of Clinical Sexual Medicine*, ed. W. W. IsHak, 359–363. Cham, Switzerland: Springer International, 2017.

IsHak, W. W., S. Clevenger, R. Pechnick, and T. Parisi. "Sex and Natural Sexual Enhancement: Sexual Techniques, Aphrodisiac Foods, and Nutraceuticals." In *The Textbook of Clinical Sexual Medicine*, ed. W. W. IsHak, 413–432. Cham, Switzerland: Springer International, 2017.

Ishak, W. W., and G. Tobia. "DSM-5 Changes in Diagnostic Criteria of Sexual Dysfunctions." *Reproductive System and Sexual Disorders* 2, no. 2 (2013): 100022 (3 pages).

Jackson, E. "Too Close for Comfort: The Challenges of Engaging with Sexuality in Work with Adolescents." *Journal of Child Psychotherapy* 43, no. 1 (2017): 6–22.

James, S., J. Herman, S. Rankin, M. Keisling, L. Mottet, and M. Anafi. *The Report of the 2015 U.S. Transgender Survey*. Washington, DC: National Center for Transgender Equality, 2016.

Jayaratne, S., T. Croxton, and D. Mattison. "Social Work Professional Standards: An Exploratory Study." *Social Work* 42, no. 2 (1997): 187–199.

Johnson, B. "Sexually Transmitted Infections and Older Adults." *Journal of Gerontological Nursing* 39, no. 11 (2013): 53–60.

Joint Commission. *Advancing Effective Communication, Cultural Competence, and Patient- and Family- Centered Care for the Lesbian, Gay, Bisexual, and Transgender (LGBT) Community: A Field Guide*. Oak Brook, IL, Oct. 2011.

Joyal, C. C., A. Cossette, and V. Lapierre. "Sexual Fantasies in the General Population." *Journal of Sexual Medicine* 12, no. 2 (2015): 328–340.

Jozifkova, E. "Consensual Sadomasochistic Sex (BDSM): The Roots, the Risks, and the Distinctions Between BDSM and Violence." *Current Psychiatric Reports* 15, no. 9 (2013): 392.

Kafka, M. "Hypersexual Disorder: A Proposed Diagnosis for DSM-V." *Archives of Sexual Behavior* 39, no. 2 (2010): 377–400.

——. "What Happened to Hypersexual Disorder?" *Archives of Sexual Behavior* 43, no. 7 (2014): 1259–1261.

Kann, L., T. McManus, W. A. Harris, S. L. Shanklin, K. H. Flint, B. Queen, R. Lowry, et al. "Youth Risk Behavior Surveillance—United States, 2017." *Morbidity and Mortality Weekly Report*, June 15, 2018. https://www.cdc.gov/healthyyouth/data/yrbs/pdf/2017/ss6708.pdf.

Kaplan, A. *Women's Self-Development in Late Adolescence*. Wellesley, MA: Stone Center for Developmental Services and Studies, Wellesley College, 1985.

Kaplan, M., and R. Krueger. "Cognitive-Behavioral Treatment for Paraphilias." *Israel Journal of Psychiatry and Related Sciences* 49, no. 4 (2012): 291–296.

Karila, L., A. Wery, A. Weinstein, O. Cottencin, A. Petit, M. Reynaud, and J. Billieux. "Sexual Addiction or Hypersexual Disorder: Different Terms for the Same Problem?" *Current Pharmaceutical Design* 20, no. 25 (2014): 4012–4020.

Karraker, A., J. Delamater, and C. R. Schwartz. "Sexual Frequency Decline from Midlife to Later Life." *Journals of Gerontology: Series B: Psychological Sciences and Social Sciences* 66, no. 4 (2011): 502–512.

Kempadoo, K. "Caribbean Sexuality: Mapping the Field." *Caribbean Review of Gender Studies* (2009): 1–24.

Kempeneers, P., R. Andrianne, M. Cuddy, and S. Blairy. "Sexual Cognitions, Trait Anxiety, Sexual Anxiety, and Distress in Men with Different Subtypes of Premature Ejaculation and in Their Partners." *Journal of Sexual and Marital Therapy* 44, no. 4 (2018): 319–332.

Kenneady, D. A., and S. B. Oswalt. "Is Cass's Model of Homosexual Identity Formation Relevant to Today's Society?" *American Journal of Sexuality Education* 9, no. 2 (2014): 229–246.

Kim, J., and K. Bolton. "Strengths Perspective." In *Encyclopedia of Social Work*, ed. L. Davis and T. Mizrahi. Online ed. Washington, DC: NASW Press, 2019.

Kinsey, A., W. Pomeroy, and C. Martin. *Sexual Behavior in the Human Male*. Philadelphia: Saunders, 1948.

Kinsey, A., W. Pomeroy, C. Martin, and P. Gebhard. *Sexual Behavior in the Human Female*. Philadelphia: Saunders, 1953.

Kirkpatrick, J. "Human Sexuality: A Survey of What Counselors Need to Know." *Counselor Education and Supervision* 19 (1980): 276–282.

Kleinplatz, P. J. "Learning from Extraordinary Lovers." *Journal of Homosexuality* 50, no. 2 (2006): 325–348.

Klesse, C. "Contesting the Culture of Monogamy: Consensual Nonmonogamies and Polyamory." In *Introducing the New Sexuality Studies*, 3rd ed., ed. N. Fischer and S. Seidman, 325–336. London: Routledge, 2016.

Koenig, T., and R. Spano. "Sex, Supervision, and Boundary Violations: Pressing Challenges and Possible Solutions." *Clinical Supervisor* 22, no. 1 (2003): 3–19.

Koike, T., H. Tanabe, S. Okazaki, E. Nakagawa, A. Sasaki, K. Shimada, and N. Sadato. "Neural Substrates of Shared Attention as Social Memory: A Hyperscanning Functional Magnetic Resonance Imaging Study." *Neuroimage* 125 (2016): 401–412.

Kolmes, K., W. Stock, and C. Moser. "Investigating Bias in Psychotherapy with BDSM Clients." *Journal of Homosexuality* 50, nos. 2–3 (2006): 301–324.

Kosciw, J. G., E. A. Greytak, A. D. Zongrone, C. M. Clark, and N. L. Truong. *The 2017 National School Climate Survey: The Experiences of Lesbian, Gay, Bisexual, Transgender, and Queer Youth in Our Nation's Schools*. New York: GLSEN, 2018.

Lahaie, M. A., R. Amsel, S. Khalife, S. Boyer, M. Faaborg-Andersen, and Y. Binik. "Can Fear, Pain, and Muscle Tension Discriminate Vaginismus from Dyspareunia/Provoked Vestibulodynia? Implications for the New DSM-5 Diagnosis of Genito-Pelvic Pain/Penetration Disorder." *Archives of Sexual Behavior* 44 (2015): 1537–1550.

Laumann, E., J. Gagnon, R. Michael, and S. Michaels. *The Social Organization of Sexuality: Sexual Practice in the United States*. Chicago: University of Chicago Press, 1994.

Leiblum, S. "Critical Overview of the New Consensus-Based Definitions and Classifications of Sexual Dysfunction." *Journal of Marital and Sex Therapy* 27, no. 2 (2001): 159–168.

Leon, L. "Texting Amor: Emerging Intimacies in Textually Mediated Romance Among Tzotzil Mayan Youth." *Ethos* 45, no. 4 (2017): 462–488.

Lev, A. I. *Transgender Emergence: Therapeutic Guidelines for Working with Gender-Variant People and Their Families*. Binghamton, NY: Haworth Press, 2004.

LeVay, S., J. I. Baldwin, and J. D. Baldwin. *Discovering Human Sexuality*. 3rd ed. Sunderland, MA: Sinauer Associates, 2015.

Levine, E., D. Herbernick, O. Martinez, T. C. Fu, and D. Dodge. "Open Relationships, Non-consensual Nonmonogamy, and Monogamy Among U.S. Adults: Findings from the 2012 National Survey of Sexual Behavior and Health." *Archives of Sexual Behavior* 47 (2018): 1439–1450.

Lindau, S. T., and N. Gavrilova. "Sex, Health, and Years of Sexually Active Life Gained Due to Good Health: Evidence from Two US Population Based Cross Sectional Surveys of Ageing." *BMJ* 340 (2010): c810.

Lindberg, S. M., J. S. Hyde, and N. M. McKinley. "A Measure of Objectified Body Consciousness for Preadolescent and Adolescent Youth." *Psychology of Women Quarterly* 30, no. 1 (2006): 65–76.

Liu, E., and M. E. Roloff. "Regret for Complaint Withholding." *Communication Quarterly* 64, no. 1 (2016): 72–92.

Manion, J. "The Performance of Transgender Inclusion: The Pronoun Go-Round and the New Gender Binary." *Public Seminar*, November 27, 2018. http://www.publicseminar.org/2018/11/the-performance-of-transgender-inclusion/.

Masters, W., and V. Johnson. *Human Sexual Response*. Bronx, NY: Ishi Press, 2010.

Mathews, T. J., and B. E. Hamilton. "Mean Age of Mothers Is on the Rise: United States, 2000–2014." NCHS Data Brief no. 232, January 2016. https://www.cdc.gov/nchs/data/databriefs/db232.pdf.

McCave, E., B. Shepard, and V. Winter. "Human Sexuality as a Critical Subfield in Social Work." *Advances in Social Work* 15, no. 2 (2014): 409–427.

McCullough, C. P., and S. E. Patterson. "'No Lectures or Stink-Eye': The Healthcare Needs of People in the Sex Trade in New York City." Persist Health Project. April 2014. http://media.wix.com/ugd/6ddedf_5c3c4b0d5fe84af89a543f8eeacead4c.pdf.

Meijer, M. L. dir., *69: Love Sex Senior* (Netherlands, 2013).

Merwin, K., L. O'Sullivan, and N. Rosen. "We Need to Talk: Disclosure of Sexual Problems Is Associated with Depression, Sexual Functioning, and Relationship Satisfaction in Women." *Journal of Sex and Marital Therapy* 43, no. 8 (2017): 786–800.

Meston, C., and A. Stanton. "Evaluation of Female Sexual Interest/Arousal Disorder." In *The Textbook of Clinical Sexual Medicine*, ed. W. W. IsHak, 155–163. Cham, Switzerland: Springer International, 2017.

——. "Treatment of Female Sexual Interest/Arousal Disorder." In *The Textbook of Clinical Sexual Medicine*, ed. W. W. IsHak, 165–168. Cham, Switzerland: Springer International, 2017.

Mileham, B. "Online Infidelity in Internet Chat Rooms: An Ethnographic Exploration." *Computers in Human Behavior* 23 (2007): 11–31.

Money, J. *The Lovemap Guidebook: A Definitive Statement*. New York: Continuum, 1999.

Monro, S., S. Hines, and A. Osborne. "Is Bisexuality Invisible? A Review of Sexualities Scholarship, 1970–2015." *Sociological Review* 65, no. 4 (2017): 663–681.

Moore, L. "Polishing the Pearl: Discoveries of the Clitoris." In *Introducing the New Sexuality Studies*, 3rd ed., ed. N. Fischer and S. Seidman, 69–73. London: Routledge, 2016.

Moore, L., T. Pincus, and D. Rodemaker. "What Professionals Need to Know About BDSM." National Coalition for Sexual Freedom. Accessed November 30, 2019. https://www .ncsfreedom.org/images/stories/pdfs/Activist/What_Professionals_Need_to_Know _About_BDSM_1.pdf.

Morin, J. *The Erotic Mind*. New York: Harper Perennial, 2012.

Mourra, S. "Sexualized Transference in Older Adults." *Psychiatric Times*, September 26, 2014, 1–4.

Murray, C. E., and E. C. Campbell. "The Pleasures and Perils of Technology in Intimate Relationships." *Journal of Couple and Relationship Therapy* 14, no. 2 (2015): 116–140.

Mustanski, B., R. Andrews, and J. A. Puckett. "The Effects of Cumulative Victimization on Mental Health Among Lesbian, Gay, Bisexual, and Transgender Adolescents and Young Adults." *American Journal of Public Health* 106, no. 3 (2016): 527–533.

Mustanski, B. S., R. Garofalo, and E. M. Emerson. "Mental Health Disorders, Psychological Distress, and Suicidality in a Diverse Sample of Lesbian, Gay, Bisexual, and Transgender Youths." *American Journal of Public Health* 100, no. 12 (2010): 2426–2432.

Mustanski, B., and R. T. Liu. "A Longitudinal Study of Predictors of Suicide Attempts Among Lesbian, Gay, Bisexual, and Transgender Youth." *Archives of Sexual Behavior* 42, no. 3 (2013): 437–448.

Mustapic, J., D. Marcinko, and P. Vargek. "Body Shame and Disordered Eating in Adolescents." *Current Psychology* 36, no. 3 (2017): 447–452.

Myers, S., and J. Milner. *Sexual Issues in Social Work*. Bristol, UK: Policy Press, 2007.

National Association of Social Workers. *Code of Ethics*. Washington, DC: National Association of Social Workers, 2017.

National Coalition of Anti-Violence Programs. *A Crisis of Hate: A Report on Homicides Against Lesbian, Gay, Bisexual and Transgender People: Emily Waters, Larissa Pham, Chelsea Convery*. New York: National Coalition of Anti-Violence Programs, 2018.

National Sexual Violence Resource Center. *Preventing Child Sexual Abuse Resources*. https:// www.nsvrc.org/preventing-child-sexual-abuse-resources.

Newman, B., P. Dannenfelser, and L. Benishek. "Assessing Beginning Social Work and Counseling Students' Acceptance of Lesbians and Gay Men." *Journal of Social Work Education* 38, no. 2 (2002): 273–288.

New York City Health Department. *Health of Older Adults in New York City*. https://www1.nyc .gov/assets/doh/downloads/pdf/episrv/2019-older-adult-health.pdf.

Nippoldt, T. B. "Is There Any Safe Way to Naturally Boost a Man's Testosterone Level?" Mayo Clinic. July 19, 2017. https://www.mayoclinic.org/healthy-lifestyle/sexual-health/expert -answers/testosterone-level/faq-20089016.

Ochs, R. "Biphobia: It Goes Both Ways." In *Bisexuality: The Identity Politics of an Invisible Minority*, ed. B. A. Firestein, 217–239. Thousand Oaks, CA: Sage, 1996.

——. "What's in a Name? Why Women Embrace or Resist Bisexual Identity." In *Becoming Visible: Counseling Bisexuals Across the Lifespan*, ed. B. A. Firestein, 72–86. New York: Columbia University Press, 2007.

Oliver, V., E. van der Meulen, J. Larkin, S. Flicker, and the Toronto Teen Survey Research Team. "If You Teach Them, They Will Come: Providers' Reactions to Incorporating Pleasure Into Youth Sexual Education." *Revue Canadienne de Sante Publique* 104, no. 2 (2013): 142–146.

Osterberg, E., A. Bernie, and R. Ramasamy. "Risks of Testosterone Replacement Therapy in Men." *Indian Journal of Urology* 30, no. 1 (January–March 2014): 2–7.

Pahwa, P., and S. Foley. "Biopsychosocial Evaluation of Sexual Dysfunctions." In *The Textbook of Clinical Sexual Medicine*, ed. W. W. IsHak, 79–94. Cham, Switzerland: Springer International, 2017.

Pardor, S., and A. Devor. "Transgender and Gender Nonconforming Identity Development. In *The Sage Encyclopedia of Psychology and Gender*, ed. K. Nadal, 1689–1692. Thousand Oaks, CA: Sage Publications, 2017.

Parsons, J., T. Starks, S. DuBois, C. Grov, and S. Golub. "Alternatives to Monogamy Among Gay Male Couples in a Community Survey: Implications for Mental Health and Sexual Risk." *Archives of Sexual Behavior* 42, no. 2 (2013): 308–312.

Peixoto, M. "Sex and Sexual Orientation." In *The Textbook of Clinical Sexual Medicine*, ed. W. W. IsHak, 433–445. Cham, Switzerland: Springer International, 2017.

Physicians' Desk Reference. 71st ed. Montvale, NJ: PDR Network, 2017.

Powls, J., and J. Davies. "A Descriptive Review of Research Relating to Sadomasochism: Considerations for Clinical Practice." *Deviant Behavior* 33, no. 3 (2012): 223–234.

Poynten, M., A. Grulich, and D. Templeton. "Sexually Transmitted Infections in Older Populations: Current Opinions." *Infectious Diseases* 26, no. 1 (2013): 80–85.

Pyne, J. "Unsuitable Bodies: Trans People and Cisnormativity in Shelter Services." *Canadian Social Work Journal* 28, no. 1 (2011): 129–138.

Rachman, A., R. Kennedy, and M. Yard. "Erotic Transference and Its Relationship to Childhood Seduction." *Psychoanalytic Social Work* 16 (2009): 12–30.

Ream, G. L. "What's Unique About Lesbian, Gay, Bisexual, and Transgender (LGBT) Youth and Young Adult Suicides? Findings from the National Violent Death Reporting System." *Journal of Adolescent Health* 64, no. 5 (2019): 602–607.

Reamer, F. "Boundary Issues in Social Work: Managing Dual Relationships." *Social Work* 48, no. 1 (2003): 121–133.

——. *Social Work Values and Ethics.* 4th ed. New York: Columbia University Press, 2013.

Reese-Weber, M. "Intimacy, Communication, and Aggressive Behaviors: Variations by Phases of Romantic Relationship Development." *Personal Relationships* 22 (2015): 204–215.

Reynolds, D. "Disability and BDSM: Bob Flanagan and the Case for Sexual Rights." *Sexuality Research and Social Policy* 4 (2007): 40–52.

Richardson, J., and M. A. Schuster. *Everything You Never Wanted Your Kids to Know About Sex (but Were Afraid They'd Ask): The Secrets to Surviving Your Child's Sexual Development from Birth to the Teens.* New York: Three Rivers Press, 2003.

Robbins, N., K. Graff Low, and A. Query. "An Exploration of the 'Coming Out' Process for Asexual Individuals." *Archives of Sexual Behavior* 45, no. 3 (2016): 751–760.

Roberts, R. "Importance of the Sexual Dimension in Psychosocial Assessment." *Australian Social Work* 45, no. 3 (1992): 37–42.

Robinson, K. "Children's Sexual Citizenship." In *Introducing the New Sexuality Studies*, 3rd ed., ed. N. Fischer and S. Seidman, 485–493. London: Routledge, 2016.

Rosenberg, K., P. Carnes, and S. O'Connor. "Evaluation and Treatment of Sex Addiction." *Journal of Sex and Marital Therapy* 40, no. 2 (2014): 77–91.

Rosier, J. G., and J. M. Tyler. "Finding the Love Guru in You: Examining the Effectiveness of a Sexual Communication Training Program for Married Couples." *Marriage and Family Review* 53, no. 1 (2017): 65–87.

Roy, C. F., D. L. Tolman, and F. Snowden. "Heterosexual Anal Intercourse Among Black and Latino Adolescents and Young Adults: A Poorly Understood High-Risk Behavior." *Journal of Sex Research* 50, no. 7 (2013): 715–722.

Russell, S. T., and J. N. Fish. "Mental Health in Lesbian, Gay, Bisexual, and Transgender (LGBT) Youth." *Annual Review of Clinical Psychology* 12 (2016): 465–487.

Sandberg, L. "Inventions of Hetero-Sex in Later Life: Beyond Dysfunction and the Coital Imperative." In *Introducing the New Sexuality Studies*, 3rd ed., ed. N. Fischer and S. Seidman, 304–312. London: Routledge, 2016.

Sarin, S., R. Amsel, and Y. Binik. "A Streetcar Named 'Derousal'? A Psychophysiological Examination of the Desire-Arousal Distinction in Sexually Functional and Dysfunctional Women." *Journal of Sex Research* 53, no. 6 (2016): 711–729.

Schmidt, A. "Prevalence, Predictors, and Negative Outcomes Associated with Discordant Sexual Identity, Sexual Attraction, and Sexual Behavior." PhD diss., City University of New York, 2010.

Schulman, J. K., and L. Erickson-Schroth. "Mental Health in Sexual Minority and Transgender Women." *Medical Clinics of North America* 103, no. 4 (2019): 723–733.

Schwartz, P., and M. Kempner. *50 Great Myths of Human Sexuality*. New York: Wiley, 2015.

Serano, J. *Outspoken: A Decade of Transgender Activism and Trans Feminism*. Oakland, CA: Switch Hitter Press, 2016.

Sheff, E. *The Polyamorists Next Door: Inside Multiple-Partner Relationships and Families*. Lanham, MD: Rowman and Littlefield, 2014.

Shelton, J., and SJ Dodd. "Beyond the Binary: Addressing Cisnormativity in the Social Work Classroom." *Journal of Social Work Education* 56, no. 1 (2020): 179–185.

Shelton, M. *Fundamentals of LGBT Substance Use Disorders: Multiple Identities, Multiple Challenges*. New York: Harrington Park Press, 2017.

Sherer, I., J. Baum, D. Ehrensaft, and S. Rosenthal. "Affirming Gender: Caring for Gender-Atypical Children and Adolescents." *Contemporary Pediatrics* 32, no. 1 (2015): 16–19.

Shilts, R. *And the Band Played On: Politics, People, and the AIDS Epidemic*. New York: St. Martin's Press, 1987.

Sitron, J., and D. Dyson. "Validation of a Sexological Worldview: A Construct for Use in the Training of Sexologists in Sexual Diversity." *SAGE Open* 2, no. 1 (2012): 1–16.

Slater, A., and M. Tiggemann. "Body Image and Disordered Eating in Adolescent Girls and Boys: A Test of Objectification Theory." *Sex Roles* 63, nos. 1–2 (2010): 42–49.

Sorrentino, R. "DSM-5 and Paraphilias: What Psychiatrists Need to Know." *Psychiatric Times* 33, no. 11. November 28, 2016. https://www.psychiatrictimes.com/dsm-5/dsm-5-and-paraphilias-what-psychiatrists-need-know.

Spade, D. "We Still Need Pronoun Go-Rounds." December 1, 2018. http://www.deanspade .net/2018/12/01/we-still-need-pronoun-go-rounds.

Spurgas, A. "Interest, Arousal, and Shifting Diagnoses of Female Sexual Dysfunction, or: How Women Learn About Desire." *Studies in Gender and Sexuality* 14, no. 3 (2013): 187–205.

——. "Low Desire, Trauma, and Femininity in the DSM-5: A Case for Sequelae." *Psychology and Sexuality* 7, no. 1 (2016): 48–67.

Steensma, T., J. McGuire, B. Kreukels, A. Beekman, and A. Cohen-Kettenis. "Factors Associated with Desistance and Persistence of Childhood Dysphoria: A Quantitative Follow-Up Study." *Journal of the American Academy of Child and Adolescent Psychiatry* 52, no. 6 (2013): 582–590.

Stefano, A. "Erotic Transference." *British Journal of Psychotherapy* 33, no. 4 (2017): 505–513.

Sternberg, R. "A Triangular Theory of Love." *Psychological Review* 93, no. 2 (1986): 119–135.

——. "Triangulating Love." In *The Psychology of Love*, ed. R. Sternberg and M. Barnes, 119–138. New Haven, CT: Yale University Press, 1988.

Strahan, E. J., A. Lafrance, A. E. Wilson, N. Ethier, S. J. Spencer, and M. P. Zanna. "Victoria's Dirty Secret: How Sociocultural Norms Influence Adolescent Girls and Women." *Personality and Social Psychology Bulletin* 34, no. 2 (2008): 288–301.

Strom-Gotfried, K. J. "Professional Boundaries: An Analysis of Violations by Social Workers." *Families in Society* 80, no. 5 (1999): 439–449.

Stryker, S., and P. Burke. "The Past, Present, and Future of an Identity Theory." *Social Psychology Quarterly* 63, no. 4 (2000): 284–297.

Taormino, T. *Opening Up: A Guide to Creating and Sustaining Open Relationships*. San Francisco: Cleis Press, 2008.

Tatkin, S. *Wired for Dating*. Oakland, CA: New Harbinger, 2016.

——. *Wired for Love*. Oakland, CA: New Harbinger, 2011.

——. *Your Brain on Love*. Audible, 2013. https://www.audible.com/pd/Your-Brain-on-Love -Audiobook/B00DMCBEOE.

Taylor, A., and M. A. Gosney. "Sexuality in Older Age: Essential Considerations for Healthcare Professionals." *Age and Ageing* 40, no. 5 (2011): 538–543.

Taylor, G. W., and J. M. Ussher. "Making Sense of S&M: A Discourse Analytic Account." *Sexualities* 4, no. 3 (2001): 293–314.

Ter Kuile, M., R. Melles, H. de Groot, C. Tuijnman-Raasveld, and J. van Lankveld. "Therapist-Aided Exposure for Women with Lifelong Vaginismus: A Randomized Waiting-List Control Trial of Efficacy." *Journal of Clinical Psychology* 81, no. 6 (2013): 1127–1136.

Timberlake, D., D. Meyer, S. Hitchings, A. Oakley, L. Stolzfus, S. Aguirre, and A. Plumb. "Sexually Compulsive Behaviors: Implications for Attachment, Early Life Stressors, and Religiosity." *Sexual Addiction and Compulsivity* 23, no. 4 (2016): 361–373.

Tolman, D. *Dilemmas of Desire: Teenage Girls Talk About Sexuality*. Cambridge, MA: Harvard University Press, 2005.

Unitarian Universalist Association. *Our Whole Lives: Lifespan Sexuality Education*. https://www .uua.org/re/owl.

U.S. Census Bureau. *American Community Survey*. U.S. Census Bureau, 2017. https://www .census.gov/library/stories/2019/09/where-same-sex-couples-live.html.

Vance, E. B., and N. N. Wagner. "Written Descriptions of Orgasm: A Study of Sex Differences." *Archives of Sexual Behavior* 5, no. 1 (1976): 87–98.

Veale, D., E. Eshkevari, N. Ellison, A. Costa, D. Robinson, A. Kavouni, and L. Cardozo. "Psychological Characteristics and Motivation of Women Seeking Labiaplasty." *Psychological Medicine* 44, no. 3 (2014): 555–566.

Veaux, F., and E. Rickert. *More than Two: A Practical Guide to Ethical Polyamory*. Portland, OR: Thorntree Press, 2014.

Wagner, A. "Making Peace with Jealousy in Polyamorous Relationships." Accessed November 29, 2019. http://www.practicalpolyamory.com/images/Jealousy_Updated_10-6-10.pdf.

Waldinger, M. "Evaluation of Rapid Ejaculation." In *The Textbook of Clinical Sexual Medicine*, ed. W. W. IsHak, 271–282. Cham, Switzerland: Springer International, 2017.

Walton, M., J. Cantor, N. Bhullar, and A. Lykins. "Hypersexuality: A Critical Review and Introduction to the 'Sexhavior Cycle.'" *Archives of Sexual Behavior* 46, no. 8 (2017): 2231–2251.

Weber, G. "Practice with Bisexual People." In *Social Work Practice with Lesbian, Gay, Bisexual and Transgender People*, 3rd ed., ed. G. P. Mallon, 30–41. New York: Routledge, 2018.

Weinberg, M. S., C. J. Williams, and C. Moser. "The Social Constituents of Sadomasochism." *Social Problems* 31, no. 4 (1984): 379–389.

Weitzman, G., J. Davidson, R. A. Phillips Jr., J. R. Fleckenstein, and C. Morotti-Meeker. "What Psychology Professionals Should Know About Polyamory." National Coalition for Sexual Freedom. Accessed November 30, 2019. https://ncsfreedom.org/images/stories/pdfs /KAP/2010_poly_web.pdf.

Whalen, K. "(In)validating Transgender Identities: Progress and Trouble in the DSM-5." National LGBTQ Task Force. Accessed November 28, 2019. https://www.thetaskforce.org /invalidating-transgender-identities-progress-and-trouble-in-the-dsm-5/.

Whipple, B., and K. Brash-McGreer. "Management of Female Sexual Dysfunction." In *Sexual Function in People with Disability and Chronic Illness: A Health Professional's Guide*, ed. M. L. Sipski and C. J. Alexander, 509–534. Gaithersburg, MD: Aspen, 1997.

Williams, D., and E. Prior. "Contemporary Polyamory: A Call for Awareness and Sensitivity in Social Work." *Social Work* 60, no. 3 (2015): 268–270.

Williams Institute. *Adult LGBT Population in the United States*. Los Angeles: University of California, Los Angeles, 2019.

Wineburg, H. R. "Social Work and Human Sexuality: An Examination of the Country's Top 25-CWSE Ranked MSW Curricula." Master's thesis, Smith College, 2015.

World Health Organization. *Defining Sexual Health: Report of a Technical Consultation on Sexual Health 28–31 January 2002, Geneva*. 2006. Author. https://www.who.int/reproductive health/publications/sexual_health/defining_sexual_health.pdf.

World Health Organization and UNAIDS. *Male Circumcision: Global Trends and Determinants of Prevalence, Safety and Acceptability*. Geneva: WHO Press, 2007. http://www.unaids.org /sites/default/files/media_asset/jc1360_male_circumcision_en_2.pdf.

Yost, M., and L. Hunter. "BDSM Practitioners' Understandings of Their Initial Attraction to BDSM Sexuality: Essentialist and Constructionist Narratives." *Journal of Psychology and Human Sexuality* 3, no. 3 (2012): 244–259.

Yule, M., L. Brotto, and B. Gorzalka. "Sexual Fantasy and Masturbation Among Asexual Individuals." *Canadian Journal of Human Sexuality* 23, no. 2 (2014): 89–95.

Zimmerman, K. "Clients in Sexually Open Relationships: Considerations for Therapists." *Journal of Feminist Family Therapy* 24, no. 3 (2012): 272–289.

Zucker, K. J. "The DSM-5 Diagnostic Criteria for Gender Dysphoria." In *Management of Gender Dysphoria: A Multidisciplinary Approach*, ed. C. Trombetta, G. Liguori, and M. Bertolotto, 33–37. Trieste, Italy: Springer-Verlag Italia, 2015.

INDEX

INDEX

Ryan White Comprehensive AIDS Resources Emergency Act (1990), 84

same-sex marriage: legalization of, 84, 85, 216; statistics of, 86
Sarin, Sabina, 182
Schwartz, Pepper, 28, 35, 91
scrotum, *39*, 40
Secretary (film), 160
Semans, James, 188
serotonin, 145
sex: cultural taboos, 187; fertility/infertility issues and, 37; *vs.* gender, 101; in Latinx culture, 57; menopause and, 38; outside of marriage, 131; plain, 156; pregnancy and, 37; relationship between love and, 139–140
sex addiction, 192, 193
sex apps, 8–9. *See also* online dating
sex hormone dehydroepiandrosterone (DHEA) peak, 124
Sexological Ecosystemic Questionnaire (Buehler), 67
sex-positive environment: creation of, 8, 12, 24, 214; physical space, 16–17, *17*
sex-positive intake forms, 18, 19–22, 59, 214
sex-positive social work: avoiding assumptions in, 171–172; biopsychosocial assessment in, 22–24; client interview techniques, 8–9, 11, 13–15, 23, 55; goal of, 216; knowledge of anatomy and physiology in, 26, 27, 53; language in, 3–4, 14–15, 45–46; practice of, 3, 213–214; relevant CSWE competencies, 7, 26, 55, 62, 77, 100, 118, 138, 156, 177, 197; role-playing technique, 15, 16
sex trades, 201, 202, 217
sexual aversion, 181, 182
sexual behavior, 20, 80, 191
sexual communication, 146, 147, 148, 149
sexual desire: and arousal, 48, 49–50, 182; difficulties with, 181–182; discrepant, 182, 183, 184; hyperactive, 182

sexual development: adolescence stage of, 67, 68, 69; adulthood stage of, 68, 69; childhood stage of, 67; cultural and social influence on, 70, 72; family influence on, 67; institutional influence on, 67, 69; preteen stage of, 67, 68; religious influence on, 67, 69
sexual dysfunctions and disorders: age factor, 185; assessment of, 178–180; characteristics of, 178, 195; lifelong and acquired, 178, 179, 186; physiological causes of, 185, 187, 190; related to arousal, 180, 182, 184, 185; related to desire, 180, 181–182, 184; related to orgasm, 180, 186–189; related to painful sex, 180, 189–190; therapy of, 184, 190
sexual education: advocacy of sex-positive, 10, 127–128, 215; evolution of, 10; gaps in, 27; media and, 28; non-gendered language of, 27; resources about, 10; on sexual-transmitted infections, 27; social norms and, 28; for social workers, 1–2, 3, 7–8; in Western culture, 32
sexual history assessment: adolescence topics, 63, 71–72; adulthood topics, 72; approaches to, 55–56, 59, 74–75; avoidance of assumption during, 58–59; background questions, 62–63; breaking the ice strategy, 57–58; CDC's approach to, 73; childhood topics, 71; dating history questions, 64; DOUPE model, 73–74, 75; exosystem questions, 67, 69; five Ps approach, 60–61, 75; macrosystem questions, 67, 70; mesosystem questions, 67, 69; microsystem questions, 67–68; narrative format for, 72–73; questions about sexual experiences, 63, 64; setting the space for, 56–57; sexological ecosystemic approach, 67–70; sexual functioning questions, 72; sexual health questions, 59; specific concerns in, 73; very structured approach, 62–66, 67; very unstructured narrative approach, 71–73

GPSR Authorized Representative: Easy Access System Europe, Mustamäe tee
50, 10621 Tallinn, Estonia, gpsr.requests@easproject.com

www.ingramcontent.com/pod-product-compliance
Lightning Source LLC
Chambersburg PA
CBHW032121020426
42334CB00016B/1027